THE

EVERYTHING®

LAWN CARE BOOK

From seed to soil, mowing
to fertilizing—hundreds of tips
for growing a beautiful lawn

Douglas Green

Adams Media Corporation
Avon, Massachusetts

An Everything® Series Book.
Everything® and everything.com® are registered trademarks of Adams Media Corporation.

Published by Adams Media Corporation
57 Littlefield Street, Avon, MA 02322. U.S.A.
www.adamsmedia.com

ISBN: 1-58062-487-1
Printed in the United States of America.

J I H G F E D C B

Library of Congress Cataloging-in-Publication Data
Green, Douglas.
Everything lawn care / Douglas Green.
p.   cm.
ISBN 1-58062-487-1
1. Lawns. I. Title.
SB433 .G74   2001
635.9'647–dc21   00-050253

Many of the designations used by manufacturers and sellers to distinguish their products are claimed as trademarks. Where those designations appear in this book and Adams Media was aware of a trademark claim, the designations have been printed in initial capital letters.

This publication is designed to provide accurate and authoritative information with regard to the subject matter covered. It is sold with the understanding that the publisher is not engaged in rendering legal, accounting, or other professional advice. If legal advice or other expert assistance is required, the services of a competent professional person should be sought.

—From a *Declaration of Principles* jointly adopted by a Committee of the American Bar Association and a Committee of Publishers and Associations

Illustrations by Barry Littmann and Kathie Kelleher.

This book is available at quantity discounts for bulk purchases.
For information, call 1-800-872-5627.

Dedication

For Nancy and John Proud—
Nancy for loving us all and John for mowing
more grass than any sane man should.

Contents

Introduction . . . . **viii**

CHAPTER ONE

The Anatomy of Grass / 1

An Anatomy Lesson **2**
Shoots 2
Buds and Propagation 3
Roots 4
Identifying Types of Grass **5**
Major Grasses and Their Features **10**
Northern Lawn Grasses 10
Southern Lawn Grasses 18
Buying Grass Seed **26**

CHAPTER TWO

How To Start a Good Lawn / 27

Level and Grade the Soil **28**
Pregrading 28
Subsurface Grading 29
Finish Grading 30
Test the Soil **33**
Prepare the Soil **34**
Compost: A Lawn's Best Friend 35
Make It Level 38
Apply Starter Fertilizer 38
Firming It Up 39

Seeding Your Lawn **39**
How to Seed Your Lawn 42
Winter Overseeding/Dormant Seeding 43
Watering 43
Using Mulch 44
After Grass Seed Germination 44
Pest Control 45
Sod—The Instant Lawn **46**
Step-by-Step Lawn Sodding 48
Laying Sod Successfully 49
Watering 52
When Can I Walk on It? 53
Other Methods **54**
Plugging 54
Strip sodding 54
Stolonizing 54

CHAPTER THREE

How to Grow a Good Lawn / 57

Sunshine **59**
Food **60**
Nitrogen 61
Phosphorus 65
Potassium 67

CONTENTS

Minor Trace Nutrients 68
Organic Fertilizers 70
When to Feed **74**
Spring 74
Summer 74
Fall 75
How Much to Feed **75**
Feeding the Warm Season Lawn 75
Feeding the Low-Maintenance Lawn 76
How to Use a Fertilizer Spreader **76**
Setting Up Your Spreader to Work
with Fertilizer 78
Getting Good Coverage 79
Different Types of Fertilizers **81**
Weed-and-Feed Products 81
Liquid Fertilizer 82
Irrigating **83**
How Much Water Does Grass Need? 83
How Often Should I Water? 83
When Should I Water? 84
Summer Drought 85
How to Reduce the Amount of Water
You Use 86
Thatch **87**
Why Is It a Problem? 87
What Causes Thatch? 87
How Do I Control Thatch? 89
Don't Roll Your Lawn **90**
Mowing **91**
How Does Mowing Affect the Grass? 92
How Long Do I Leave the Grass? 94
Kinds of Lawn Mowers **94**
Rotary Mowers 94
Reel Mowers 97
Sickle Bar Mowers 97
Flail or Hammer Knife Mowers 98
What About the Clippings? **100**

CHAPTER FOUR
How to Repair or Renovate a Lawn /101

Repair **102**
Sodding 103
Reseeding 105
Renovation **105**
Kill the Existing Grass 106
Mow and Sow 108
The Organic Approach 109
The Easy System of Lawncare:
Have Someone Else Do It **112**

CHAPTER FIVE
Weeds / 115

Cultural Controls **117**
Mowing 117
Fertilization 117
Irrigation 118
Seed 118
Cultivation 119
Chemical Controls **119**
Pre-Emergence Herbicides 119
Post-Emergence Herbicides 120
Nonselective Controls 120
Chemical Mixes 120
Organic Controls **122**
How to Control Moss **122**
Commonly Available Herbicides **123**
The Lawn Weed Hall of Fame **124**
White Clover 124
Clover 124
Plantains 128
Sorrels 128
Spurges 128

Chickweed 128
Knotweed 130
Bunch-Type Grasses 130
Spreading Grasses 131
Nut Sedge 132

CHAPTER SIX
Lawn Diseases and Their Cures / 135

Diagnosis: The First Step **137**
   Usually It's Fungi 140
Identifying Diseases **141**
   Anthracnose 142
   Bermuda Grass Decline 142
   Brown Patch 143
   Centipede Decline 144
   Cercospora Leaf Spot 144
   Crown and Root Rot 144
   Curvularia Blight 146
   Dollar Spot 146
   Fairy Ring 147
   Fusarium Blight 148
   Fusarium Patch or Pink Snow Mold 148
   Gray Leaf Spot 148
   Leaf Blotch 150
   Leaf Spot 151
   Melting Out 151
   Necrotic Ring Spot 152
   Nigrospora Blight 154
   Pink Patch 154
   Powdery mildew 155
   Pythium Blight 155
   Red Thread 156
   Rusts 156

St. Augustine Decline 157
Sclerotium Blight (or Southern Blight) . . . 158
Slime Mold 158
Spring Dead Spot 158
Stripe Smut and Flag Smut 159
Summer Patch 159
Take-All Patch 160
Take-All Root Rot 160
Typhula Blight (Gray Snow Mold)
   Typhula Species 161
White Patch 161
Yellow Patch 162
Zonate Leaf Spot 162
Pesticide and Spray Injury **163**
Identifying Problems Other than Diseases . . . **166**

CHAPTER SEVEN
Lawn Pests and Cures / 175

The Five Stages of the Disease Cycle **178**
Monitoring Techniques **180**
   The Famous Coffee Can Technique 181
   The Soap Solution Technique 181
   The Cup Changer Trick 182
An Important Pest Control Point **182**
   Biological Controls 184
   Foliar or Drenching Sprays: Insecticides . . 184
Pests That Hurt Grass:
Chemical and Organic Controls **186**
   Grubs 187
   Chewing Insects 198
   Webworms 200
   Cutworms 203

Armyworms 205
Mole Crickets 206
Aphids 209
Chinch Bugs 209
Mites 212
Scale 215
Other 216

**Nuisance Pests: Chemical and Organic
Problem Solving** **218**
Ants 218
Earwigs 225
Fleas 225
Wasps 225

Rodent Pests **226**
Moles and Voles 226

Large Animal Pests **227**
Skunks and Raccoons 227
Armadillos 228

CHAPTER EIGHT
Specialty Lawn Areas / 229

Golf Greens **230**
Soil 230
Grass 232
Play Areas **233**
Shade Lawns **234**
Pathways **236**
Seats **237**
Containers **237**
Tennis Courts **237**
Croquet Lawns **238**
Mazes and Labyrinths **239**

CHAPTER NINE
Alternatives to Lawns / 241

Ground Covers **242**
Myths 242
Selecting a Good Ground Cover 244
Preparing the Bed 244
Planting 245
Hardiness and Winter Protection 247
Watering 247
Controlling Weeds 248
Feeding 248
Pruning 249
Ornamental Grass **254**
Wildflower Lawn **255**
Moss **257**
Shrubs **258**
Herbs **260**
Vines **260**
Hardscape **261**

Glossary **262**

Resources / 267

General Internet Sites **268**
Books **269**

Index **270**

Introduction

I wish I had a penny for every lawn-growing question I've answered over the years in my nursery, gardening radio phone-in program, Internet newsletter, and newspaper columns. You know, I get more questions about growing grass than just about any other kind of gardening. It seems almost everybody wants to grow a good lawn.

My own lawn started out as a hayfield and pasture and the first few years we were on the farm, it was inhabited by cows. While they were great fertilizers, my wife decided that she'd rather look at a lawn than a cow herd. So after the cows were fenced out, I started the process of creating a good lawn, using organic techniques that would meet my needs for a low mainte-nance lawn. I'm not a fan of heavy-duty spraying, hours of cut-ting grass and constant raking out in the hot sun. Let's face it, I'm a lazy gardener and I don't have a lot of time to spend taking care of grass. Any lawn that was going to live outside my front window had to be easy to care for as well as decent to look at.

It had to be a good looking lawn because I was a garden writer with a nursery. All the people coming to the nursery in the spring wanted to see good gardens and lawns. I wrote about lawns and I had better walk the walk as far as my readers and customers were concerned. This trend will even be worse now that I've written a book about lawn care; every spring-yellow dandelion will be an indictment.

This book is my way of collecting all the questions I get asked and answering them in one place. I've mined my radio and Internet question notes to find all the beginner questions I could and made sure they were answered here using easy-to-learn techniques. For example, I share all the tricks and techniques for weed control I've picked up over the years because I hate weeding and I always look for the easy way out. I can almost guarantee that if there is an easy way to have a good looking lawn, it's in this book.

I should also emphasize that I'm not a fan of chemical sprays on the lawn so this book outlines both organic as well as chemical treatments for lawn problems. Your lawn can make a contribution to our environment in a positive way and this book describes how you can accomplish this. Organic lawns are safe and healthy places for kids and pets to play. I also note that many lawns are plagued with insects and grubs. While I don't have too many problems with pests on my lawn because of the soil building techniques I use (I describe those too), I've spent some time making sure the simple and effective organic treatments for lawn pests are fully described. You'll be able to control grubs, mole and voles, and most other lawn pests once you read the book. There are summary charts throughout the book to help you find and identify the specific techniques that are useful to your garden zone.

So, if you're a beginner to lawn care or even an experienced gardener trying to improve your lawn, this book will help you grow better grass.

Doug Green

Athens, Ontario
www.simplegiftsfarm.com

CHAPTER ONE

The Anatomy of Grass

This chapter explains how to identify the grass you have in your lawn and what kind of grass will grow well in your area. It is a little technical, but it just might make you a turf expert. At the very least, you'll be able to sound like one at the next neighborhood barbecue. If you don't care what kind of grass is living in your lawn, skip ahead to the maintenance chapter—and get another iced tea out of the fridge while you're at it. (Better yet, get one for me too, and we'll watch the grass grow together.)

Still with me? All right, let's get started.

An Anatomy Lesson

To begin with, grasses are called monocots or monocotyledons. That's because when the seed germinates, only one (mono) baby leaf (cotyledon) comes out of it, hence "monocot." Weedy plants, such as dandelions or clover, are dicotyledons because they have more than one seed leaf (normally two). Knowing this difference in seed behavior is helpful if you are checking the grass seed you bought for weed content. If you see too many two-leafed plants germinating along with the one-leafed plants, you know you are planting weed seed along with your grass seed.

Shoots

Grass anatomy is not particularly difficult to master. Anything above the ground is called a "shoot." The shoot is composed of a central stem and leaves. The leaves have two parts: the blade (that's the flat leafy part) and the sheath (the rounded part just below the blade). The stem supports the leaves, and roots support the entire structure underground. I told you it was simple.

The interesting thing about the stem is that at intervals along its length, it develops swollen areas called "nodes." You can feel them if you run your fingers gently along the stem. It is at these nodes that new "buds" develop. This is a good thing because if you cut the top off the stem by mowing, the bud will develop into a new leafy top. Without these buds, you'd only get to cut your lawn once. Hmm . . . Although a single mowing might strike your fancy, the grass would probably die shortly afterward because it

WHAT IF YOU'RE PLANTING WEED SEED TOO?

Some authors will tell you that you might find yourself planting weed seed along with the grass seed when you are sowing a lawn. Really inexperienced authors will tell you to stop and return the seed if you discover weed seed. In real life, there is no way any gardener is going to know that this is happening. I know only one gardener who can identify seeds at a glance, and she runs a specialist seed company and handles seeds all day long. The rest of us have to trust that what we are planting is grass and not weed seed. Also, seeds like mustard (a common weed in grass seed) are so small that we can hardly see them in the mix anyway.

The end result of a good healthy stand of grass has more to do with how you establish the grass than with the odd bit of weed seed in the mixture. So relax!

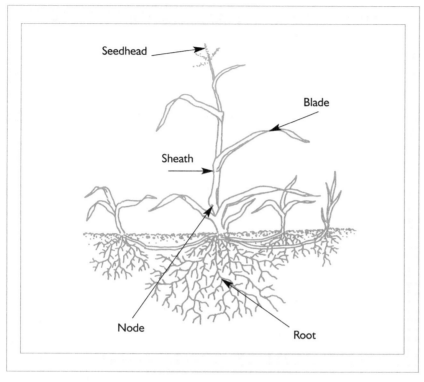

PARTS OF A GRASS SHOOT

wouldn't be able to obtain enough food to live. The success of our entire grassland structure depends on the existence of these nodes and developing buds.

Buds and Propagation

The way the new bud grows determines how the grass plant spreads in your lawn. This can be a good thing to understand, especially if you're trying to eliminate one of the weedy grass species from an otherwise picture-perfect lawn. If the bud grows up through the sheath area of the mother plant, it looks a bit like a new plant attached to the old plant and is called a "tiller." Plants that spread by tillering are sometimes referred to as bunchgrass; some weed species on your lawn may do this. The second way buds have of creating new plants is to begin growing, but then they cut through the sheath of the mother plant to form a new *aboveground* stem called a

TWO DISTINCT SYSTEMS

Think of a grass plant as two distinct systems. The root system absorbs oxygen and nutrients from the soil and produces carbon dioxide as a waste product. It also takes nutrients from the leaves and stores them. The leaves, on the other hand, use carbon dioxide and the sunlight to produce energy and give off oxygen as a waste product. Together, leaves and roots form a complete biological system.

KEEP OFF THE GRASS

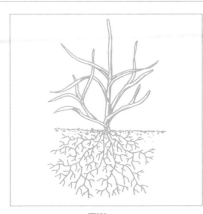

Tillers

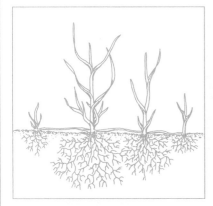

Stolons

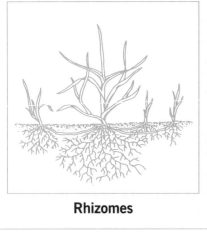

Rhizomes

ROOTS

"stolon." Nodes develop along the length of this aboveground stem, and each node can produce a perfect clone of the mother plant. The third method of propagation is for the bud to penetrate the other sheath and stay belowground to form a new *underground* stem called a "rhizome." Although they may look like long white roots, rhizomes are in fact stems because they develop nodes from which new shoots pop to the surface. (You can tell the difference between roots and underground stems because roots do not have nodes.)

Genetic coding determines which of these methods a grass type uses. Many use more than one. We'll describe genetic coding in the specific grass section that follows. And yes, it does seem that the really weedy ones use rhizomes!

Roots

You don't have to be a gardener very long to figure out that roots are pretty important things for plants. Roots are the anchors that keep the plant firmly in the ground regardless of the effects of wind and rain. They absorb the food and water the plant requires for survival. Roots store the carbohydrates that allow the plant to go **dormant** for long periods without dying. They also produce and use hormones to communicate with the rest of the plant about its overall health and requirements. This relationship with the rest of the plant is quite interesting; the leaves produce the carbohydrates needed for plant growth, but the roots store them. If you remember your basic botany class, roots do not have any chlorophyll (the green in plant leaves) and as a result can't produce their own food.

When compared to other plants, grass roots are very fibrous and heavily branched. This large root mass allows the grass plant to be very efficient in collecting water and food. This is why garden plants such as tall phlox **wilt** in drought conditions while the weedy grass underneath them seems to grow quite happily. The dense root system is also good at collecting food. This is well illustrated by comparing the different ways in which grass and garden perennials obtain phosphorus. Phosphorus does not move readily in the soil, unlike nitrogen, which is water-soluble and moves with the water as it percolates downward. Grass can obtain phosphorus easily because its roots reach into more soil areas, but the less densely rooted plants, the garden perennials, are less efficient. The less root area, the less efficient a feeder the plant is. This is why fertilizers for general garden use have proportionately higher phosphorus levels than do lawn foods. It is not that the grass needs any less phosphorus, it is simply that it can find and use all available sources better than garden plants, which waste a lot because they can't get their roots over to it.

Unfortunately, this dense root mass is not typically deep. Grass roots normally penetrate 12 inches into the soil, so while they are quite efficient at collecting nutrients in the topsoil layers, plants with deeper roots have the advantage at the deeper levels. This is particularly true with water use. Grasses are very efficient water collectors in the top 12 inches of soil but are unable to make use of subsurface water.

Identifying Types of Grass

Sometimes, lawn lovers want to know whether the grass they are growing in their lawn is a lawn plant or a weed grass. My experience is that most garden center staff really cannot help with this problem because they are not trained in grass or turf management. What follows here is a basic course in grass leaf identification that will let you go out to your garden and identify all the different kinds of grass you are growing. Each of the grasses listed in the rest of this chapter is described using these anatomical structures, so you can take the book outside, lie down on the grass, and sort things out. To accomplish this job, however, you do have to stay awake while lying on the grass.

Let's start with the *collar*. This is where the blade of grass and sheath meet on the individual grass leaf. You can almost forget the collar because on most grass species, you won't be able to see it unless you're a trained botanist with a hand lens. I include it only because it's there and because on some species, it can be useful. If it is important, it will be listed under the appropriate grass species.

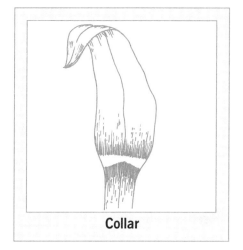

GOOD ROOTS =
GOOD GROWTH

Good roots on a plant almost always equal good tops and good growth. Emphasize the gardening techniques that grow good roots and you'll automatically have a good plant. This is as true for grass plants as it is for any other plant in your garden. You have to remember that your lawn is not a single thing; it is composed of thousands of individual grass plants, each with its own specific needs for growth and health. You are growing a lot of individual plants in that lawn so you have to take good care of them. Start with the roots.

Collar

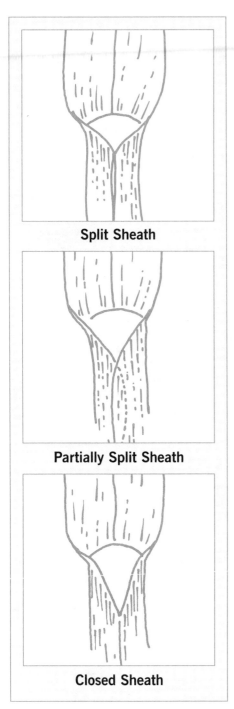

Split Sheath

Partially Split Sheath

Closed Sheath

The *sheath*, the rounded part of the grass leaf, runs between the collar and the leaf node. There are three kinds of sheaths: (1) split down its entire length, (2) split part of the way, or (3) closed along its entire length. Most good turfgrasses have sheaths that are split down their entire length. A split sheath will not help you identify which good grass you've got. However, if a sheath is not split along its entire length, you know it's probably a weed species. This is your first clue to weed grasses.

Look on the inner side of the grass leaf where the blade meets the sheath (the collar area). This is where you'll find the *ligule*. This tiny bit of botany is our first important feature. It will distinguish between the kinds of grass you want to grow in a grass family and those you don't. There are three kinds of ligule distinctions: (1) a "hairy" ligule with small hairs (the hairs are different lengths for different grass species), (2) a membrane ligule that resembles a small bit of skin, or (3) the complete absence of one.

Again, look at the collar area of your grass plant. There are three ways that the collar can join at the front of the sheath to form the *auricle*. This front of the collar area is quite distinctive and very useful in identifying grass species. Again, there are three choices: (1) long auricles that overlap, (2) short auricles that do not overlap, and (3) no auricle at all. In men's dress shirts, the analogy would be to the long pointed collars of the '70s, the button-down, non-overlapping collars of the '80s prep school, or the no-collar look of the '90s.

THE WONDERS OF TURF

A good lawn not only looks good, it provides other benefits when compared with surfaces such as pavement, artificial turf, or even flower gardens.

- *Improved water infiltration.* Water is more easily able to penetrate into soil when turf is present as opposed to hard packed bare soils. Grass roots help "open up" the soil for the water.
- *Erosion prevention.* The aboveground grass leaves and stems slow down the mad rush of water over the soil, preventing erosion. Grass roots with their dense, interlocking growth habit "lock" the soil particles together, preventing temporary, fast moving water streams from picking up soil particles and digging trenches. Run a stream of water at your lawn and then try it on bare garden soil to see the way grass prevents erosion.
- *Reduced surface temperatures.* Leaves have an evaporative cooling effect, so areas with lawns will be cooler than areas that have no vegetation.
- *Improved air quality.* Grass releases oxygen and absorbs carbon dioxide. The cumulative effect of a lawn is often understated;

thousands of plants on the average-size lawn are a good air production system.

- *Noise reduction.* The sound-buffering effect of thousands of blades of grass is considerable.
- *Absorption of pollutants.* Grass absorbs pollutants from the air, giving us cleaner air to breathe.
- *Excellent surface for sports.* If you've ever fallen on turf and compared it to being tackled on Astroturf, you'll understand why professional athletes would rather play on grass. It's softer, more resilient, and doesn't create ankle and knee injuries as frequently as do artificial surfaces. Also, how could you be a kid and not enjoy the mud of a good football game in the rain?
- *Oxygen production.* The end product of respiration in plants is oxygen. Tens of thousands of grass plants on your lawn are producing oxygen for you to breathe.

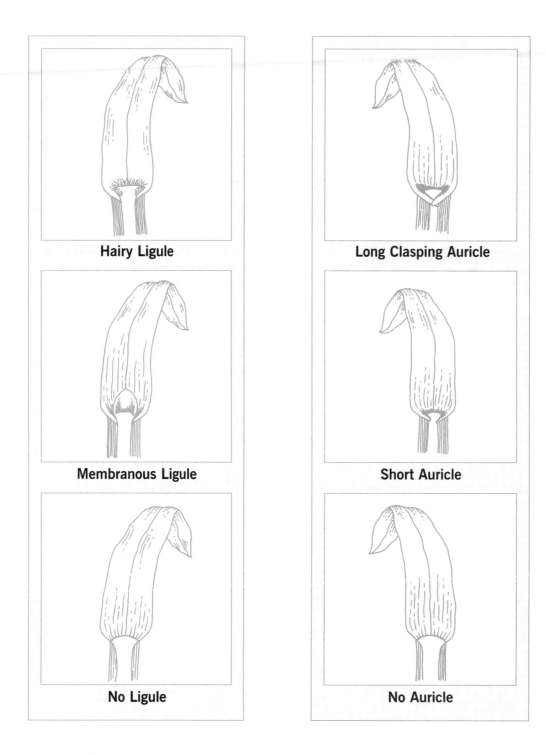

Hairy Ligule

Long Clasping Auricle

Membranous Ligule

Short Auricle

No Ligule

No Auricle

The *tip* of the leaf sometimes provides good identification clues. The first type is a pointed tip that looks like the sharp end of a pencil. The second type has tips shaped like the bow of a boat, with a rounded edge leading to an upfacing point, or simply two parallel sides coming together. A small trick to keep in mind if you are having trouble determining whether a leaf is boat shaped or pointed is to hold the tip of the grass leaf between your thumb and forefinger very gently and slowly apply pressure. If the leaf is boat-shaped, it will likely split into two parts under increasing pressure, while a pointed leaf will simply crush.

Vernation is the last characteristic to be considered. Again, this is very helpful when trying to distinguish between the good guys and the bad guys in a particular grass family. Vernation describes how the new grass blade comes out of the sheath. Is it folded or rolled? That's the difference, and you'll use it to tell the weedy grasses from the good grasses.

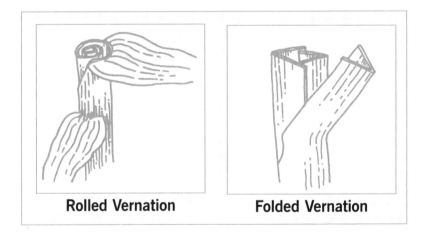

Rolled Vernation **Folded Vernation**

Now, that wasn't hard, was it? Time to play Sherlock Holmes.

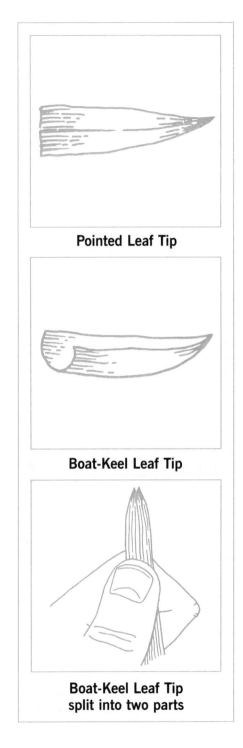

Pointed Leaf Tip

Boat-Keel Leaf Tip

Boat-Keel Leaf Tip split into two parts

Major Grasses and Their Features

Now that you know the basics of grass anatomy, you're ready to learn about the different varieties of grass plants. This section identifies the main grass plants that we find (or hope we find among the weeds) on our lawns. Each of these plants is botanically described and then the key growing features are outlined. If you're starting a lawn from scratch, this should help you decide on the kinds of grass you'll need for the lawn area you have in mind. Be sure to check the map to see whether you need northern or southern grasses. We'll cover specific details for growing these grasses later on.

Northern Lawn Grasses

Fescues

Tall Fescue *(Festuca arundinacea)*

Key Identification: Rolled vernation and pointed leaf tips. Possibly short ligules and auricles on species; sometimes the cultivars lack these last two characteristics.

Spreading System: Sometimes has short rhizomes, but is spread primarily by tillers.

Uses: Tall fescue grows in a wide range of soil types and is especially good in areas that are too cold for warm season grass and too hot for cold season grass. It has good shade tolerance, and, if irrigated, will stay green year round in warmer areas. It is extremely wear tolerant and well suited for athletic fields.

Advantages: If the temperatures are right and it has enough water, this grass will grow almost anywhere. It has excellent shade tolerance. It tolerates low fertility but responds well to minimal amounts of nitrogen—3 pounds per 1,000 square feet per year is adequate.

Disadvantages: It dies out in cold areas and has high water needs. In hot areas, its wear tolerance is not as good as Bermuda grass, so it is not used in playing fields in the southern part of the United States.

Cultivars: Adventure, Alta-Kenwell, Falcon, Kenhy, Kentucky-31, Olympic, Rebel. Bonsai is a dwarf variety.

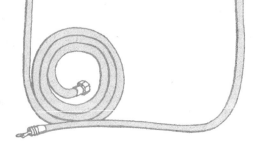

MAP OF GRASS GROWING ZONES

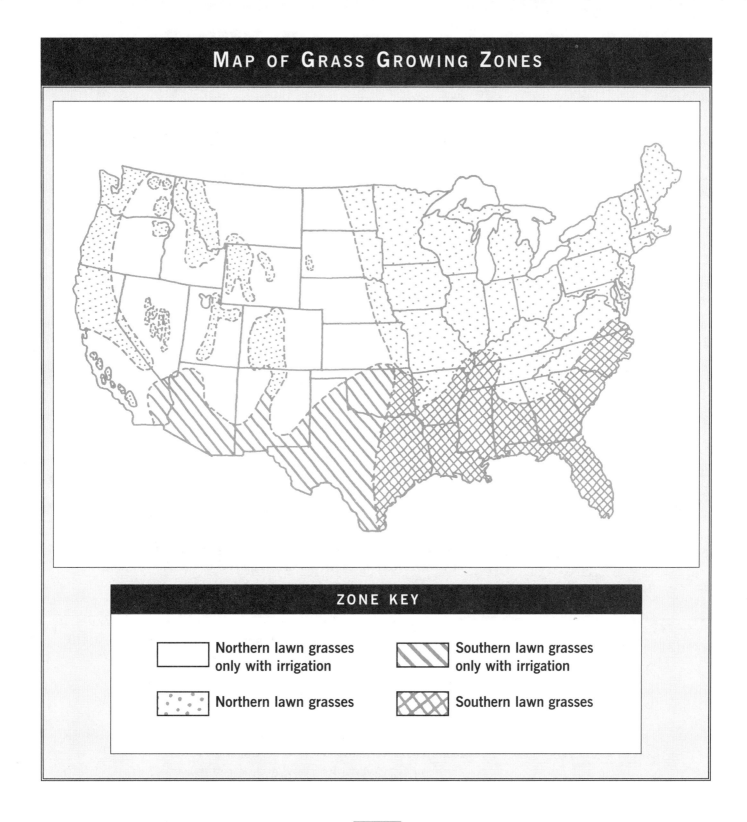

ZONE KEY

	Northern lawn grasses only with irrigation		Southern lawn grasses only with irrigation
	Northern lawn grasses		Southern lawn grasses

Cultivation Comments: Mow this grass at 2 inches during the fall and spring. If growing in shade or under drought conditions, mow to 3 inches tall. This grass requires frequent watering during high heat conditions. Thorough deep waterings are better than shallow watering. If there are dead patches, reseed in the fall, at 2 to 3 pounds of seed per 1,000 square feet.

Creeping Red Fescue *(Festuca rubra)*

Key Identification: Sheath is slightly wider than blade.

Spreading System: Short rhizomes.

Uses: It is well adapted to cool, moist situations or where humidity is high. Creeping red fescue is also very cold tolerant.

Advantages: It has good shade tolerance.

Disadvantages: It is susceptible to heat and drought.

Cultivars: Bargena, Boreal, Cindy, Dawson, Durlawn, Ensylva, Flyer, Fortress, Franklin, Herald, Jasper, Jasper E, Marker, Merlin, Medallion, Pennlawn, Recent, Reptans, Shademaster, SR 5200E, Vista.

Cultivation Comments: Although more tolerant than most of dry shade, this grass does better in sun with water and fertilizer. It does not grow back quickly when damaged, so it's probably not a good idea to make creeping red fescue into a children's play area. Do not overfeed it, or the quality of the turf will go down. Three pounds of nitrogen per 1,000 square feet per season is adequate for most purposes.

Chewings Fescue *(Festuca rubra* subspecies *fallax)*

Key Identification: Same as creeping red fescue but without rhizomes. Sheaths split upon maturity.

Spreading System: Seed.

Uses: This is one of best fescues for shade growing. It tolerates heat and drought stress a bit better than creeping red fescue.

Advantages: Similar to red fescue.

Disadvantages: Similar to red fescue.

Cultivars: Banner, Barfalla, Bridgeport, Center, Dignity, Enjoy, Epsom, Highlight, Jamestown, Koket, Longfellow, Luster, Mary, Menuet, Molinda, Rudax, Shadow, Southport, SR5000, SR5100, Tatiana, Treazure, Victory, Victory E, Waldorf, Wilma.

Growing Conditions: As per creeping red fescue.

GRASS WORD OF THE DAY

You can impress your neighbors at the next block party by using the word *topdress* properly. **Topdressing** means to put new seed, special feed, sand, or compost on top of the existing lawn without killing off the old grass. You *topdress* new seed or compost. On the other hand, you *apply* or *put* chemical fertilizer on your lawn. The only exception to this is if you are working on your backyard putting green and then *any* seed or feed you put on is topdressing.

KEEP OFF THE GRASS

NORTHERN LAWN GRASS SPECIES

Name	Propagation	Use	Advantages	Disadvantages
Tall fescue	Short rhizomes or tillers	Grows almost anywhere	Excellent shade tolerance	High water needs, can die out in very cold or hot areas
Creeping red fescue	Short rhizomes	Cool, moist turf areas	Tolerates shade and moist soils, winter hardy	Susceptible to heat and drought
Chewings fescue	Seed	Shady turf areas	Tolerates shade	Susceptible to heat and drought
Kentucky bluegrass	Rhizomes and tillers	General turf use	Fast recovery from wear or abuse, dense turf	Poor shade tolerance, requires regular watering
Rough bluegrass	Stolons	Lawns, golf courses	Winter hardy, low mowing tolerance	Poor wear tolerance, dense patchy growth
Annual bluegrass	Seed	Weed grass	Aggressive	Dies in winter, leaving brown patches
Canada bluegrass	Short rhizomes	Parks, low-maintenance areas	Tolerates wet or dry soils, some shade tolerance	No wear tolerance
Bent grass	Stolons	Weed or putting greens	Takes short mowing, reasonable wear	Very invasive, needs high maintenance to grow well
Red top	Rhizomes	Rough conditions	Tolerates wet soils	Short lived, does not withstand high temperatures or shade
Annual ryegrass	Seed	Temporary nurse crops	Fast germination	Short lived, does not mow
Perennial ryegrass	Seed	General turf areas	Fast establishment, good wear tolerance	Doesn't like poor drainage

HORTICULTURAL LATIN

Horticultural Latin uses two words to describe specific plants. A family name identifies all the grasses in a genetic family. In the case of bluegrass, the family name is *Poa*. To identify it as *Kentucky* bluegrass, we need another name—a specific name—and this is *pratensis*. Kentucky bluegrass is *Poa pratensis*. Rough bluegrass is *Poa trivialis*. Both bluegrass species are named *Poa*, but botanists and those involved in the turf industry can discuss them, and positively identify them in their discussions, by using the Latin specific descriptive name as well.

Aren't the common names good enough? The short answer is that common names vary from area to area. Although grass common names are not as variable as flower common names, there is still enough of a difference to make using the Latin worthwhile for those in the industry. For example, there are at least two different grass families commonly called crabgrass—depending on whether you live in North America or South America.

Both hard fescue (*Festuca brevipila*) and sheep fescue (*Festuca ovina*) perform much like red fescue and chewings fescue when it comes to household lawn management.

Bluegrasses

Kentucky Bluegrass (*Poa pratensis*)

Key Identification: Boat-shaped leaf tip and folded vernation. Kentucky bluegrass has a visible ligule and rhizomes; annual bluegrass is almost identical, except that it has neither a ligule nor rhizomes.

Spreading System: Rhizomes and tillers. A Kentucky bluegrass plant that is allowed to set seed will die soon after the seed has matured. Mature plants only live for two to three years at best. Encourage the rhizomes.

Uses: Lawns, golf courses, or anywhere a dense mat of turf is desired.

Advantages: The reason Kentucky bluegrass is so widely used is that it recovers quickly from cutting or abuse, and it survives drought and greens up quickly. The rhizomes grow and repair the turf area itself. It is a dense grass so that when it is mowed at a higher level (2½ to 3 inches) it prevents weed establishment. It has good disease and cold weather tolerance. When cut with a sharp mower, it cuts cleanly with little ripping.

Disadvantages: Kentucky bluegrass has a relatively shallow root system and a subsequent high demand for regular watering. It also has a poor tolerance for shade.

Cultivars: There are over three hundred cultivars in use. Planting a blend of different cultivars is often a good idea if a pure Kentucky bluegrass lawn is desired. The cultivars that are best adapted for shade with moderate tolerance include Bristol, Glad, Nugget, and Touchdown. Those best for warm areas are Adelphi, Baron, Fylking, Glade, and Midnight.

Cultivation Comments: High nitrogen fertilizers and frequent mowing will drastically reduce the root growth and the rhizome production of Kentucky bluegrass. High soil temperatures stop this grass from growing; with temperatures over 80°F, growth is virtually nonexistent.

Rough Bluegrass (*Poa trivialis*)

Key Identification: Boat-shaped leaf tip and folded vernation. Long membrane ligule, partly split sheath.

Spreading System: Stolons, seed if allowed to set.

Uses: Rough bluegrass can be used on lawns if it is irrigated and fertilized regularly. Golf courses use it because of its low mowing ability.

Advantages: It is very winter hardy and grows quickly in spring and fall. Rough bluegrass tolerates lower mowing heights and more shade than Kentucky bluegrass.

Disadvantages: It has poor wearing tolerance, recovers slowly from abuse, and is slow growing in the high heat of summer. Rough bluegrass has a dense patchy growth so it does not mix well with Kentucky bluegrass.

Cultivars: Colt, Cypress, Dark Horse, Laser, Sabre, Snowbird.

Cultivation Comments: Regular mowings, feeding, and irrigating are necessary to grow this species properly. Avoid light irrigations. When water is applied, do so heavily and then wait until the soil is dry to water again. Mowing can be as low as ½ inch. It is an excellent grass for topdressing because it establishes well from seed.

Annual Bluegrass (*Poa annua*)

Key Identification: Boat-shaped leaf tip and folded vernation. Membranous ligule.

Spreading System: Seed that germinates in the fall. The plant lives over the winter and sets seed in the spring.

Uses: This is a weed grass. Don't encourage it. It dies out in early summer leaving large brown patches in areas it has heavily colonized.

Advantages: This is aggressive grass will easily take over large areas if the grass is kept short, particularly in wetter and cooler climates. As taller turf, it shades and retards seed germination.

Canada Bluegrass (*Poa compressa*)

Key Identification: Flat compressed stems, boat shaped leaf tip, folded vernation and membranous ligule.

Spreading System: Short rhizomes.

LATIN AND BLUEGRASS: DESCRIPTIVE TRANSLATIONS

trivialis = "ordinary"
pratensis = "of the meadows"
annua = "annual"
compressa = "flattened"

KEEP OFF THE GRASS

PHOTOSYNTHESIS

Photosynthesis is a term we all heard about in grade school science class. Here's a quick refresher course:

Energy from the sun combines with carbon dioxide from the atmosphere, hydrogen and oxygen from water, and all the minerals and nutrients absorbed by a plant's roots to produce a series of products. These products include starches, proteins, sugars, fats, waxes, lignin, cellulose, hormones, and a multitude of enzymes.

The photosynthesis happens in the plant leaves where energy from the sun sets off a very complicated chemical process. The end products are a series of carbon products that contain energy. These products can be used either by the plant or by any other of Earth's inhabitants that use grass as a food source.

The entire world's population, both animal and human, depends on photosynthesis for life.

Uses: A loose turf for low-maintenance areas used in parks and in low traffic areas.

Advantages: It grows better than most on wet, poorly drained, or dry soils. Soils that are wet in spring and fall but dry during the summer are good candidates. It is tolerant of some shade.

Disadvantages: This grass does not recover well from wear. It has loose turf, not thick and dense.

Cultivars: Canon, Reubens

Cultivation Comments: Mow this species high, at 2 inches or more. Its recuperative ability is better at higher cuts than under intensive cutting. It is a good grass for poor areas of fertility or light where a thick turf is not needed. Annual bluegrass responds well to a low-maintenance system of feeding (3 pounds of nitrogen per 1,000 square feet of turf per year).

Bent grass (*Agrostis palustris*)
Creeping Bent grass

Key Identification: Rolled vernation and pointed tip. Membranous ligule and prominent veins on upper side of leaf.

Spreading System: Stolons—and lots of them.

Uses: Golf putting greens, specialty turf areas.

Advantages: Creeping bent grass has a fine texture and takes low cutting very well. It is winter hardy and has very good recuperative ability when damaged.

Disadvantages: It is a major weed in home lawns and requires high maintenance to grow well on golf courses. Creeping bent grass is disease prone, has high requirements for water and feeding, and a high tendency to thatch.

Cultivation Comments: Feed $1/3$ pound of nitrogen per 1,000 square feet per month for high maintenance golf greens. Mow every two to three days. Water regularly, at least $1\frac{1}{2}$ inches of water a week, by irrigation or natural sources. Watch for molds, especially in spring. To eliminate it from lawns, mow very high and topdress in the fall with aggressive grass species such as perennial rye.

Red Top (*Agrostis alba*)

Key Identification: Similar to creeping bent grass. Pointed leaf tip, rolled vernation. Upper side of leaf has very visible veins. Membranous ligule is rounded and quite visible.

Spreading System: Rhizomes.

Uses: Roadsides, ditches.

Advantages: Red top grows in rough conditions, tolerates wet soils, and has no shade tolerance. Because of its fast germination, it is sometimes used as a nurse grass.

Disadvantages: It is a rough, open, short lived grass. If used as a nurse grass, it tends to die out after a few years except for a tuft or two here and there on the lawn. Red top does not withstand high temperatures or shade.

Cultivation Comments: Tall or infrequent mowing will keep it alive and turn into a perennial lawn. Feed at 2 pounds per 1,000 square feet per year. Short mowing, under 3 inches, will shorten its life. Intensive lawn management will eliminate red top from a Kentucky bluegrass lawn.

Ryegrass

Annual Ryegrass (*Lolium multiflorum*)

Key Identification: Rolled vernation (note: perennial ryegrass is folded) and a pointed leaf tip. Extended, clawlike auricles and a very broad collar. The upper side of the leaf has prominent veins.

Spreading System: Seed.

Uses: Temporary nurse crops for better species, particularly on rough ground. No use in good turf areas.

Advantages: Fast germination.

Disadvantages: Annual ryegrass does not mow well. It shreds rather than cuts It is also short-lived.

Cultivation Comments: Do not grow annual ryegrass; cheap grass mixtures are often 50 percent annual ryegrass and are a waste of money: the grass will die out, and until it does, it will look ugly.

Thatch is a dense layer of living and dead organic matter that accumulates between the soil surface and green matter. If it is too thick, it can create unfavorable conditions for grass.

• • •

Nurse grass is a term used by gardeners to describe a fast growing, short lived grass species that is planted with a slow growing, long lived species. The nurse grass establishes itself quickly to prevent water erosion and soil compaction or blowing. As the nurse grass is dying out over the winter or in its second or third growing season, the long-term grass is establishing itself in the good soil environment that has been protected by the "nurse" grass.

PLANT A MIX

When choosing a lawn grass, keep in mind that a lawn with a large mix of grass species will do better than a single-species lawn. Why? Because when summer conditions are right for a fescue, the fescue grass will thrive and give you a good-looking lawn. If conditions change to favor bluegrass, then the bluegrass will thrive. Planting a mix is like planting an insurance policy.

Most homeowners seem to think that they want a Kentucky bluegrass lawn. The reality is that unless you are a turf expert, you won't be able to tell the difference between Kentucky bluegrass and perennial ryegrass. They're both green and they're both grass.

Plant a mix to find out what grows best in your lawn. Mother Nature will help you choose your lawn species.

Perennial Ryegrass (*Lolium perenne*)

Key Identification: Folded vernation, pointed leaf tip. Prominent veins on upper side of leaf. Membranous ligule and short auricles. (To confuse the issue, many of the new cultivars have no visible ligule and short auricles.) Broad collar.

Spreading System: Seed.

Uses: Lawns, fairways, playing fields. Perennial ryegrass blends well with Kentucky bluegrass on home lawns.

Advantages: Fast establishment, good tolerance to wear and traffic, some shade tolerance. It germinates at low temperatures and establishes well if sown directly into established turf. It is less susceptible to some diseases than Kentucky bluegrass.

Disadvantages: Perennial ryegrass is not as cold tolerant as Kentucky bluegrass, especially if grown poorly or on poorly drained soils. It can develop into clumpy grass tufts unless density is maintained by overseeding.

Cultivation Comments: Grow it as you would Kentucky bluegrass. Do not mow lower than 1½ inches for best results. Overseed the area every spring at 2 pounds per 1,000 square feet to keep the turf filled in and growing densely. Feed nitrogen at 2 to 3 pounds per 1,000 square feet per season.

Southern Lawn Grasses

Bermuda Grass (*Cynodon* species)

Key Identification: Folded vernation and a fringe of hairs at the ligule. No auricles.

Spreading System: Vigorous rhizomes and stolons.

Uses: Lawns, parks, school grounds, playing fields, golf courses in tropical or subtropical areas.

Advantages: This grass is very tolerant of low mowing. It also has good tolerance to compaction and wear and tear. Bermuda grass responds well to moderate fertilizing, frequent mowing, and average moisture conditions. It will tolerate droughts but does best where rainfall is 25 to 100 inches per year. It is salt tolerant.

Disadvantages: Easily killed by cool temperatures (under 30°F). Bermuda grass will stop growing when soil temperatures reach 50°F.

It has poor shade tolerance. This species needs less water than culti-vars (as a rule of thumb) and cultivars may thin out during a drought.

Cultivars: Champion, Floradwarf, Midiron, Midlawn, Midfield, Nu-Mex Sahara, Princess, Texturf, Tiffine, Tifgreen, Tifdwarf, TifEagle, Tiflawn, Tifway, U-3.

Cultivation Comments: Though Bermuda grass survives drought, it does go brown, so regular irrigation is best. This grass has a very dense root system and is capable of using whatever water is available. Water deeply to encourage deep and drought-resistant root growth. Drainage must be good; it does not tolerate poorly drained areas. This is a greedy feeder and to keep it growing thickly, apply 1 to 1½ pounds of nitrogen per 1,000 square feet per month while it is actively growing. Do not apply any less than ½ pound of nitrogen or the grass will start to thin out.

St. Augustine Grass (*Stenotaphrum secundatum*)

Key Identification: Boat-tip leaf, folded leaf blades, short fringe of hairs on ligules. The blade normally turns 90 degrees from the sheath at the collar.

Spreading System: Stolons, can be quite long.

Uses: This grass is adapted for moist, coastal areas with mild winters. Assuming good fertility and water availability, it will survive in almost any soil. General lawn use.

Advantages: It tolerates more shade than other warm season grasses and stays green longer under stress, particularly heat stress. It thrives in damp spots.

Disadvantages: St. Augustine grass is not at all cold tolerant. Will not survive drought conditions.

Cultivars: Bitter Blue, Floratam, Floratine, Raleigh, Seville, Texas Common. Mostly propagated from stolons, plugs, or sod, so seeding is not an option.

Cultivation Comments: In early spring and later summer or fall when the temperatures are lower, this grass is a slow grower requiring mowing every two weeks. As the temperatures rise to midsummer values, the growth rate increases and mowing will become an every five-day chore. The more shade this grass is given, the higher the

GOOD GRASS FROM THE GROUND UP

The reality of growing good grass is that the more time and effort you put into estab-lishing the belowground environment, the easier it will be to grow the above-ground portion of the plant. Get the soil right and the grass will follow.

KEEP OFF THE GRASS

mower deck should be set, up to 3 inches for any shade over a few hours a day. Increase the mowing height in the fall to increase the amount of energy the roots can store to assist in overwintering. During the growing season, fertilize at 1 pound of nitrogen per 1,000 square feet per month. Any more than this will lead to excessive growth rates that lead to insect infestations. This grass is sensitive to iron deficiency. On alkaline soils, spraying iron sulfate on the leaves will reduce the pale green, chlorotic symptoms. If the mower deck is kept too short, the stolons will be cut and the thick growth of the grass will be checked. Thin grass stands are prone to invasion by weeds.

Zoysia Grass (*Zoysia* species)

Key Identification: Ligule fringed like Bermuda grass, but with a rolled vernation. No auricles. Leaf blades are generally smooth, sometimes with small hairs near the base.

Spreading System: Both stolons and rhizomes.

Uses: General turf grass.

Advantages: Tolerates moderate shade, salt, and wear. Extremely drought tolerant and while it does go yellow brown under drought, it responds quickly to water by greening up again.

Disadvantages: Recovers slowly from excessive wear. Zoysia grass makes a good baseball field, but a poor football field. The football wear area is concentrated in a limited area and with that damage, zoysia grass will not recover well. It does not tolerate poorly drained areas.

Cultivars: Belair, El Toro, Emerald, Meyer.

Cultivation Comments: This grass requires at least 1 inch of water per week in summer to keep it growing and green. Its fertilizer needs are not as intensive as other southern grasses. Feeding 1 pound of nitrogen per 1,000 square feet of turf every two to three months will keep this grass growing well. Under these watering and feeding conditions, the grass will require mowing to 2 inches once every five to seven days. If you're growing zoysia grass in the shade, mow at least 1 inch higher to allow the grass to store energy from the increased leaf surface. Zoysia grass does tend to develop thatch conditions under excessive fertilizing. Consider removing the grass clippings if this is a problem.

DOG'S TOOTH GRASS

Bermuda grass is named *Cynodon* in Horticultural Latin; this translates from the Greek as dog's tooth. (*kyon* = dog and *odous* = tooth)

Can you imagine why anyone would call this grass a dog's tooth?

For northern gardeners, it's because of the sharp pointed tips and stiff blades.

KEEP OFF THE GRASS

As a last note on this important grass, you can always be the hit of a neighborhood barbecue when you point out that zoysia grass was named after Karl von Zoys, an Austrian botanist who lived between 1756 and 1800.

Bahia Grass (*Paspalum* species)

Key Identification: May have rolled as well as folded vernation on same plant. Short, membranous ligule. Very broad blades and widely spaced covering of hair on sheaths.

Spreading System: Short woody rhizomes, but can set seed.

Uses: Low maintenance on roadsides and slope stabilization. Lawns, golf courses

Advantages: Very salt tolerant. Very aggressive; it will crowd out other grass species. This grass also thrives in moist sites.

Disadvantages: Bahia grass forms a thick thatch quite easily. It is not cold tolerant.

Cultivars: Agrentine, Pensacola.

Cultivation Comments: Bahia grass an be mowed to almost any height (even 1 inch or less) if the watering needs are met. Feed it in the spring and fall but not during the height of the summer heat.

Centipede Grass (*Eremochloa ophiuroides*)

Key Identification: Membranous ligule with short hairs on top of ligule. Hairy collar and hairs along the edges of the lower part of the leaves.

Spreading System: Stolons as well as seed if allowed to set seed.

Uses: Golf courses and parks, but not on playing fields or child play areas because it does not tolerate high rates of abuse. Use where you don't want to mow often (e.g., on slopes or ditch areas).

Advantages: It grows quite slowly and requires less mowing than other warm season grasses. Centipede grass is easy to establish.

Disadvantages: This grass is severely knocked back or killed by cold temperatures. Varying temperatures between frosty nights and warm days are particularly hard on this plant. It will come back from one or two frosts, but after that, the root energy reserves are spent and so is the grass.

Cultivars: Oaklawn, Tifblair

SPECIAL CARE FOR SOUTHERN SOIL

One of the problems with tropical soil and organic matter is that as soon as soil temperatures go over 88°F, the soil's organic matter is destroyed faster than it can be produced. Therefore, tropical soils are usually devoid of organic matter, and the plants hold all the organic matter in living tissue. Tropical soil's lack of organic matter can have a profound influence on the ability of southern areas to grow a good stand of turfgrass. Without organic matter and the reserves of nutrients, water, and its pest-fighting abilities, southern turf can be drastically influenced in times of stress.

To alleviate this problem, mow southern grasses taller than normal. The extra height allows the extra leaf surface to shade the soil, reducing the soil temperature. The extra blade length also leads to the production and storage of more nutrients in the leaves. If the clippings are left where they fall instead of being picked up, they will also help shade the soil surface, as well as add to the organic matter of the soil.

Cultivation Comments: A very warm season grass, centipede grass is currently found in northern Florida and the Gulf Coast states. It prefers a sandy, acidic soil although it thrives on moderate feeding. Do not exceed 3 pounds of nitrogen per 1,000 square feet. Low fertilization rates (1 pound of nitrogen per 1,000 square feet in the spring and again in the fall) and barely enough water to keep this grass from wilting create a low maintenance area. Mow tall (2 to 3 inches); it does not tolerate short mowing.

Carpetgrass (*Axonopus affinis*)

Key Identification: Folded vernation and a fringe of short hairs on the ligule. Wide leaves with blunt rounded tips. Nodes may be covered with dense hairs.

Spreading System: Flat stolons that root at every node.

Uses: Low-maintenance areas and roadsides.

Advantages: Good on sandy and moist soils. Carpetgrass tolerates more shade and moisture than Bermuda grass.

Disadvantages: This grass does not thicken up like Bermuda grass. It produces a lot of seedstalks very quickly and at low heights creating a visually ugly lawn, which necessitates frequent mowing as prevention. It does not grow well in drought conditions.

Cultivation Comments: While carpetgrass does well under conditions of poor fertility, feeding at 1 pound of nitrogen per 1,000 square feet per month will keep it growing well and assist it to fill in. Mow frequently (weekly) to keep the seedheads cut off and mow to 1 to 2 inches in height.

Kikuyu Grass (*Pennisetum clandestinum*)

Key Identification: Light green in color, a fringe of hairs on the ligule, and a folded vernation. Sheaths are covered with fine hairs, with slightly longer hairs on the collar area.

Spreading System: Rhizomes and stolons mostly, although does set seed and is very aggressive.

Uses: This is a weed grass that can crowd out other desirable species in tropical areas.

GRASS IN HISTORY

In the English countryside, children who ran into stinging nettles were quick to pull a handful of grass and briskly rub it onto their stinging flesh while chanting,

"Nettle come out—grass go in."

It comes highly recommended in books of folklore.

• • •

SEEDHEAD

Seedhead is one of those gardening terms that is as simple as it sounds. It's the flower part of the grass that has gone to seed. The flower is found on top of the stalk. And no, you're not really going to get brownie points if you give a bouquet of grass flowers for Valentine's Day.

WHISTLING WITH GRASS LEAVES

Every school-age child growing up in the country learned to whistle with grass leaves. As a boy, I would regularly grab a particularly attractive leaf blade for our musical ensembles. I taught all my children how to whistle and still manage a few "tunes" every spring just to keep my hand in.

It is much easier to learn to do this as a child but a childlike attitude will suffice. Here goes.

Hold your hands as if in prayer, with your thumbs and thumb pads pressed together. Slightly rotate your thumbs until the thumbs are squarely facing you without losing contact with each other. If you have good grass whistle–blowing hands, there will be a slight space between the first and second knuckle joints on your thumbs.

Slightly bend your thumbs. Put the long blade of grass—thin side toward you—on the pads of your thumbs and then hold the other end firmly with the ends of your bent thumbs. By straightening your thumbs you can increase the tension on the grass stalk. You need to create a reasonable tension because you are going to blow across the stalk into the small space created by your thumbs.

If you get the tension just right and blow just right—you can make a wonderful squacking noise. And that is whistling with grass leaves.

It is a particularly delightful activity to indulge in while lying on a huge expanse of long grass on a sunny, cloudless day. Two or more grass whistlers are needed for a good grass band—and a good time.

THE GRASS OF THE FUTURE

Buffalo grass is currently the darling of the no-work lawn crowd, and it bears investigating. This grass is a native plains grass and grows to about 6 inches tall before it simply stops growing. The new cultivars are extremely heat *and* cold tolerant as well as drought tolerant. The sure way to kill buffalo grass is to water it like a normal lawn! Another way to kill it is to mow it too short, too often.

So no watering and no mowing! Hmmm, I'll have to think about this one.

Buffalo grass also requires minimal fertilization. Plan on using plugs that contain only female plants; they do not produce pollen. No grass pollen equals no allergies to the lawn. Once established, buffalo grass forms a tight sod that resists weed infestations, and who wouldn't want one of those.

This grass will survive in the dry South, the cold Midwest, and even in the Northeast if the area is not one of high rainfall. This could be the grass of the future.

Advantages: An aggressive grass that takes short mowing well.

Disadvantages: It forms thatch quickly and needs extensive aeration to form a good turf. This grass does not survive in any cold temperatures. It also tends to form unsightly seedheads immediately after mowing.

Buffalo Grass (*Buchloe dactyloides*)

Key Identification: Fine hairs on both sides of the blade. Curled and twisted leaves. Hair fringe on ligule and rolled vernation.

Spreading System: Stolons and seed.

Uses: Adapted to low rainfall areas, buffalo grass is ideal as a grass for naturalizing wildflowers because it makes an open, thin turf area. It is a low-maintenance grass for low-use areas.

Advantages: Very drought tolerant.

Disadvantages: Cannot stand traffic or short cutting. Does not tolerate shade.

Cultivation Comments: Do not irrigate this grass or feed it. It is best adapted to receiving 15 to 30 inches of water per year. Mow when needed to 2 to 3 inches tall. Shorter mowing weakens this grass. Do not feed any more than 2 pounds of nitrogen per 1,000 square feet per year. If watered at 1 inch per week in the heat of the summer, it will stay green through the summer months; otherwise it browns.

Bluegrama (*Bouteloua gracilis*)

Key Identification: Folded vernation and fringe of hairs at the ligule. Leaves come to a sharp point.

Spreading System: Short rhizomes.

Uses: Low-maintenance turf area in dry areas.

Advantages: Bluegrama forms a low, open turf used in low-maintenance areas such as roadsides. It tolerates dry conditions very well.

Disadvantages: Open turf that is not dense.

SOUTHERN LAWN GRASS SPECIES

NAME	PROPAGATION	USE	ADVANTAGES	DISADVANTAGES
Bermuda Grass	Vigorous rhizomes and stolons	General turf areas	Tolerant of low mowing and wear and tear	Poor shade tolerance
St. Augustine Grass	Stolons	General lawn grass, especially in moist coastal areas	Shade, heat, and moist soil tolerant	No cold tolerance, not drought tolerant
Zoysia Grass	Stolons and rhizomes	General turf grass	Tolerates moderate shade and salt, very wear tolerant, extremely drought tolerant	Slow recovery from excessive wear, not tolerant of wet soils
Bahia Grass	Rhizomes and seed	Low maintenance and slope stabilization	Salt tolerant, very aggressive, tolerates moist soils	Not cold tolerant, forms thatch very easily
Centipede Grass	Stolons and seed	Good turf on sandy, acidic soils	Slow growing, easy to establish	Cold weather kills it easily
Carpet Grass	Stolons	Low-maintenance areas and roadsides	Tolerates shade and moist soils	Thin turf, not drought tolerant, forms ugly seedheads right after mowing
Kikuyu Grass	Rhizomes and stolons	Weed grass	Can take short mowing, aggressive spreader	Needs intensive management to make good turf
Buffalo Grass	Stolons and seed	Dry areas, for naturalizing wildflowers	Drought tolerant	Doesn't wear well, can't tolerate shade
Bluegrama	Rhizomes	Low maintenance for dry areas	Tolerates dry conditions	Not a dense turf

Buying Grass Seed

There are not all that many tricks to reading a grass seed label once you know what all the numbers really mean.

- Examine the list of seed varieties and see whether the varieties are listed or whether the seed is simply generic. For example, does the label say "Liberty Kentucky bluegrass" or simply "Kentucky bluegrass"? Cheaper seed mixes will not identify the variety.

- Ensure the germination percentages are the highest possible. At least 75 percent for Kentucky bluegrass and 85 percent for all others.

- Under "other ingredients" check for weed seed. The lower the percentage, the better. Anything over .5 percent is best left on the shelf for both weed seed and other crop seed categories.

- Inert matter (stuff that is organic but will not grow) should be no more than 5 percent of the total package.

- Avoid packages that have annual grasses in them, particularly if you are establishing a perennial lawn. Annual ryegrass is the one exception. It is sometimes used as a nurse grass or erosion control grass; if listed, the amount should be 5 percent or lower.

XYZ Brand
Lawn Seed Mixture

PURE SEED	SEED VARIETY	GERMINATION
60%	Liberty Kentucky bluegrass	85%
15%	Jamestown Chewings fescue	85%
24.55%	Manhattan II perennial ryegrass	90%

OTHER INGREDIENTS

0.26%	Other crop seed	
0.10%	Weed seed	
	No noxious weed seed	
0.09%	Inert matter	

Tested January 1993
Lot No. 1002

XYZ Super Seed Co., Anytown, OH 44118

CHAPTER TWO

How To Start a Good Lawn

There are a few magical steps in establishing a good lawn area. Like cooking with a good recipe, you have to accomplish each step properly in order for the final product to come out right. So, here's the step-by-step method of establishing a good lawn from scratch.

Level and Grade the Soil

As with any form of gardening, the soil is the key to success. Good soil grows good grass plants, and this is how to get your soil right. The very first step is to ensure that the grading around your home is done correctly. To get this right, do the grading in several steps: pregrading, subsurface grading, and finish grading.

Pregrading

The first step, sometimes known as *pregrading,* is when you remove all the rocks, sticks, and any other debris. All rocks larger than three-quarters of an inch should be removed from the lawn because they will interfere with mowing and cultivation. If you have quite a few of these small rocks, rock-picking machines can be rented from the local rental company. These machines work wonders with small stones and save countless hours of backbreaking work. As a kid, when my brother and I handpicked all the rocks in the backyard so my Dad could have a proper lawn instead of a hayfield, I would have killed for one of those machines.

If your home is new construction or renovation, there will inevitably be wood debris scattered around. These remnants must be removed. On my radio program, I get quite a few calls asking why mushrooms are growing in the middle of the lawn of new homes. Just about every time, they can be traced back to some old, leftover lumber that has been buried in the backfill rather than removed. Decaying wood is the preferred host to a variety of mushrooms, providing all the nutrition they need for good growth in your lawn. Not only that, but often a problem will happen season after season in one particular part of the lawn. Only after digging up the chunk of plywood does the homeowner realize that the drainage and fertility of this area were nonexistent because of the wood barrier between the turf and the soil.

STOP WEEDS BEFORE THEY START

Control weeds at the pregrading stage. If you get rid of the perennial weeds at pregrading it is a lot easier to establish grass plants. As you dig and cultivate the soil, be sure to remove all existing roots. This will ensure that weeds will not compete with your newly emerging baby grass plants.

Southern homeowners should be aware that allowing old construction wood to stay in the ground is like leaving dinner invitations out for termites. Remove this wood now or face problems in the future.

Once all the wood, sticks, stones, and weeds are removed, it's time for the real work to begin. Subsurface and surface grading are at the bottom of lawn construction (literally) and are two of the unseen causes of lawn problems and failures. Let's deal with them individually.

Subsurface Grading

The operating rule of thumb for grading is that all grades should slope away from buildings at a minimum slope of one degree. Any contours should be gradual, so that once the lawn grows in, mowing machines can easily work the slopes and curves. Any slope over 33 degrees should not be considered for grass but should be treated as an alternative turf area.

The subsurface grading (subgrading) should establish the grading contours for the finishing grading to follow. That is, the subgrade should look exactly like the finished grading (only lower). Do not plan on leaving high spots with less topsoil or filling low spots with extra topsoil, because the drainage will be changed by doing so. If the planned finished gradient away from the building is 5 degrees, then the subgrading should be 5 degrees too.

This is more important than you might think at first glance. Water moves downward in soil and even if the surface water moves away from the building because of proper surface grading, the water that is absorbed by the soil is still moving downward. When this absorbed water hits the subsoil or subgrade layer, it will tend to follow along the grading of the subsoil rather than continuing downward. If this subgrade layer has a different gradient or direction than the surface layer, the water will follow the lower gradient. In other words, if the subgrade has a puddle or sunken area, the water will congregate in this area. It will show up as a wet spot in the lawn or an area that does not dry as quickly as the rest of the lawn. The grass will always be greener and taller in this area.

ALTERNATIVE TURF AREA

An **alternative turf area** is a fancy way of saying that you'll have trouble growing grass in that area. You might already know the problem. It may be too much shade, too steep a slope, or too much water—to name a few conditions under which lawn grass will not thrive. Alternative turf areas get their own chapter—see Chapter 9—to solve the problem of not being able to support good grass growth.

The worst scenario is if the subgrade slopes toward the house while the finish grading slopes away from it. The water will percolate down through the finish grading and then will follow the lower gradient right into the basement! And, to make matters worse, you won't know why. To avoid problems, you have to ensure that the subsoil gradient moves away from the house at the same slope as the final topsoil gradient.

Before we go on to finish grading and soil preparation, be sure to read the sidebar about drainage. If you have problems moving water away from the house because of natural factors such as nearby swamps or clay subsoil, you should install drainage tiles before you think about finish grading.

Finish Grading

As the name suggests, finish grading is laying down good topsoil to create the final layer of soil that will support your lawn. There are several important points to consider in this process.

- The topsoil should be equally applied throughout the lawn area to correspond to the subgrading.
- A minimum of 8 inches of good topsoil is necessary for a good lawn if the subsoil is heavy clay or fill sand. If the subsoil is better, then as little as 4 inches of topsoil is acceptable. Rule of thumb for topsoil: *More is better.*
- Add an inch of topsoil and then rototill it deeply (as deeply as the tines of your tiller will reach—a minimum of 6 inches) into the subsoil. Add a second inch and repeat the rototilling to a depth of 4 to 6 inches. Add the third inch of topsoil and till to 2 to 3 inches. This reduces the stratification between the subsoil and the topsoil layers. This is one of the most important steps you'll take in preparing your soil. The success and failure of the drainage on your lawn will largely depend on this step.
- After tilling in 2 to 3 inches of topsoil, add the remainder of the topsoil to the lawn area. Rake it out and remove any rocks, weeds, or debris to get a good level planting surface. This is the last chance to get rid of any imperfections

DRAINAGE

If your future lawn is in a low-lying area or features poorly drained soils such as clay, it will benefit considerably from the installation of drainage tiles or pipes. This is a job for a contractor with a laser level (water has to run downhill) and a trench-digging machine (unless you think hand-digging 30-inch deep trenches is interesting work). The tiles should be laid 30 inches deep and covered with at least 1 inch of washed gravel. Using long lengths of perforated plastic tile is much easier than the old clay tiles we used to see in the industry—the only thing you have to remember about plastic is to lay it so the holes face down.

There are plastic joints you can buy to join the pieces of tile together, but a sheet of plastic taped over the joint with black electrical tape works quite well, too. And, although the distance between trenches on any given lawn will be equal, different lawns will require different distances between the trenches. These will range from 15 feet on lawns that are quite wet or very heavy clay to 25 feet for drier or sandier soils. The tiles should all run toward the lowest spot on the lawn and be plumbed out to a catch basin or underground reservoir system. Some more elaborate systems use pumps to move the water up and off the property via surface drainage routes. If possible, the drainage tiles should be opened up to a boundary ditch where the water can run off by natural surface drainage.

The time of construction of a drainage system is also the time to consider an irrigation system. It is much cheaper to install one during construction than it is to dig up an established lawn to lay down an irrigation system.

A good drainage contractor will understand and can deal with all drainage problems and municipal requirements. These people will save you money in the long run.

(bumps and miniature lakes) in the lawn grading. Do not rush this step. Remember that you're laying the surface for mowing. The better the surface at this step, the easier and smoother your mowing will be after the grass is established.

- If you've gotten this far, relax in the shade with a cool drink. You've earned it.

BOUNDARY ZONE IN A FLOWER POT

The boundary zone problem with water is why we never put rocks in the bottom of a flower pot as the old wives' tale used to tell us to do. The rocks actually stop the water from moving rather than improve the drainage. Lawns work (on a bigger scale) in exactly the same manner.

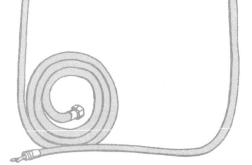

The boundary layer between soil types (topsoil and subsoil) is important to understand. Water doesn't just move downward through the soil; it is influenced by the physics of that soil. Water moves downward through the topsoil to the subsoil; and when it hits a layer that has different drainage properties than the one it is in, it stops. We call these areas of soil change *boundary zones*. They occur even when water is moving from topsoil to sand (you'd think the water would speed up, but it doesn't) and from sand to topsoil. Believe it or not, the change from topsoil to a rock drainage area is a boundary zone, and there will even be a wet zone around drainage tiles.

The movement of water through these boundary zones is determined by many factors. Without going into the physics of water movement, let's just say that the water stops and creates a wet layer every time it hits a soil boundary zone. Once the amount of draining water backs up and is heavy enough to overcome the resistance to moving through the layer, the water will begin draining again. This creates several considerations for our lawns and drainage.

First, if the topsoil is shallow and not enough water is applied to force it past the shallow boundary zone, root growth in the drier area below the wet boundary zone will be effectively stopped. There will be reduced water levels below the boundary, and the grass roots will not grow through to a drier soil. When drought hits, the grass will be in a weakened state with a reduced root zone.

Second, this boundary zone between the good topsoil and the subsoil becomes a conduit of water movement. Water does not percolate downward but instead moves along the boundary zone and is lost to lower tree roots and shrub roots as well. Water will take the path of least resistance.

This is why we till in the first several inches of topsoil. By mixing the two layers, we are creating a transition layer in which the soil is neither topsoil nor subsoil. This process will eliminate the abrupt transition layer that would have stopped the water, and will improve drainage.

Water will percolate downward to be made available to deep grass roots and even deeper roots of other plants in the garden area.

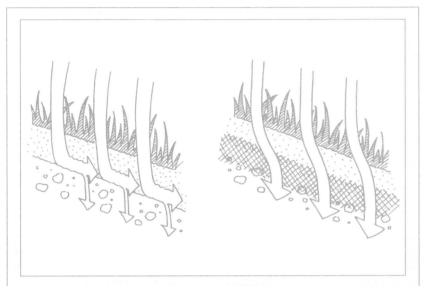

STEEP BOUNDARY ZONES

Test the Soil

No matter what method you choose to establish your lawn—seed or sod—you'll want to have a soil test done first. A soil test will give you the correct amounts of nutrients and amendments needed by the soil to get your lawn started properly.

Make sure you test the topsoil, not the subsoil. Subsoil tests will not be accurate for growing good turf.

To take a representative sample of your lawn, follow these directions:

- Use a clean plastic bucket. Metal buckets will interfere with the sample.
- Dig a small hole about 9 inches deep or the depth of your shovel blade. With your shovel, slice another thin section of dirt from the side of the hole from top to bottom. This sliced-off soil layer (like the side of a cake) is your sample. Put it into a clean bucket.
- Fill in the hole with the remaining soil. You only took a slice from the hole, top to bottom, to give a representative sample of the entire 9-inch depth.
- Use at least two samples from each 1,000 square feet of lawn.
- Put all samples into the same bucket.
- Mix all the samples together with your hand or a plastic tool. This will give a representative sample of the entire area.
- Do not use a rusty shovel to do the digging. Rust or iron particles in the sample will ruin the results.
- After the soil is well mixed, fill the sample bag or bags with the mixed soil, depending on the instructions in the soil test kit.
- Send the sample to the lab as soon as possible. Do not allow it to dry out or sit around on a counter.

Prepare the Soil

Now that the grading has been done and everything is almost ready to go, it is time to do the final preparation. The final preparation makes sure that:

- Organic matter is tilled in.
- The ground is level.
- Starter fertilizer is applied.
- The soil is firmed up for seeding or sodding.

PLANNING MAKES PERFECT

Planning is very important in getting the soil test done on time. It will take several weeks to get the sample to the lab and to get the results back. You'll have to take this into account in your work schedule. As soon as any topsoil is brought to your property, take a sample and send it off.

• • •

IF YOU SKIP THE SOIL TEST

If you do not want to take a soil test, then you can add 10 pounds of 10-20-20 fertilizer to every 1,000 square feet and call it a day. This is not as good as taking a soil test, but it is the standard extension service recommendation for lawn establishment in average soils.

Compost: A Lawn's Best Friend

Throughout this book, I'll advise adding organic matter or compost to the soil. Before we progress further, I'd like to discuss this for a moment. In nature, all of the organic debris from the forest to the prairies is recycled back into the soil. Everything—dead leaves, animal residues—you name it—gets recycled. In our modern urban world, we've lost that recycled health. We send out leaves and grass clippings to be recycled somewhere else other than our own lawn; flower tops and waste from our kitchens are still not recycled in the majority of North American homes. We go out of our way to dispose of organic matter improperly, when compost is the most wonderful fertilizer around. Our soil needs compost for our plants to be healthy and grow properly. We're taking away more than fertility when we do not add compost, we're taking away soil health. If you want healthy grass, you have to have healthy soil underneath it, and compost is an essential part of that.

Compost research is revealing some incredible things. Not only does compost feed plants, it fights diseases, kills soil **pathogens**, encourages beneficial organisms, and plays a significant part in creating and maintaining healthy plants. You can indeed grow your entire lawn on compost (I'll tell you how later in the book) without having to use any other fertilizers.

Compost is used to improve the soil's biological, chemical, and physical properties. It is particularly good when added to sandy or heavy clay soils. By the way, compost is simply organic matter that is in a more advanced state of decomposition. Finished compost has a dark brown, crumbly texture, almost like good topsoil. You can add finished compost or you can add the raw organic matter such as peat moss or chopped up leaves to the lawn. I add leaves to the lawn in the fall when, in my lazy gardener mode, I chop up the leaves with my lawn mower. Then, I either blow them back onto the surrounding gardens to let them decompose there, or I spread them (all chopped up of course) on the lawn to be naturally composted over the winter. The key to leaving them on the lawn over the winter is to ensure they are well chopped up. Do not let whole leaves (particularly maple or other leaves that form a thick wet mat) sit on the turf over the winter or you'll kill the grass under the leaf mat.

ADD ORGANIC MATTER TO YOUR TOPSOIL

Topsoil will benefit from an addition of organic matter. Adding 8 cubic feet of peat moss and one bushel (or two large bags, 50 pounds) of purchased composted manure per 1,000 square feet, will give you a good start. Till this into the top 4 to 6 inches of soil.

Peat moss is often recommended as organic matter because that's exactly what it is. Peat is the partially decomposed remnants of reeds and sedge bog plants and is particularly useful in lawns because it holds up to thirty times its weight in water. It has little fertilizer value, but performs well as an organic matter addition to soil.

Those of you who have suburban homes will likely find that your topsoil is quite thin and underneath is a layer of fill-sand that was used as a cheap way to create the grades and contours after the homes were built. Adding compost is one way to help this thin layer of topsoil support good growth and begin the process of making even more topsoil. In clay soils, the organic matter separates the small clay particles, helping water and oxygen to move down into the soil. As you'll find when we get into growing grass, both of these elements (water and oxygen) are critical for good grass success. Adding compost improves the soil's Cation Exchange Capacity (or CEC). This is the way in which a soil feeds plants and without going into the scientific basis of this process, it is enough to say that the single best way to improve CEC is to add compost to the soil.

Adding compost and organic matter to the lawn also improves soil texture, making it easier for young grass plants to become established. More and more research suggests that many lawn weeds do not like compost and the soil conditions it creates. Therefore, when you add compost to your lawn, you'll find that your weed population may be less of a problem. Soil temperatures are modified on soils with higher organic content than on mineral soils with reduced organic matter content. Without organic matter, the soil gets slightly colder in the winter and much hotter in the summer heat. This can particularly be a problem in more southerly gardens (we talk about this a bit later on as well). Heat is not good for grass roots, and compost and organic matter are key players that help alleviate this problem.

Compost feeds worms, and these subterranean soil enhancers are tremendous resources for the lawn owner. You can even pick your own fishing worms from your lawn once you start using compost. By using compost and allowing the worms to build your soil, you'll never burn your lawn with excess fertilizers or pollute nearby water courses with runoff fertilizers.

Compost is the single most important ingredient for a good lawn recipe. We'll come back to it time and time again

COMPOST MAKING

Composting is the decomposition of organic matter, and gardeners want to be able to accomplish this task as efficiently as possible. Here's the short and sweet way to make compost.

- Ignore the small plastic containers and "instant" compost makers. They're more trouble than they're worth and often don't work at all.
- Pick a spot that is out of the way of your garden sight lines to make your pile. (Compost piles aren't scenic; they're just useful.)
- The minimum size for a good compost pile is 4 feet by 4 feet and as high as you can easily pile the material. There is no maximum size.
- Fancy compost piles are contained by wire fencing material, or any material that will hold the weight of the pile of organic material. I've never bothered to contain mine. I just pile it up to chest height. Fenced piles will take less room and likely look neater.
- Any organic matter can be put into the pile. Don't add animal or fish scraps, and no fatty products. Citrus peelings will decompose, but very slowly. Leaves are wonderful.
- Add a layer of garden soil every foot or so when you make your pile. This layer need only be a few inches thick. The soil provides all the micro-organisms you need to get the compost working.
- The soil "inoculates" the pile with good bacteria to get it decomposing.
- The pile should be damp but not soaking wet. Sometimes, this is a hard thing for beginners to get right. Once the pile is large enough, water it thoroughly. Then leave it alone unless you are in a very dry climate. If you can squeeze water out of the partially decomposed matter at the bottom of the pile, it is too wet. The material should feel wet to your touch but should not hold enough water to squeeze out. You can cover or uncover your pile to allow natural watering, depending on your sense of the dampness of the pile. I don't worry about it. I ignore the water content, and while my pile may take a bit longer to make compost, it does it eventually all by itself.
- Some authors recommend turning the pile. This will speed up the compost making quite a bit, but it's too much work for me. I let the pile sit, and it does its thing and I do mine, quite independently and happily.
- Compost can be made in three months if you turn and water the pile properly. My make-a-pile-and-walk-away system takes two years.
- I harvest the compost by removing the top uncomposted material and starting a new pile with this material at its bottom. Once I've removed all the uncomposted matter, I put the remaining finished compost onto the garden.

throughout this book. I just wanted to warn you ahead of time to get your compost pile started.

This is also an excellent time to mix in any lime or acidification material called for in the results of the soil test. You should also till in the fertilizer called for in the soil test or the general application at this stage.

Make It Level

All you need to level the ground and make sure it is a perfect seedbed are rakes, shovels, and a strong back. A little attention to detail here will pay off during the mowing season.

If you find that you've missed getting the lawn perfectly level and that puddles form during a heavy rain, fill up the puddles with topsoil and reseed that area. It's much better to fix the problems right at the beginning than to wait to see where the excess water will go or how waterlogged grass will (or will not) grow.

Apply Starter Fertilizer

Apply your starter fertilizer after the ground is tilled and given a final raking and leveling. Starter fertilizer is different from the general fertilizer we applied and tilled in to bring the soil up to good fertility levels for growing grass. As its name implies, starter fertilizer is used to give the grass plants a good start and encourage strong root growth. For this purpose, we use a plant food that is high in phosphorus and low in nitrogen.

The thinking behind this is that phosphorus doesn't move very well in the soil; it gets bound up in the soil's chemistry and isn't water soluble like nitrogen. Our newly emerging seedlings can use an extra dose of phosphorus, and if there's a good source nearby, they'll benefit. The nitrogen level is low because it is quite easy to burn tender roots with excess levels of nitrogen. Keeping it low while the seedling develops is just common sense.

Spread the starter fertilizer on the surface of the soil. *Do not work it in.* A good choice would be a formula with the phosphorus levels that are twice that of nitrogen. Something like 12-25-10 (that is, 12 percent nitrogen, 25 percent phosphorous, and 10 percent potassium) would be ideal. In the absence of a soil test,

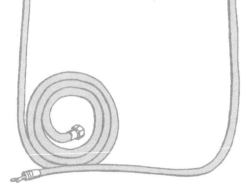

FOR PEAT'S SAKE

Some topsoil companies sell topsoil that has already been modified with peat moss to improve its texture and sales appeal. You can incorporate the peat and compost yourself or you can pay a company to do it for you.

apply this fertilizer at approximately 8 pounds per 1,000 square feet of ground. If the soil test says that the phosphorus levels in the topsoil are quite low, do not hesitate to use a formula that is closer to a 10-52-10, where the phosphorus number is significantly higher than the nitrogen number. Again, if you did not do a soil test, your best bet is to apply this formula at 8 pounds per 1,000 square feet.

Firming It Up

The very last step before seeding or laying sod is to firm up the soil. We do not want to crush the soil, flattening and compacting it beyond the means of any tender root to penetrate. We just want to firm up the soil a bit so we can walk on it without leaving too much of a footprint. The rule of thumb is to fill a small lawn roller a quarter to half full with water and then gently roll the soil.

Seeding Your Lawn

Once the soil is ready and the starter fertilizer is laid down, you can begin the seeding process. Using seed to establish a lawn is a time-honored method. And, like any other aspect of gardening there is a good way and a not-so-good way to seed a new lawn. To begin with, there is a difference between the warm weather lawn and the cool weather lawn.

- Warm season grasses are best established in the spring as soon as the soil temperatures are right for germination. Generally, soil temperatures of 78° to 85°F. are best.
- Cool season grasses are best established in the fall or late summer when the soil temperatures are 60° to 75°F. The second choice is early April to mid-May.

The reason for these differences is in the growing habits of the grasses being used. Warm season grasses thrive in the heat of summer and make most of their growth at this time. In the fall, the warm season grasses go dormant. Cool season grasses, on the other hand, make their best growth in the cool air temperatures and warm soil temperatures of late summer and early fall. They do

YOUR LAWN ROLLER AND YOU

A lawn roller looks like a barrel that you pull with a handle. The handle is attached at the ends of the barrel so it will roll behind you. The roller is hollow, and you fill it with water to add weight. Be sure to fill it *after* you get it sitting on flat ground. The weighted roller flattens everything it rolls over. We use it to get a good smooth surface for sowing seed and ensuring the seed is in contact with the soil.

Fill it about a quarter full and run it over the edge of the lawn. Then see how much of a footprint you leave in sneakers or other soft soled shoes. If you still sink in, fill the roller with a bit more water. Rake the rolled area lightly and roll it again with the heavier weight. Any footprint that is less than a quarter-inch deep is as good as it gets. Don't add any more water once this depth of imprint is achieved.

Too much weight compacts the soil and makes it very difficult for the seedlings to get established.

Too little weight, and you will still have bumps and ridges. Keep experimenting until you get it right.

not grow as well during the high heat of summer. Competition from weeds and crabgrass is much less in a fall seeding. I've seen spring sown lawns that were mostly weeds by the end of the summer; the small grass seedlings could not compete with the fast-to-establish crabgrass and broadleaf weeds. Weed grass species and broadleaf weeds will not grow as well in the fall as in the early spring.

I can hear the question forming in your mind right now. "Why don't you just use a spray on the lawn to stop the crabgrass from germinating?" Well, you can, but—and it's a big BUT—any spray that will stop crabgrass from germinating will also stop the desirable lawn grasses from germinating.

Many seed mixes will contain a nurse grass along with the desired blend. For example, a ryegrass nurse grass is often used in a Kentucky bluegrass and red fescue mix. The rapid growth rate of the perennial ryegrass will bind the soil and prevent it from being blown away (mostly into the kitchen, my wife notes) by the wind; its quick growth will shade the soil reducing water loss and the soil surface temperature. These actions allow the desirable grasses to become established much easier and without a reduction in soil quality.

Why is this important? Well, as you'll see as you keep reading this chapter, seed mixtures give us good lawns no matter what the season does. Each different species of grass performs well in slightly different seasons. With different species, it doesn't matter whether you have a hot, dry season or a cool, wet season. One of the grass species will grow well enough so you'll have a good lawn without any action on your part. The other species will struggle for that season but will live and perform for you the following year when the weather changes.

With a blend, you get different varieties of the same grass. So, although you have some diversity in performance, if the weather is dry and you have a grass species that likes water, you'll have to supply water by irrigating. Blends are for finer lawns and those people who like to fuss over things.

SOWING YOUR LAWN

Sowing grass seed is not difficult, and it is not an exact science. But try to stay within the recommended seeding guidelines or at least close to them. Drastically increasing the amounts sown will not give you a better or thicker lawn. If you plant far too much seed, you will create a too-large population of grass seedlings fighting to live. The survivors will be weaker than if you had sown the proper number of seeds and fed them properly. Stay close to the guidelines, and the grass plants themselves will thicken up and close in to give you a good lawn. The general amounts for sowing lawns from seed are summarized in the following table. This table also indicates how long you will have wait until you see seed germinating.

Seeding Rates and Time to Germination

GRASS SPECIES	POUNDS OF SEED (PER 1,000 SQUARE FEET)	DAYS TO GERMINATION
Kentucky bluegrass	1–1½	6–28
Creeping bluegrass	2	5–6
Rough bluegrass	1–1½	6–21
Annual ryegrass	7–10	3–8
Perennial ryegrass	7–9	3–10
Hard fescue	3½–4½	5–12
Chewings fescue	3½–4½	5–12
Creeping red fescue	3½–4½	5–12
Tall fescue	7–9	4–12
Creeping bent grass	¼–1	6–10
Colonial bent grass	½–1	7–14
Idaho bent grass	1½–3	6–10
Bahia grass	7–10	8–15
Bermuda grass	1–1½	7–15
Buffalo grass	3 burrs*	7–14
Centipede grass	4–6	7–14
Zoysia grass	2–3	10–14

* Buffalo grass seed comes in **burrs**, like the burrs that stick onto your clothes. (A burr is not a fancy new form of measurement.)

Nick Christian, *Fundamentals of Turf Management* (Chelsea, MI: Ann Arbor Press, 1998), p. 76.

SOWING THE PROFESSIONAL WAY

Professionals use different technology to apply grass seed than homeowners. If you have a professional lawn team do a large lawn, they may very well use a hydroseeder. This machine applies the seed, mulch, fertilizer, and a soil binder all in one operation. The slurry mix is agitated in a large tank and then blown onto the lawn. Truck-mounted units can carry 5,000 gallons of liquid (that's a lot of seed).

Professionals will also use culti-packer spreaders. This machine lays down the seed, buries it, and covers it to the correct depth. They also leave the soil lightly rolled for good germination. Cultipackers come in a variety of sizes and if you have a very large lawn, this is the machine you might rent to do the best job of sowing lawn seed.

Are these professional methods better than what you'll use as a homeowner? Nope. They just work better and faster when you have a lot of acreage. Your small seeder will work fine for the average city, suburban, or small country lot.

Having said all that, I have to tell you that the average person can't tell the difference between a blend and a mixture when they look at a lawn. Mixtures are the easiest lawns for most of us to keep.

How to Seed Your Lawn

Sowing grass seed is not difficult. The key to success is to achieve a uniform distribution of seed, and any way you can do that is acceptable. There are two sowing machines that work quite well for grass seed. The first is a hand-seeder. A small hopper feeds the seed into a whirling sprocket that shoots the seed away from the walking gardener. Normally, the seed is distributed by hand-cranking a small lever to set the spreading sprocket whirling. I have seen battery-powered ones but the old hand-crank models are superior and will last far longer than any modern battery-powered machine.

Larger machines resemble fertilizer spreaders. If you've got a really large lawn, you can rent farm-type machinery that will do an excellent job. Most of the time, a garden center will rent or loan you the equipment when you purchase the seed and fertilizer from them.

When you're ready to sow, divide the grass seed into two equal amounts. Apply the first portion by going up the lawn area and then turning 180 degrees to return—just like you're mowing. Make sure that the grass seed overlaps just a little bit from the spreader. It is better to have a little extra grass in one area than a bare patch.

Once you've covered the whole lawn area with half your seed, apply the remainder by going up and down the lawn at right angles to the original direction. This will prevent any banding or striped look from appearing as the grass seed germinates.

After you spread the seed and lightly rake it, rolling the lawn with a quarter-filled roller is a good idea. This rolling presses the seed into contact with the soil, and as long as the soil is kept damp, germination will follow. The seed does not have to be covered—in darkness—to germinate. It requires only a steady and consistent supply of moisture.

Winter Overseeding/Dormant Seeding

Some garden authors have recommended sowing during the winter or dormant period. Their thinking is that the seed will be naturally ready to germinate first thing in the spring and a good fast start will result. Although there is merit to this thinking, research has shown that better lawns are obtained by spring sowing in warm grass areas and fall sowing in cool grass areas.

By sowing, covering, and rolling at the appropriate time, you are keeping your seed unavailable to birds, mice, and ants. Also, it will take a bit of time in the spring for the soil to warm up to germination temperatures and no amount of hoping for early germination will give you a thicker lawn.

If you sow your grass seed before the soil temperatures have reached the germination temperatures, the grass seed will simply sit there and wait for the correct temperature. Some homeowners apply the seed too early, wait a few days, and then figure that the seed must have been dead. They continue to apply new seed (sometimes more than once or twice). Suddenly, the soil temperatures warm up, all the seed germinates, and they think, "Finally we got good seed!" But you know better, and will avoid this little pitfall.

Watering

If you've been reading carefully, one of the critical elements in getting good seed germination is the sufficient availability of water. Without water, the seed is not going to germinate. If the seed starts to germinate because there is enough water and then the watering ceases and the soil dries out, the newly emerged seedling will quickly dry out and die. The most critical time, then, is just after the seed has germinated but before it has grown a full root system capable of sustaining itself. This is where you as the homeowner-in-charge come in.

The objective is to keep the lawn "just" damp, not dried out and not swampy. If you apply too much water, the soil will begin to float up into the water. If there is the slightest gradient for the water to carry the soil away, the soil will erode.

FOR FASTER GERMINATION

If you want slightly faster germination rates, then pregermination is the technique to use. Put your seed into a small nylon sack (the toe and foot ends of old pantyhose work really well) and immerse it in a bucket of warm water. Change the water every day for four days. Pat the seed dry on paper towels, and then immediately sow the seed normally. Do not let soaked seed dry out or it will die. Pregerminated seed starts faster than seed that has not been treated. This is not an advantage with fast germinating seed such as ryegrass, but it is with the slower forms such as Kentucky bluegrass.

If possible, set up a sprinkler system to provide several short bursts of water (5- to 10-minute duration) during the day, particularly during the heat of the day. If no sprinkler is available and you have to go to work, turn on the sprinklers for at least 15 minutes before you leave and then again at night when you return. If the lawn is dry when you return from work, apply the sprinkler for more than 15 minutes. If it's still wet, apply the sprinkler for fewer than 15 minutes. There is no rule here; each and every lawn and soil condition will differ.

Using Mulch

One of the tricks of the trade is to use a mulch over the seedlings to preserve the critical moisture level around the seedlings. Some garden centers carry straw for this purpose, and it is usually the cheapest and best mulch around. Apply it at the rate of one to one and a half bales per 1,000 square feet of lawn. It doesn't have to be too thick to do the job. Do not apply more or you'll have to take it off again when the grass starts to germinate. If applied thinly, straw can be chopped up with the first mowing. The disadvantage of straw is that it often contains seeds of the plant involved (i.e., oat straw contains oat seeds) and sometimes broadleaf weeds.

Garden centers or lawn care companies will also be able to sell you excelsior, the shredded wood fiber material that is used in packaging. Sometimes this is available to the lawn care industry in rolled fiber mats that degrade after the grass grows up and through the mat. These rolled mats are particularly good if you are trying to establish grass on a steep slope. The mat stops erosion from wind and water and gets the seedlings off to a good start.

I've also seen shredded newspaper used in this way. Again, it degrades with water and does not have to be removed if applied thinly.

After Grass Seed Germination

After your grass seed has germinated, follow these steps:

- Do not walk on it for the first six to eight weeks after it starts to sprout. Grass cannot handle traffic during this establishment time. If you absolutely have to walk on newly emerged grass,

A NOTE OF CAUTION

When we mulch our lawns, we are not trying to stop plant growth as we are when we mulch our gardens for weed control. A very thin layer will stop evaporation (our objective with lawns) so do not apply more than the recommended bale to a bale and a half per 1,000 square feet or you'll stop the grass seed from germinating.

lay down a straw mulch to absorb some of the foot pressure. Go around the lawn area, not over it.

- Do not mow until the grass leaves are at least one-third higher than you want them to be after mowing. In other words, if your final grass height is to be 2 inches, then do not mow until the grass is thickened up and roughly 3 inches tall. There is an old wives' tale that grass should be allowed to reach 6 inches before mowing. The old wives are wrong.

- As the grass starts to grow, don't irrigate the new grass plants as often. When you do, apply more water in each irrigation. Instead of several times a day, move to once a day. Then, every second day, moving to every third day, and finally twice a week. By the six- to eight-week mark, you should be watering the grass as you would a mature lawn. It doesn't hurt new grass to be a bit water hungry once it is 1 to 2 inches tall. Being water hungry will force the roots to grow deeper in search of water.

- Do not apply any postemergent herbicides to the lawn area until the grass is at least six to eight weeks old. Do not apply pre-emergent herbicides at all. If you are tempted to apply an herbicide—read the label carefully to ensure it is suitable for new seedlings (most aren't).

- Grass areas that will receive maximum wear (i.e., children's play areas) should have as long as possible before traffic is allowed. In professional sports turf areas, the recommendation is for one full year without traffic. You probably won't be able to meet that requirement, but eight to ten weeks is the absolute minimum. You will see damage if you have traffic on lawns before this time is over.

Pest Control

This is a bit of a tricky problem. Birds will eat the seeds you've worked so hard to lay down. Think of it from the bird's perspective: it's a massive free lunch scattered there before its very eyes. Hard to go wrong here if you're a bird. Additives that are sometimes touted as foul tasting do not seem to work on birds. Sometimes they work on squirrels when they are eating at bird feeders, and they may work on the mice that are going to enjoy some of the seed you've sown, but they don't work on birds.

Birds can be deterred by several methods. The most useful is a large plastic beach ball painted with several large eyes. These eyes, yellow with a large black dot in the middle, deter birds for a few days (they think it's a big predator). Then you have to move the ball around the lawn. Once the birds get used to it, the deterrent value plummets, so you have to keep it on the move. If you can attach some flashing Mylar streamers (available at better garden centers as bird deterrents) to the ball, you'll have even better luck with it. These "eyes" are sometimes available through garden centers.

The second thing that works extremely well is to use a bird-in-distress recording. Commercial fruit farmers use them to deter birds such as starlings from ruining their fruit crops. They are quite effective if not played constantly. You can also use electric and propane "bangers" (like miniature cannons on timers). Unfortunately, the birds get used to them in a short time, and they are guaranteed to annoy the neighbors with their constant explosions. Of course, if the neighbors are walking on your lawn, perhaps one of these propane cannons would be exactly what you want!

All said, the easiest thing to do is relax and apply an extra half pound of grass seed over what is required. The birds will get some, the ants and mice will get some, and you'll have enough left over to grow a good lawn. Everybody is happy and you haven't worried about the situation at all. In gardening, it is better to work with Mother Nature instead of against her.

Sod—The Instant Lawn

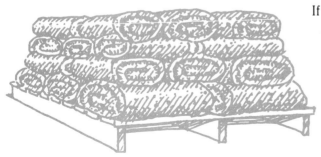

If you want an instant lawn, there's no easier way to achieve it than by using sod. It's fast, clean, and easy, and doesn't require technical expertise to lay it successfully. See the "Seed Versus Sod" sidebar for a side-by-side comparison.

Having an instant lawn is the main advantage of sod; the major disadvantage is its higher cost. You are paying somebody else to grow the turf for

SEED VERSUS SOD

FACTORS TO CONSIDER	SEED	SOD
Time of year to install	Fall in cool winter areas; spring in warm winter areas	Year-round installation although frozen ground can be tricky
Soil preparation	Same for both seed and sod	Same for both seed and sod; it must be done for sod or rooting can be reduced
Water requirements	Slightly higher for seed; bare ground will dry faster than covered ground	Less than seed; water heavily at installation and then keep damp for 2 to 3 weeks
Seed quality	Can be variable with weed seed depending on retailer	Usually highest quality available used by sod growers
Weed control	Weeds may germinate and compete with newly germinating grass plants	Usually weed free when installed because grown weed free
Uniformity of coverage	Depends on sowing method and care taken by gardener	Excellent if you can put two pieces of sod together
Runoff	Erosion can occur in heavy rains until grass is established	Runoff can occur under the sod but it is normally not as great a problem
Visual impacts	Slow to establish that green look (3 to 6 weeks)	Instant lawn
Wait to use	6 to 8 weeks for moderate use	2 to 3 weeks for moderate use
Costs to install	Lowest cost	2 to 3 times the cost of seed

you, and as I'm sure you know, convenience never comes cheap. Also, sod is pretty much restricted to those grass varieties that form stolons or rhizomes as their method of spreading. Ryegrass and fescues, for example, do not make great sod because they are mainly spread by bunching and seeding (see Chapter 1). Kentucky bluegrass and zoysia grass, on the other hand, make an excellent sod.

Step-by-Step Lawn Sodding

To sod your lawn, first

- Take its measurements using a tape measure. This step may sound pretty obvious, but garden center customers regularly try to purchase sod without knowing the measurements of their lawn. They say pleasantly, "Oh, just give me enough to do the average-size lawn." Don't be one of them.

  Better yet, make a sketch of your lawn (especially if it is an irregular shape). Put as many measurements in as possible to help your sod supplier calculate the square footage you'll need. Let the supplier calculate how many rolls you'll require. They have the experience.

- Prepare the soil *exactly* as you would have done for seed sowing before your sod is delivered. The only difference in having grass plants from a sod farm and having grass plants from seed is that the sod farm does the initial growing for you. The success or failure of *your* lawn is still intimately tied into the soil. You can start with the best sod in the world and if you put it onto terrible soil, pretty soon you'll have a terrible lawn.

  Too many homeowners simply kill off the old grass or rake off the major debris from construction and lay on the sod without any other preparation of the soil. This moves the soil boundary layer right up to the sod. Grass roots will have difficulty getting established and the resulting lawn will be unsatisfactory. There have been examples of this short cut on rather steep slopes; after several months of tending the sod, a heavy rain actually washed the sod off the slope because the roots had not penetrated deeply enough to hold.

- Schedule the delivery of your sod for after all the soil preparation work is finished. Do not have sod sitting around for several days waiting for you to finish preparing the soil. Sod is a living thing, and sitting around will kill it. Install it immediately on delivery. It is an excellent idea to have the delivery people put the sod in the shade or out of the hot noon sun. Covering it with moist burlap or having the sprinkler give it regular shots of water will also extend its storage time.

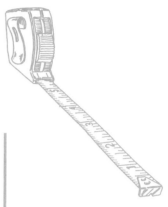

Laying Sod Successfully

To make laying sod as successful and easy as possible, follow these steps.

- Moisten the soil before laying sod. Don't turn it into a swamp, but ensure the soil is damp
- Lay the sod in a bricklike pattern as shown so the ends of the sod rolls do not line up across the lawn.
- On slopes, lay the sod horizontally across the slope—never in the same direction as the slope. Sod laid with the slope is more easily eroded and is harder to lay in a straight line.
- On steep slopes greater than 10 degrees, peg the sod roll. This means driving a wooden stake (two per roll) through the sod into the ground to hold the sod to the ground until roots can form. Remove the pegs after three to four weeks when the roots have established themselves or just before your first mowing. Make your own pegs by cutting 1-by-2-foot lumber into 12-inch lengths. There is no need to sharpen the pegs, just drive them into the soil with a hammer. Drive the peg 8 inches into the soil, leaving 4 inches to grab onto when you remove the pegs.

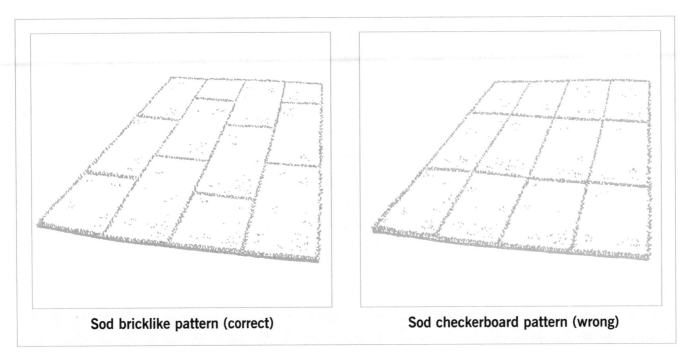

Sod bricklike pattern (correct)   Sod checkerboard pattern (wrong)

LAWN SODDING

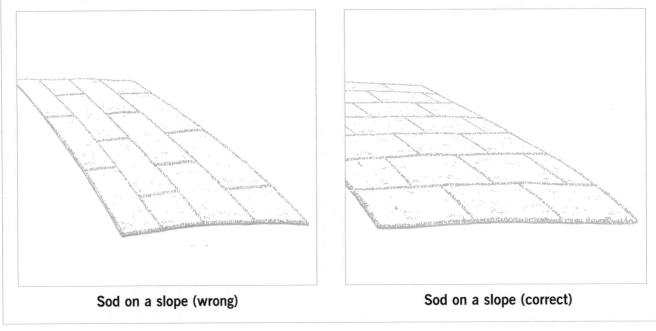

Sod on a slope (wrong)   Sod on a slope (correct)

LAYING SOD

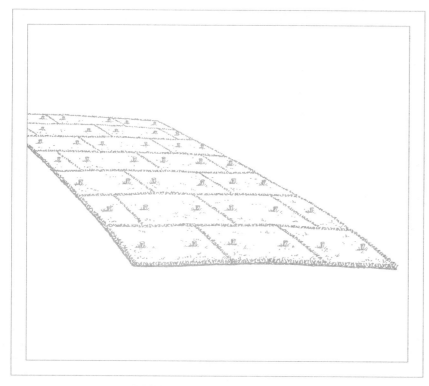

PEGGING SOD TO A SLOPE

- Find the longest straight line to begin installing the sod. Lay this line first. For example, along the driveway or house entrance walkway is a good starting point. After this first line of sod is done, all other sod rolls can be laid with this as a reference point.
- Butt and push the ends of the sod rolls together to ensure they fit snugly.
- Avoid gaps or overlays. Gaps give weeds an open invitation to move in, and overlays create bumps in the lawn. Use a serrated knife to cut off chunks that are too long or to create angles around flowerbeds, mailboxes, walkways, and so on. Do not plan on using this knife in the kitchen again; it will be quite dull when you've finished hacking soil and plant roots.

- Do not stretch the sod turf to cover more area. Rookies do this, thinking they are saving money. They're actually damaging the grass roots and setting back the sod so the lawn is of poorer quality.
- After laying the sod, roll it lightly to ensure the roots are in contact with the soil. Use a roller that is approximately a quarter to a third full of water.
- Begin watering as described in the next section.

Watering

The first watering a newly laid sod receives is the most important one it will ever receive. *Begin watering immediately after you install the sod.* This first watering will determine how the grass plants perform for the next few years; this is one product you do not want to dry out.

Here are a few tips on proper watering.

- Avoid hand sprinkling. You won't be as even and objective in your watering as will an automatic sprinkler. You also won't have the patience to wet down each and every blade of grass. Your automatic sprinkler has enough patience for both of you.
- After you've watered for an hour, pull back the corner of a section of sod and push a screwdriver (or some other sharp tool) down into the soil. The blade should go in quite easily. When you pull it out, the blade should be wet and show moisture along its first 3 to 4 inches. If not, keep watering.
- You have to be absolutely certain that water is getting to all areas of the newly sodded lawn. If there is a problem, it is almost certainly to be at the corners and edges where sprinkler patterns don't reach or don't reach well. These areas do not receive as much water as the middle of the sod, so this is where problems occur first. Also, the areas closest to the house can be a problem; they dry out faster due to the reflected heat from the home. Watch these areas for drying and give them extra water.

- Sometimes if the sod is laid on a slope, you'll see water runoff before the underlying soil is adequately watered, as measured by your "high-tech" screwdriver water measuring device. If runoff occurs, stop the sprinkler or move it to another area for 30 to 45 minutes. After the water has had a chance to soak in, test it with your screwdriver and start watering again if necessary. You may have to repeat this several times to get a good soaking, particularly on a steep slope.

- Keep the soil under the sod wet for at least two weeks to give the new roots a chance to penetrate and start growing properly.

- After a few days, it is not a good idea to move the corner of the sod back to check the soil moisture levels. If you move the sod, you'll be pulling up newly established roots. Simply stick your screwdriver into the ground and take into account the thickness of the sod when assessing the soil moisture levels.

- Water as early in the morning as possible to take advantage of the growing cycle. Grass starts to grow very early (right after sunup), and if it has adequate water, it will grow faster. You'll also save water if you apply it in the early morning.

When Can I Walk on It?

It will take at least two to three weeks before you can walk on your newly sodded lawn. While it may look solid before that time, it is still sending roots down and establishing itself. Mow when the grass grows to 3 inches and cut it down to 2 inches. As with seed, no more than 30 percent of the grass leaf should be cut off at any one mowing.

Other Methods

Plugging

Plugging is like using a mini-sod system. Very small pieces of sod are planted at regular intervals in the prepared soil. These plugs are either small bits of cut-up sod or plugs cut from an established turf area. The entire area is not covered but bare soil is left between the plugs; the plugs will grow out to fill in the bare soil. Generally, the 4-inch plugs are planted 6 to 16 inches apart.

The main advantage of plugging is cost. A sod of 100 square feet can produce enough plugs to cover 1,000 square feet of lawn. A tenfold reduction in the price of the sod! This advantage sometimes outweighs the disadvantage of the lawn taking two years to fill in and having some weeds getting established in the spaces left between plugs.

Plugs can be used on new lawns or for renovating old lawns. Any spreading grass—from Kentucky bluegrass to zoysia grass and St. Augustine grass (the latter two grasses are the most commonly used in plugs)—can be used as a plug grass.

The establishment of plugs is exactly the same as establishing a lawn from sod. To be successful, you must be sure that all the same steps are carried out.

Strip sodding

Strip sodding is a modification on plugs and sodding. It involves nothing more than laying sod down with 6- to 10-inch wide bare soil strips between the sod rolls. It's easy, it's fast, and it's cheaper than a full sod coverage, but the disadvantage of having bare ground is the same. It will take at least an extra year to grow in fully.

Stolonizing

Using stolons to create a new lawn is technically possible and sometimes used with Bermuda grass on southern lawns by professional turf experts. As the old saying goes, "If you're a beginner, don't try this at home!" Stolonizing is used for some of the newer hybrids that have specific characteristics that may not be consistently passed on through seeding.

CHECKLIST:
STEPS TO STARTING A GOOD LAWN

1. Grading
- ❏ Level and grade the subsoil exactly as the topsoil will be laid.
- ❏ Level and grade the topsoil.
- ❏ Rototill to reduce the boundary zone.
- ❏ Make sure the drainage is good.

2. Soil
- ❏ Get a soil test done on the topsoil.
- ❏ Add fertilizer as recommended by the soil test.
- ❏ Add organic matter and till it in.
- ❏ Perform a final raking to ensure the ground is level.
- ❏ Apply starter fertilizer.
- ❏ Firm up the soil by lightly rolling it before seeding or sodding.

3. Seeding
- ❏ Choose the right seed for the job (see Chapter 1).
- ❏ Obtain the proper amounts of seed (see page 41).
- ❏ To avoid lawn patterns, use a seeder to spread the seed in two directions.

4. Watering
- ❏ Apply mulch to conserve moisture around the newly developing seedlings.
- ❏ Apply water properly depending on the stage of growth. Move from frequent irrigations to less frequent but deeper waterings.

5. Post–Seed Germination Care
- ❏ Do not walk on the lawn for six to eight weeks.
- ❏ Do not mow until the lawn is at least 3 inches tall.
- ❏ Only remove 1 inch of grass blade (or 30 percent of height) of any lawn on any mowing.
- ❏ Do not apply herbicides.

6. Sodding the Lawn
- ❏ Prepare the soil exactly as if you were seeding it.
- ❏ Do not have the sod arrive until you are ready to lay it immediately on delivery.
- ❏ Follow all rules for laying sod—in particular, do not stretch it.
- ❏ Do not overlap or leave gaps.
- ❏ Lay the sod in bricklike patterns and up and down slopes, not across them.
- ❏ Water immediately, within 30 minutes of laying the sod.
- ❏ The soil below the sod cannot dry out for two weeks or until the roots are well established.
- ❏ Do not walk on the sod for at least two to three weeks and, even then, avoid heavy use.

Remember that a stolon is an aboveground stem that forms nodes along its length. These nodes form baby plants identical to the mother plant. To create a lawn using stolons, you have to spread these stems equally over the lawn. Roll them gently to ensure they are in contact with the soil, and then maintain a high humidity around the nodes (usually with mulch, sometimes with fine sprinkler systems) until they form new grass plants. It is not a job for beginners or casual do-it-yourselfers.

The advantage to this system is that it gives a very uniform turf (remember, it is composed of one plant multiplied millions of times) and usually one of very high quality. One disadvantage is that if a disease gets established on the lawn, the entire lawn is prone to that disease because every plant is genetically identical. A second disadvantage is that the high cost of stolons makes it an expensive way to create a lawn.

CHAPTER THREE

How to Grow a Good Lawn

There are fewer smells more wonderfully reminiscent of summer than freshly mown lawns. That heavy, green, fresh fragrance is a balm to summer evenings after a hard day of work. Now that you've created a good lawn, this chapter will describe how to feed, cut, and maintain it.

Before charging off with the lawn mower to do battle, you need to make a few decisions. First, decide exactly what kind of lawn you are going to have. High-maintenance lawns mean lawns that you mow short, mow often, irrigate and feed regularly, and practice regular pest and weed control. These are the kinds of lawns that are found on golf courses and lawn fanatics' front yards. As the name indicates, it is a lot of work to maintain this kind of lawn.

Medium-maintenance lawns are a notch down from the fanatic's intensity. Irrigation and feeding are reduced so the lawn does not need as much mowing. However, weeds and insects are still controlled, often by chemical means.

My own backyard is best described as low-maintenance lawn. I mow it once a week or so but I never water it. I control the weeds organically; I feed the grass but I never use chemicals to kill pests. I prefer to control weeds and pests naturally, and I do not get upset at a bit of dead grass here and there from the dogs. It's green, and I can go out and lie on it whenever I want and if a dandelion or three poke their heads up in the spring—well, life still goes on. My lawn looks good, it's all natural, and it doesn't require using lots of resources, financial or environmental, to maintain.

What you intend to do with your lawn and how much effort you want to put into it will determine the level of feeding, watering, and other maintenance practices. The higher the maintenance, the closer the lawn will resemble a golf course. But it will take work to get it to look that good and keep it looking that good. Most homeowners fall somewhere between the golf course and the hay field. We all make our decisions based on our own needs; mostly these fall somewhere at the medium- to low-maintenance systems of care.

Sunshine

The first requirement of a good lawn is a minimum of six full hours of hot sunshine a day. Anything less than that and you had better start thinking shady lawn care. And let's dispel a garden center myth right here and now. You don't grow great lawns in the shade of trees, particularly evergreen trees. Their dense shade can reduce available light by as much as 95 percent. The fewer hours of sunshine you give your turf, the poorer the turf will be. The more complete and dense the shade, the weaker the grass. This is, unfortunately, a pretty hard and fast rule in horticulture regardless of what the lawn seed package says.

The problems you have to overcome are presented in the following list. Luckily, there are some techniques that we can use to grow reasonable lawns in varying amounts of shade. If the following techniques don't work for you, you'll need to read the section on turf alternatives for shady areas.

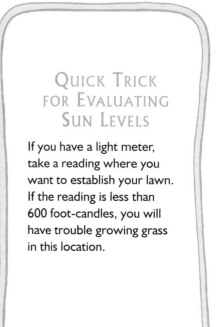

QUICK TRICK FOR EVALUATING SUN LEVELS

If you have a light meter, take a reading where you want to establish your lawn. If the reading is less than 600 foot-candles, you will have trouble growing grass in this location.

1. Pick a variety of grass that tolerates shade and that thrives in your climate. This is the first and most important rule. See Chapter 1 for grass varieties that will do this. The grass breeders are constantly coming up with new cultivars that will tolerate even more shade. Ask at a quality garden center for this seed.

2. In shady areas that don't get enough sunlight, the grass is not able to replace the food they used in growing. Without replacing the consumed food by photosynthesis, the grass will become weaker and weaker. The root systems will become shorter and thinner and will branch out less. Grass in shade requires a good feeding and watering system if it is going to stay alive.

3. Air movement under trees is generally less than in open areas, which means that the dew does not dry as quickly. Combine this moisture with dark, motionless air conditions, and you have a perfect environment for diseases. People with high-maintenance lawns will spray with chemicals when these conditions occur; the rest of us

will simply increase the compost application to help the plant fight off infection.

4. Grass growing in the shade tends to grow more upright than grass grown in sunnier spots. This means that if you don't increase the height of your mower deck when you cut the shady spots, you'll be cutting more of the blade off the shade grass than the sun grass. This will weaken the shade plants that are struggling to survive because of increased competition for nutrients from the trees and decreased sunlight. Low mowing contributes to the problem, so increase the height of your mower deck for shady spots.

5. Weaker grass and subsequent thinning out is an invitation to weeds to colonize the lawn. Annual topdressing with shade-tolerant grass cultivars is a necessity if the lawn is to be maintained at an acceptable level of thickness. See page 105 for my recipe for spring topdressing.

6. Trees are very efficient collectors of moisture. Their huge root system sucks up darn near everything that falls. A large maple tree can use upward of 300 gallons of water a day. A poor grass plant trying to live under this tree has to compete with the tree for water. If you want your grass to thrive in shade, make sure you follow an irrigation program.

Food

You have to feed your lawn. Well, maybe you don't *have* to . . . BUT if you want good growth and healthy plants, you want to provide adequate nutrition for all those tender little friends out there. Proper nutrition is as important for our lawn as it is for us, and just like our own diet (or lack thereof) we can get our lawn into trouble by underfeeding or overfeeding it. Underfeeding weakens the turf; and a weak, thin turf allows weeds to become established. Overfeeding gives lush, soft growth that is an open invitation for diseases and insects to wreak havoc. Providing the right amount of food for the grass plants is not all that difficult if you follow a few simple rules.

Nitrogen

Let's begin with nitrogen, the engine of plant growth. In the normal course of its growing cycle, grass uses more nitrogen than any other substance. From a practical standpoint, this means that gardeners apply more nitrogen and spend more money on it than on any other fertilizer. By understanding how it works and what it does, you can save money *and* get better grass performance.

Nitrogen is a vital part of most growth processes in grass plants. Chlorophyll depends largely on nitrogen for its existence and operation in producing carbohydrates to support the grass plant. Amino acids and proteins for plant growth depend on adequate amounts of nitrogen as well, as do the enzymes that transport the vitamins, which also depend on nitrogen within the plant. In short, if a grass part or function does not need nitrogen directly as part of its building-block or functioning system, it does require nitrogen indirectly as part of the process by which it was constructed. Nitrogen is a basic building block in this grass playground.

Symptoms of Nitrogen Deficiency or Overfeeding

If the grass does not have the right amount of nitrogen for growth or maintenance, there are serious disruptions in the plant life cycle. The first symptom that you'd see in an underfed lawn is a yellowing of the grass plants—and subsequent yellowing of the lawn. The lawn loses its deep green sheen and starts to look sickly and pale, or chlorotic, due to a lack of chlorophyll. The second symptom is that the lawn growth rate will slow down. The grass will not grow as quickly, even though the time of year indicates it should be sending all kinds of growth skyward. If you save your clippings or rake a predetermined area of grass after every mowing, you'll quickly see any decrease or increase in the amount of clippings produced. A decrease in clippings may reflect the lack of available nitrogen.

Another less visible change in the grass as a result of insufficient nitrogen is reduced root growth. Grass that lacks chlorophyll is producing fewer carbohydrates. This reduction in carbohydrates (energy) limits the ability of the roots to grow and regenerate. So, if the tops look sickly and light green to yellowish, you can bet that the roots are equally unhappy.

DOUG'S FIRST RULE OF GARDENING

This rule states: "You only have to feed your plants if you want flowers, fruit, or growth." Remember that lawns are composed of thousands of individual grass plants. If you want them to grow, you have to feed them.

KEEP OFF THE GRASS

Does this mean that a gardener should just load the nitrogen right to the lawn and the problems will be over? Nope. It doesn't work that way. If you overload nitrogen onto the lawn, several things might happen. To begin with, if you really overload it, nitrogen will burn the existing grass plants and they'll die. If you don't go that far but you give the plant more than it needs to eat, it will get fat. You can probably imagine people as fat, but can you imagine a fat grass plant? Try this thought. If you overfeed your lawn with nitrogen, each individual grass plant will grow so quickly it will develop a thin outer cell layer (the **cuticle** for you scientific types). This layer of cells is responsible for keeping bacteria and other pathogens out of the plant; when it is thin and weak from overfeeding, it does a poor job of guarding the gates—keeping diseases out of the grass plant. Thin cuticles equal plants that are

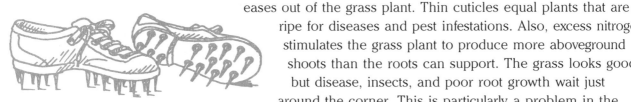

ripe for diseases and pest infestations. Also, excess nitrogen stimulates the grass plant to produce more aboveground shoots than the roots can support. The grass looks good, but disease, insects, and poor root growth wait just around the corner. This is particularly a problem in the spring when gardeners overfeed their lawns. Initially, the lawn looks good, but the weak grass has problems with disease and insects during early and midsummer.

The solution, as in many things, is to find the correct balance for feeding nitrogen. Not too little and not too much.

Sources of Nitrogen

The advertisements for lawn fertilizers are truly confusing. The manufacturers try to convince you that one form of nitrogen is better for your plants than another or that an organic source is more readily available to your plants than a chemical source. You've heard or read these kinds of ads. Here's the basic information about the kinds of nitrogen found in the packages and what this means to you as a homeowner.

Inorganic sources of nitrogen are rarely found in fertilizers meant for the home trade. Compounds such as ammonium nitrate, ammonium sulfate, and potassium nitrate can easily burn the grass if applied even slightly over the recommended rates. These chemicals also absorb moisture from the air; if left in an open bag, they would form clumps and become unusable. If you see a bag of fertilizer with an inorganic source of nitrogen listed on the label, do not buy it. It may be cheaper than other fertilizer products; but if you make a mistake and burn your grass, the cost is much greater than the cost of a good bag of fertilizer.

You will see other kinds of nitrogen advertised. Each company is trying to sell you a product based on one of two criteria: the excellence of its product or the cost. Unfortunately, you can't have it both ways in the nitrogen business. These are the basic products you'll find as the source of nitrogen in most bagged fertilizers. I'll start with the most expensive and work to the cheapest.

1. IBDU (Isobutyledenediurea). This is a mouthful of a name, but it does have some useful characteristics. To begin with, IBDU is relatively insoluble with cold water. This means that when you apply it to your garden, it will not decompose immediately and give the plants a flush of food. IBDU decomposes slowly and is available to the grass plants over a long period. As a result of the manufacturing process, each molecule of this product is the same size and contains 32 percent nitrogen. This uniformity creates a product that is easy to work with and brings no surprises for the homeowner. Fertilizer manufacturers combine these molecules into different-size particles (more molecules for larger particles) so the particles will break down at different times in order to feed the lawn over a long period of time.

IBDU is the most expensive product because of its uniformity and method of manufacture. It also has some disadvantages depending on the weather. IBDU releases its product quite slowly. If it is the only source of fertilizer you use, there will be a time lag between application and availability to the plants, perhaps as long as two to three weeks. If you see IBDU in the analysis on the label, you'll often see urea added as well to increase the speed of its availability to the plants. Also, if you live in a cool area, you'll find that the breakdown rate of this product is slow; cool temperatures slow down the breakdown process. However, cool spells do not bother IBDU as much as other slow-release forms, so it is

SYMPTOMS OF NITROGEN DEFICIENCY

- Leaves turn a yellow or yellow-green color.
- Older leaves die quickly and new shoots are pale green.
- Plants are stunted in growth and do not grow quickly.
- Diseases such as dollar spot, rusts, and red thread are more prevalent.
- Turf is thinner, not as luxuriant. There is increased weed competition.
- Some grass may go reddish or reddish purple in color, particularly in cool weather.

often the fertilizer of choice in cool spring areas. Also, if there is no water to dissolve the nitrogen particles, then the fertilizer will not be available to the plants. Dry springs with no irrigation can leave the fertilizer sitting on the lawn waiting for the proper conditions to dissolve.

2. Sulfur-Coated Urea (SCU). This product is one of the most commonly found ingredients in lawn fertilizer bags. It is about one-third cheaper to produce than IBDU and does the same job. The urea or nitrogen source is sprayed with molten sulfur and formed into little "prills," or tiny beads. When the sulfur hardens, the encapsulated urea is safely enclosed in an almost waterproof coating. To prevent these particles from sticking together, manufacturers will add a silica such as diatomaceous earth to the product, which allows each individual bead to resist clumping in the bag. As you might imagine, the thickness of the sulfur coat determines how fast or slow the urea is made available to the grass plants as food. Different manufacturers will advertise their products as having different lengths of time over which they will feed your lawn and will try to convince you that their product is the best on the market. Each bag will have a wide mix of different-size beads to enable the fertilizer to make itself available to the lawn plants over a predetermined period.

The release of SCU is determined by temperature (the higher the temperature, the faster it releases), available water (the wetter, the faster) and the health of the lawn. The overall health of the lawn determines how many micro-organisms are present. The more micro-organisms that are available to assist the sulfur to decompose, the faster the SCU will be made available to the grass plants. In other words, the healthier your lawn, the better the SCU will work. Of course, remember that the fastest way to increase the number of micro-organisms in any soil is to add compost.

3. Urea. Urea is the fastest acting nitrogen source found in home lawn fertilizer bags. It is also the cheapest to produce, making it tremendously popular with manufacturers. Urea is almost completely available as you apply it to your lawn, so the turf will have an almost overnight response to the fertilizer.

This has several important consequences. First, if you overapply urea, you will burn your lawn with the excess nitrogen. The grass will die and you'll have to replace it with a renovation program. Second, irrigation or rainfall will quickly dissolve urea and leach it down through the soil, carrying it away from the grass root zone. Urea's normal active working life in the garden is measured in days or a week or two depending on moisture conditions.

Urea is not available to plants when the soil temperatures are cold. If you apply it too early in the spring before the grass has started to grow actively, it will likely be dissolved and leached out before the grass roots can make use of it. So, if the majority of the nitrogen in the bag is urea, apply it carefully after the grass has started to grow actively.

Phosphorus

Phosphorus is necessary to the growth systems that move and store energy within the plant; if the amounts of phosphorus are limited, so are the growth rates. It is also a primary component of the plant cell membrane, both in the leaf and in the root. Its role in root growth is well known throughout the gardening world. Just as it is important to flowering plants and trees, phosphorus is important to grass plants for root establishment. Seed development also depends on phosphorus since DNA contains phosphorus. So if the grass species you are growing spreads by seed, having adequate phosphorus available is a good tactic for maintaining a thick lawn.

There is some research to show that adding phosphorus to the soil reduces disease attacks on turfgrass, although the research is not consistent on this point. It very well may be that soils lacking in phosphorus invite diseases to attack grass plants, and that bringing the phosphorus levels up to optimum levels reduces the diseases that can attack the grass plant. In any case, having enough phosphorus in the soil is a good idea.

NITROGEN TIPS

- Do not add a bit extra to help the grass grow faster. This only creates problems with nitrogen overfeeding.
- Follow the directions for spreading fertilizer. Be prepared to give the lawn more frequent, but smaller, feedings during the growing season.

KEEP OFF THE GRASS

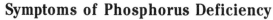

Symptoms of Phosphorus Deficiency

The first symptom of phosphorus deficiency is that the grass blades turn a dark, green color. This is *not* the color of healthy grass. It is much darker—a sickly green shade rather than a healthy green shade. Another way of describing it would be to say that there are purple tones in the green. Do not confuse this with cold injury that occurs in the fall when the soil temperatures start to plummet. Luckily for both of us, phosphorus deficiency is a rare event in the home lawn. There is normally more than enough phosphorus present for all lawn needs.

Secondary symptoms are much less noticeable and do not respond quickly to fertilizer application. Phosphorus deficiency lowers the grass's resistance to diseases and negatively affects its resistance to heat stress, drought, and its overwintering ability in cold climates. Unlike a nitrogen deficiency when improvements can be seen overnight, phosphorus deficiencies are not so quickly remedied or clearly identified.

Symptoms of Phosphorus Overdose

On the positive side of the coin, the interesting fact is that grass plants do not react to overdoses of phosphorus in the same way they react to overdoses of nitrogen (by dying). In fact, they hardly react at all to extremely high levels so the major problem is economic. I remember getting a soil test back for a lawn area and seeing extremely high levels of phosphorus in the result. It was a pleasure to find out I could save money for several years by not applying any phosphorus. You will simply waste your money if you apply too much phosphorus to your lawn, but you will have a hard time finding any negative health symptoms on the grass plants.

A second consequence (after your excess spending) of excess levels is that annual bluegrass will become established on your lawn. It loves high levels of phosphorus. If you want to grow this weed species, feed high phosphorus levels.

A third concern is pollution. Excess levels of phosphorus are associated with high algae levels in natural water areas. Although most of this comes from big users and producers of phosphorus such as golf courses and livestock farms, urban lawn owners cannot escape some responsibility. If the fertilizer spreader puts any prills (tiny beads) onto the street, they will be washed down into storm drains and local watercourses. If the lawn is next to water areas, as in cottages and camps, then spreading and careless handling can lead to runoff or fertilizer landing into or next to the water area. Reducing pollution is everyone's responsibility.

Potassium

Potassium is not found in any of the important cell constituents of grass plants. It is not found in cell walls, proteins, or chlorophyll. Although this may, on the surface, suggest that it is not as important as the other major plant nutrients, nothing could be further from the truth. Think of potassium as the gasoline that drives the grass growth engine. You don't find gasoline inside the walls of the engine, but without it, you can't drive very far. Plant scientists name a substance that performs this kind of activity a cofactor. Potassium has to be present for just about everything in the grass plant to work properly and is consumed in these processes but it is not used as a building block by the grass plant. Another way that potassium is used as an energy source is in opening and closing the stomata, or sweat glands. Found mostly on the underside of the leaves, stomata must open and close to allow the plant to sweat— and that takes energy. Potassium is involved in this process. Without it, the plant is not as efficient at opening and closing the stomata.

This leads us into the deficiency symptoms for potassium, and quite frankly, this is a problem. Unlike nitrogen with its very visible symptoms and phosphorus with its subtle but still distinct symptoms, potassium does not have a clearly or easily seen deficiency symptom. The grass doesn't grow as well as healthy grass. It is stressed because it cannot use its stomata efficiently; it is more prone to diseases and insects but it appears to be green healthy grass.

Older fertilizer blends tended to have lower potassium levels because turf scientists could not identify exactly what role it played. Now, even if they cannot pinpoint the exact functions of potassium, they understand its overall importance and fertilizer content reflects this importance. Older nutrient formulas might have been something like 35-10-10 or 25-5-5. Now the bags will have a higher third number. The percentage of potassium is usually higher than that of phosphorus, so the bags will read 35-15-30 or 25-5-15.

Minor Trace Nutrients

Sometimes, if grass is pale green and not growing very well, you'll be told to add micronutrients to the lawn. The quick answer to this is "yes and no"—it all depends on the micronutrient being recommended. If the grass is pale green, you should first add nitrogen to the lawn. If this does not cure the problem within 24 hours, then your lawn probably has a micronutrient problem. Let's examine the most common problems and their cures.

Iron

The absence of this micronutrient is most likely to cause yellowing of the grass. Iron is one of the main components of chlorophyll (the substance that makes the grass "green"), so if it is absent, there will be reduction in chlorophyll and a yellowing of the grass leaf. Iron is rarely deficient in soils that have a pH lower than 7.0. It *can* happen but it is quite rare. When the soil pH is above 7.0, the iron changes its form to one that is not as readily available to the plant. This is when we see the problem. You have two possible options if you suspect iron deficiency. You can send a soil sample to the extension services and wait a month for the results. Or, you can go to a good garden center, buy a bottle of fertilizer or micronutrient product that contains iron, and apply it to a small section of the lawn. Iron-deficient grass is very responsive to iron; you'll see a change within 24 hours if this is the problem.

Iron is usually sprayed onto the grass leaves to be directly absorbed by the plant. If you apply it to the soil as a powder, because of the soil pH that caused the problem in the first place, the iron will quickly change into the unavailable form. So if you have a choice at the garden center shelves, pick the spray. If your grass turns dark green overnight, you know that iron was the

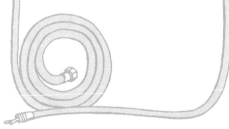

READING A FERTILIZER LABEL

Reading a fertilizer label is covered in more detail on page 26, but the most important thing to understand is the way the three major fertilizer elements are listed. The three numbers prominently displayed on every label represent the percentage of that element in the mix. So a 35-10-15 analysis would represent 35 percent nitrogen, 10 percent phosphorus, and 15 percent potassium. After you total the percentages of fertilizer, any leftover amounts are composed of fillers.

problem, and you also know that your soil is too basic (pH higher than 7.0). A long-term solution is to lower the soil pH, or make your soil more acidic.

Magnesium

If the nitrogen and iron treatments have not worked to darken the lawn, your grass may be lacking magnesium. This micronutrient might be to blame when the soil is acidic or if there is a high proportion of sand in the soil. Acidic soils have a chemistry that prevents the magnesium ion from attaching itself to the cations; this is a fancy way of saying that the plants can't absorb the magnesium. Adding magnesium makes it more available to the plant. But the long-term solution is to increase the pH of the soil, so there is room for the magnesium to get into the soil chemical mix. Sandy soil has the wrong electrical charges to attract and hold magnesium so it becomes deficient. Adding magnesium is a short-term, but effective, method of solving sandy soil deficiencies.

Luckily, we don't have to go far to obtain some magnesium: get out the Epsom salts. If you want to run a small test, mix a teaspoon of Epsom salts into a pint of warm water. Shake the mixture to dissolve the salts and then spray it on a small section of turf. It won't take much to turn the grass green if there's not enough magnesium, so only lightly spray the grass leaves. If the spray starts to run off the leaves, you are applying too much. Spray a little less so there is no runoff. If the grass greens up overnight or within 24 hours, magnesium deficiency is the culprit. Apply Epsom salts at the rate of 1 pound per 1,000 square feet of lawn. The easiest way is to mix this amount of salts into 3 or 4 gallons of warm water and apply the mix through a hand sprayer. Don't overapply the magnesium. A single pound per 1,000 square feet is enough to cure the problem.

Sulfur

I've seen TV advertisements touting the existence of sulfur in fertilizer as a wonder drug for the lawn. Well, maybe . . . Sulfur deficiencies will indeed cause a chlorosis or yellowing of the grass, but for the majority of lawns in North America, sulfur is not the culprit. I have seen reports that suggest that much of the continent

GREEN GRASS ON COOL FAIRWAYS

Golf course turf managers routinely spray iron onto the fairways in the fall when the temperatures start dropping. Nitrogen (particularly urea forms) becomes inactive when soil temperatures drop, and the grass cannot absorb it. A spray of iron helps hold the green color and the player's peace of mind.

KEEP OFF THE GRASS

receives between 10 and 15 pounds of sulfur per acre per year from rain. Only in areas where the rain comes directly from the sea (such as the West Coast) will sulfur deficiencies be a real problem. Having said that, sometimes, depending on the soil, sulfur will be the immediate cure for lawn yellowing.

Other Micronutrients

There are a variety of other micronutrients that rarely create problems because of their universal availability in soils. Some, such as boron, can create problems if there is an excess. For example, applying boron to the soil is the recommendation for controlling creeping charlie. If the gardener gets too enthusiastic about applying boron, the grass also might stop growing. This is why staying within recommended guidelines is so important. Chlorine, particularly from swimming pools, is always a concern for homeowners. At this point, I've never seen a report of chlorine damage from swimming pool water. The levels of chlorine are usually too low to hurt turf. If you can swim in it, the grass will not be bothered.

Organic Fertilizers

The use of compost or animal manure on our lawns has a long and distinguished history. Although not many of us apply 3 to 4 inches of fresh manure in the fall the way our gardening ancestors recommended, there is no reason compost shouldn't take a prominent role in our lawn care routines.

Most of us know that compost has food value. We use it on our flowering plants and vegetables. You might think that its low nitrogen content would suggest that it is not worth putting on the lawn, that there just is not enough food value in it to be worth the effort. However, the opposite is true. Compost has many more benefits for our lawns that just as a source of nitrogen.

To begin with, compost does provide food value but in ways that are not commonly understood by nonorganic gardeners. Compost feeds the micro-organisms that live in the soil, and it is these small inhabitants that unlock the nutrient value for our plants. Organic gardeners have a useful saying that many more gardeners should take to heart—"feed the soil, not the plants." As one example, if you feed compost to your soil, you will, by a roundabout process, be encouraging earthworms to move in. These earthworms chew through all manner of organic matter and soil particles, leaving wonderfully aerated and fertilized soil behind them. It is estimated that earthworms leave several hundred pounds of nitrogen per acre of turf per year behind as they work. If you object to the small piles that earthworms leave during their nocturnal activities, you are mowing your lawn too short. Increase the mowing height and you'll never know worms are helping you grow great grass.

If lawn diseases are a concern for you and you want to avoid having to spray **fungicides** or other chemicals, use compost. In modern university research, compost has been shown to fight most of the major fungus problems on a wide variety of crops. It does so in two ways. First, it actively suppresses the disease because of different chemicals contained in the compost. The phenol oils wipe out problems such as botrytis (a gray mold) with ease. Second, compost provides a nutrient base for other problem-suppressing agents. By feeding and encouraging the microscopic predators that eat and compete with disease **spores**, compost prevents diseases from even becoming established.

There is an entire world competing for nutrients and life under your lawn, and applying compost is an easy way to help the good guys beat the bad guys. The more you feed, the better. There is no such thing as too much compost.

Is there a downside to applying compost? Yes, there is. For some reason, annual bluegrass thrives more than any other grass in lawns that rely on compost feeding. This annual weed grass is a problem for golf courses (particularly the intensively managed greens) and those who take their lawns very seriously. I just look at annual bluegrass as a green grass that doesn't stick around too long but is much better looking than dandelions and their leaves. My only problem is that I don't always have enough compost to do everything I need and want to do.

COMPOST APPLICATION AMOUNT

Depth of Compost	Per 1,000 square feet
1/8 inch	10 1/4 cubic feet
1/4 inch	20 cubic feet
1/2 inch	40 cubic feet
1 inch	83 cubic feet

Milorganite

Milorganite (MILwaukee ORGAnic NITrogEn—get it?) is essentially aerobically composted sewage sludge from Milwaukee. Way back in 1879, the town fathers decided to build a sewage treatment plant that would eliminate pollution and the first Milorganite came off the line in 1926. The method chosen was quite innovative, and today, Milwaukee produces over fifty thousand tons of compost per year.

The city hired researchers to determine what the solid product was good for. They discovered that the analysis of the compost was 6-2-0, or 6 percent nitrogen and 2 percent phosphorus (there is some potassium but too little to label). It was an excellent fertilizer and much more economical to apply than manure. Milorganite became extremely popular with golf course superintendents who were relieved of the problems, and attendant complaints, caused by spreading manure on intensively managed turf. Would you like to stroll up to the tee surrounded by the aroma of fresh manure and have to use the foot scraper at every hole, not just before you entered the nineteenth tee?

By solving this problem for golf courses, Milorganite's role in the turf industry was assured. An added benefit is that it will not burn the grass if you apply too much, unlike regular lawn fertilizers that will quickly burn and brown green turf if spilled. Milorganite is still available today at garden centers. See the Compost Application Instructions sidebar if you use Milorganite or your own compost product.

For cool season grasses (see Chapter 1) apply 40 pounds of Milorganite per 2,500 square feet of lawn three times each season: early spring, midsummer, and very late fall just before the freeze. The early-spring application gets the food value to the lawn when the grass has just finished its first flush of growth and is looking for food. The midsummer feeding, done in early July, keeps the grass healthy and growing. The late-fall feeding goes directly to the roots and to increase winter and early-spring performance.

For warm season grasses, increase the number of applications to four per year. Apply 40 pounds, or one bag, per 2,500 square feet of lawn in the early spring, very early summer, late summer, and late fall. Do not apply the late-summer feeding within one

COMPOST APPLICATION INSTRUCTIONS

1. To handle Milorganite, set the opening at the bottom of your fertilizer the spreader to three-quarters open.
2. Put 8 pounds of Milorganite into the hopper. Note 3 cups of Milorganite equals 1 pound. Do not use your spouse's good measuring cups!
3. Start fertilizing your lawn. Begin at an outer edge and when the spreader runs out, leave it where it ran out.
4. Measure the area of lawn you covered. If this area (width x length) is close to 500 square feet, then you have the spreader set correctly and can continue fertilizing.
   - If you have covered more than 500 square feet, you'll have to slightly close the opening to slow down the flow. Repeat step 3 on an unfertilized area.
   - If you have covered fewer than 500 square feet, you'll have to widen the spreader opening to increase the flow rate. Repeat step 3 on an unfertilized area.
   - If you have one of the following spreaders, the settings have already been worked out for you. Just set it and away you go. If your spreader is not listed here, you'll have to go through the steps just described.

Spreader Settings

ROTARY SPREADER	REGULAR FEEDING 40 LBS. PER 2,500 SQ. FT.	NEW LAWNS 40 LBS. PER 1,250 SQ. FT.
Ames/Earthway	25	25, make two passes
LawnCrafter (Quaker)	6	6, make two passes
Red Devil	19	19, make two passes
Republic EZ Grow	12, make two passes	14, make two passes
Republic EZ	16	16, make two passes
Scotts EasyGreen	32	32, make two passes
Scotts SpeedyGreen	9, make two passes	12, make three passes

DROP SPREADER	REGULAR FEEDING 40 LBS. PER 2,500 SQ. FT.	NEW LAWNS 40 LBS. PER 1,250 SQ. FT.
Ames/Earthway	23	26
LawnCrafter	9	15
Red Devil	12	14
Republic EZ Grow	9	12
Scotts AccuGreen	11	18

month of any expected frost in your area. Stimulating plants to grow and having this new growth immediately killed before it can contribute to the overall health of the plant is a waste of plant food and is detrimental to the overall health of the plant. This is as true for grass plants as it is for flowering garden plants.

When to Feed

Spring

The objective of fertilizing in the spring is to give the overwintering grass roots a bit of help but not to force them into growth. If you are following the proper fall feeding rates, then the grass will start off quite nicely on its own without being forced. The lower rates of fertilizing in the spring are to ensure maximum chlorophyll production, not to "get that grass growing."

Having said that, if the spring is quite wet, it is advisable to cut back on the fertilizer even more. Excessively wet soils will not promote good grass growth and overfeeding with nitrogen puts stress on the plant. On the other hand, if you have a very sandy soil with high drainage rates, the lawn will benefit from a bit more nitrogen than the normal rate. Do not, however, go above $3/4$ pound of nitrogen per 1,000 square feet on sandy soils.

Summer

Avoid fertilizing during the high heat of summer. The temperatures are too hot for good grass growth, and feeding at this time just adds stress to the plant. However, feeding is a good idea later in the summer, when the night temperatures begin to cool down and the grass really starts to grow again. A mid- to late-summer feeding will hold the grass until the important fall feeding.

The exception to this is if you apply a slow-release fertilizer in early summer. The release of nitrogen is controlled by the temperature or moisture levels and will meet the growing needs of the grass without supplemental feeding during the mid- to late-summer period. Follow the directions on the label and do not exceed the recommended rates.

A TYPICAL FERTILIZER PROGRAM

When to Apply	How Much to Apply (lbs. of nitrogen per 1,000 sq.ft.)
March/April	$1/2$
June	$1/2$
Early to mid-August	1
Late fall	1 to $1 1/2$

Fall

Many turf experts recommend feeding the lawn a large dose of nitrogen in late fall. The best grass *root* growth takes place when the soil temperature is between 58° and 65°F. So even when the air temperatures are cooling down, the soil temperatures stay high enough to encourage good root growth. Keep in mind that the grass tops grow best between 65° and 75°F, and that when air temperatures get cool, new shoot development stops. The roots get to keep all this food energy, store it, overwinter in better condition, and are much healthier the following spring when they produce new shoots.

Regardless of why it works, many professional turf managers are using this practice because it does work. It's a great idea for the home lawn too.

How Much to Feed

Feeding the Warm Season Lawn

In most of the United States, all turf goes dormant during the winter months. Warm season grasses are not an exception, and their straw brown color is due to a loss of chlorophyll. No photosynthesis takes place to green up the shoots and no carbohydrates are produced to feed the roots. Growth starts to take off again in the spring when temperatures start to warm up and hits its peak during the midsummer heat.

There are differences in rates of application depending on how the grass is being used; heavier usage, such as in playgrounds, will need heavier feedings. The rule of thumb, however, is to apply 1 pound of nitrogen fertilizer for every 1,000 square feet of lawn for every month the grass is actively growing. That's pretty easy.

The only exception to this is in the tropical areas where the grass never stops growing. There, feeding becomes a bit of a balancing act. If you feed a pound of nitrogen every month, you'll be mowing more than you ever thought possible. If you cut that in half, the grass might start to yellow. It depends on how much rain you get, the nature of the soil, and numerous other factors. So, the rule of thumb here is to feed 1 pound of nitrogen the first month and

DON'T OVERFEED

A word of caution here. If you decide to feed your lawn 2 pounds of nitrogen every second month instead of once per month, you'll be mowing grass every second night for a few weeks until the grass absorbs the excess. A weakened lawn will burn and die with all that fertilizer.

Don't be tempted to overfeed a southern lawn unless you really, really like mowing the lawn.

KEEP OFF THE GRASS

then wait until the turf starts to turn the slightest bit yellow. Feed the lawn another pound of nitrogen per 1,000 square feet to green it up. Wait. Feed. Wait. Pretty soon you'll have a good picture of how often you have to feed your lawn area to get it to stay green and growing.

Even though the grass never really goes dormant, there will be a time during the low-light winter months when its growth will slow. The shorter days and lowered light levels signal the plant to take a bit of a break. Reduce the feeding during these slow growth periods. I recommend feeding only when the grass starts to look a bit peaked or off-color. You'll hold back feeding at some times and increase at others. Experience will tell you when to push for growth and when to hold off.

Feeding the Low-Maintenance Lawn

If you are unsure how much to feed, the University of Guelph in Ontario, Canada recommends the following program for a cool season, low-maintenance lawn. The total nitrogen to be applied to the lawn is 2 pounds per 1,000 square feet per year. This is applied in three doses: (1) a half pound at the end of April or early May when the grass begins to green up and start growing, (2) a second half pound in midsummer—the end of June or middle of July, and (3) the last full pound in late October after the grass leaves have gone dormant for the season (but the roots are still very active). If you are unsure what analysis of fertilizer to use, try to obtain one that has as close to a 4-1-2 ratio as possible.

How to Use a Fertilizer Spreader

No matter which spreader you buy, uniform coverage is the key to success. And that, as in many things, comes down to the quality of the spreader. Using cheap, plastic spreaders often produces cheap spreading results. And those are a waste of seed, fertilizer, and money. Buy the best you can afford.

There are two kinds of spreaders on the market: rotary and drop spreaders. Rotary spreaders measure the granules or seed and throw

NITROGEN AND THE LOW-MAINTENANCE LAWN

Timing	How Much to Apply (lbs. of nitrogen per 1,000 sq. ft.)
April	½
End of June to July	½
End of October	1

HOW TO CALCULATE THE AMOUNT
OF NITROGEN IN FERTILIZER TO APPLY

The numbers on a fertilizer bag represent the percent of the nutrient in the mix.
So, a 40-15-30 number series would indicate that 40 percent of the mix is
nitrogen, 15 percent is phosphorus, and 30 percent is potassium. This means
that if you want to apply 1 pound of fertilizer, you have to do some basic math.
Here's the easy formula:

$$\text{Amount of bagged fertilizer to apply} = \frac{\text{Amount of nitrogen the crop needs}}{\text{Percentage of nitrogen in the fertilizer}} \times 100$$

So, to apply 1 pound of nitrogen of a 40-15-30 blend, the formula would
look like this:

$$\text{Amount of bagged fertilizer to apply} = \frac{1}{40} \times 100.$$
The answer is 2.5 pounds.

In this example, we'll use 2½ pounds of fertilizer per 1,000 square feet
to apply 1 pound of nitrogen to the lawn.

them out in a broad swath that is usually several feet wide. Consider purchasing or renting a rotary spreader if:

- You have a very large lawn.
- You don't have flower beds or other garden areas in the middle of the lawn that will be fertilized by the swath of fertilizer.
- You like to get the job done as quickly as possible.

Drop spreaders measure out the fertilizer and then drop it in as wide a band as the spreader is wide. You'll find a drop spreader is good if:

- You have a small lawn.
- You have gardens or other areas in the middle of your lawn and you need precise fertilizer placement.
- You can take the time to do a precise placement. Drop spreaders are a bit slower, and they don't cover as much area in a single pass.

Setting Up Your Spreader to Work with Fertilizer

If your lawn fertilizer label has the recommendations for setting your spreader, do the following:

- Turn the spreader setting to OFF.
- Turn the setting to that recommended by the manufacturer. (Turning the setting to OFF first ensures the fertilizer gate is closing and opening properly.)
- Fill the spreader. Do this on a driveway or walkway, *not* on the lawn. If you spill fertilizer, you'll burn the lawn.
- Use the following guidelines for your spreader pattern.

Setting up a fertilizer spreader for granular fertilizer is very similar to adjusting it for Milorganite (see page 72). If your label does not have directions, follow these steps:

Calculate how much fertilizer you have to apply to achieve the amount of nitrogen you need to put on 1,000 square feet of lawn. Divide

SPREADER CHOICES

When comparing spreaders of equal dollar value and manufacture, the drop spreader will normally give better accuracy for the dollar value than will the rotary. In other words, if you have to buy a cheap spreader—buy the drop spreader.

KEEP OFF
THE
GRASS

this figure by 2. So, for example, if you were to put 5 pounds of fertilizer on the lawn per 1,000 square feet, put 2½ pounds in the hopper.

Step 1: Set the bottom of the spreader to half open.

Step 2: Put the fertilizer into the hopper.

Step 3: Start fertilizing your lawn. As with the Milorganite, start at an outer edge and when the spreader runs out, leave it where it ran out.

Step 4: Measure the area of the lawn you covered. If this area (width *x* length) is close to 500 square feet, then you have it set correctly and can continue fertilizing.

- If you've covered less than 500 square feet, you'll have to close the opening slightly to slow down the flow. Repeat step 3 on an unfertilized area.
- If you've covered more than 500 square feet, you'll have to open the spreader opening to increase the flow rate. Repeat step 3 on an unfertilized area.

Getting Good Coverage

If you have a rectangular lawn, follow these guidelines:

- Make two header strips. This means pushing two passes with the spreader at each end of the lawn (see the illustration on the next page). This two-spreader width gives you a turnaround space at each end of the lawn.
- Push the spreader back and forth between the header strips. Shut off the spreader just before you enter the header strip and turn it on again after you make your turn and just before you leave the header strip.
- Remember, if you are using a drop spreader, your spreader is wider than your dropping section. So make sure the wheel marks just overlap.
- If you're using a rotary spreader, be sure to create a small overlap along the previous drop area to prevent streaky applications.

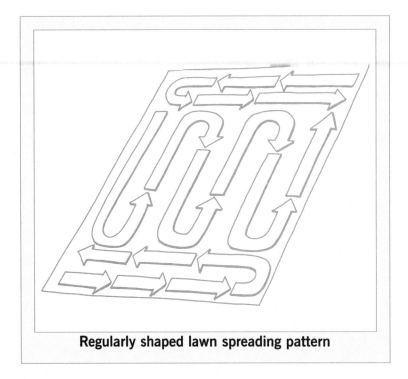

Regularly shaped lawn spreading pattern

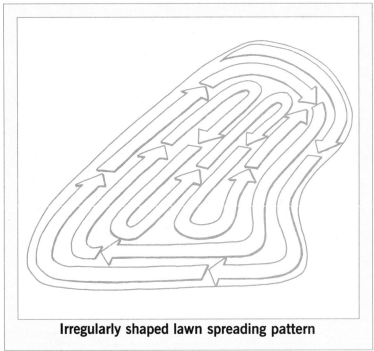

Irregularly shaped lawn spreading pattern

If you have an irregularly shaped lawn, follow these guidelines:

- Make a header strip two passes wide around the edge of the lawn.
- Go back and forth with the spreader along the longest direction (see the illustration). Again, turn off the spreader before hitting the turnaround header strip, and turn it on again just before leaving the strip.

Different Types of Fertilizers

Weed-and-Feed Products

Weed-and-feed products are big sellers in the spring and have been sold by the chemical industry to homeowners as the magic bullet of turf care. I'm not a fan of these products. I believe that feeding a lawn is one activity and taking care of the weeds is a separate activity. When you combine them, you tend to get the worst of both worlds. To obtain adequate weed control, you typically have to feed your lawn very high levels of nitrogen, and we've seen what this does to the lawn and to the soil life. Similarly, if you feed nitrogen at recommended rates for lawn health, you may not obtain good weed control because your chemical application rates are too low.

From an economic standpoint, two-action products are also expensive. They are much more costly than purchasing the fertilizer and herbicide products separately and applying them as you require them.

Weed-and-feed products are also not particularly environmentally friendly. We'll discuss environmentally friendly products in Chapter 5.

If you have to feed your lawn, do so. If you have to control weeds, do so. Don't get the activities confused. There are no magic bullets in gardening.

EVAPOTRANSPIRATION

Evapotranspiration is one of those two-word combinations beloved by academics. In this case, *evaporation* (water loss from the soil's surface) and *transpiration* (water loss from the plant) are combined. Evapotranspiration is the amount of water lost by both the soil and the plant combined.

This is only important if you want to apply water in a scientific way. Each grass variety has a specific measurement of how much water it requires. This number is called a *crop coefficient*. It is normally a decimal number less than 1. For example, Bermuda grass has a crop coefficient of 0.6.

The second thing you need to know to precisely measure the amount of irrigation water is a pan evaporation rate. To determine this rate, measure the evaporation amount in inches over the course of a week (from a circular pan).

Now, to obtain the amount of water the lawn needs, multiply the pan evaporation rate by the crop coefficient. The resulting number will be the number of inches of water that has to be applied to replace that lost by evapotranspiration.

Liquid Fertilizer

There are many excellent liquid plant food products on the market specifically for lawns. They work well particularly if you read and follow the directions. It is just as easy to burn your lawn with a liquid food (some garden experts say, "easier") as it is with granular fertilizers.

A few tips will make your job easier.

- Make sure the lawn is not suffering from drought when you apply liquid fertilizer. If drought is a problem, the grasses will be under even more stress when fed.
- Be very careful about following the mixing directions. Make sure the products are fully dissolved before you start to spray. Otherwise, there will be an uneven application of nitrogen—the early spray will be weak and the latter too strong.
- Set up a spray pattern similar to that of your granular fertilizer spreading. Do not overlap the liquid. Overlapping will create sections of very heavy growth and your lawn will have grass stripes with taller grass along the stripes.
- Do not use high-nitrogen liquid lawn fertilizers around trees and shrubs. The roots from a shrub or tree go out past the drip line of the plant (the edge of the extent of the branches and foliage). If the distance from the trunk to the drip line is 10 feet, then the roots are out another 10 feet. Do not spray within 20 feet of the trunk of this tree. Overstimulating trees and shrubs with high nitrogen fertilizers will create problems for the tree.
- After fertilizing, water the lawn to wash off the leaves and drive the fertilizer down to the root level. This prevents the leaves from "burning." Sometimes, when the water carrying the fertilizer evaporates, the remaining fertilizer on the leaf blade will burn the leaves.

Irrigating

How Much Water Does Grass Need?

Unfortunately, there is no hard-and-fast answer to this question. It's one of those *it depends* kind of answers. You know, "It depends on the soil; it depends on the sunshine levels; it depends on where you live." A good rule of thumb though is that turf requires between 1 and 1½ inches of water a week to thrive. It doesn't matter whether the water comes from irrigation or natural rainfall—or a combination of both. Let's look at a few key concepts to understand watering and what you can do to improve your turf.

How Often Should I Water?

Another of those *it depends* questions. Fortunately, even though there are all manner of factors to consider, there is a general rule of thumb that is accepted throughout the turf industry:

Water deeply and infrequently.

You are trying to wet the soil just enough so that the roots of the grass get enough water but no deeper. If you water too much, the water goes below the level of the roots. If they can't reach it, the water is wasted. If you do not water enough, the grass roots congregate in the shallow water level and do not go down very deeply. Shallow rooted grass is prone to more problems (particularly drought) than deeply rooted grass plants.

Assuming that you are going to apply between 1 to 1½ inches of water per week, apply it as a single dose on regular soils or at most split it into two equal applications. Do not water a little bit every night or three or four times a week. This promotes shallow rooting. On sandy soils, the irrigation should be split into two equal applications because the fast draining nature of sandy soils means the water will quickly move downward and out of the reach of thirsty roots.

The one soil that presents more problems with irrigation than any other is a heavy clay. It is almost impossible to say, "water once or twice a week" with these water-repelling soils. If you have

HOW TO MEASURE THE WATER APPLIED BY SPRINKLERS

Set up widemouthed margarine tubs or metal cans around your sprinkler pattern. One tub is fine, although using three equally spaced tubs will help measure whether your sprinkler is spreading water properly. Set the sprinkler going and measure the length of time it takes the sprinkler to put ½ inch of water into the tub.

This is the length of time your sprinkler system has to run (twice a week) to provide the lawn with 1 inch of water per week.

Similarly, if you decide to apply 1½ inches of water per week, you'll have to set the timer to measure how long it takes to fill the tubs with ¾ inch of water.

heavy clay, and if the soil is dry, you're going to have to water more frequently than once a week because the small particles of clay won't allow much water to penetrate before it starts to puddle and run off. With dried-out heavy clay soils, plan on watering three times a week. Once the soil is wet, apply water until it starts to puddle. Measure this amount of water and adjust your watering frequency to ensure the grass gets its inch of water.

One last note. Shallow or too frequent watering promotes the growth of weed species of grass such as creeping bent grass and rough bluegrass. It also aids in the germination and establishment of broadleaf weeds such as dandelions.

When Should I Water?

If you water at night, the turf canopy will stay wet longer. Keeping the grass leaves wet can lead to increased levels of disease, so avoid night watering if at all possible.

Daytime watering has its own problem: evaporation. On a hot day, approximately half of the water coming out of the sprinkler nozzle will evaporate before it reaches the soil. This is costly if you are on a metered municipal water system. Some of that water will evaporate in the air and some will disappear after it has hit the grass leaves. One consolation is that the water that reaches the grass leaves is cleaning the grass blades (which makes them more efficient) and discouraging insects such as spider mites that do not like excess moisture.

The *best* time to water is first thing in the morning when there is already dew on the ground. The cooler temperatures reduce the evaporation loss and the grass leaves will dry off as soon as the sun hits them. If your sprinkler system can be set on a timer, set it for sunrise.

Oh, one last thing, it's OK to run your sprinkler during a rain shower if you forget to turn off the timer. It won't hurt the grass, but it will ruin your reputation with the neighbors. There are few funnier sights in gardening than a sprinkler system running full tilt in the middle of a good downpour.

Summer Drought

At some point in the middle of the summer, your grass might start to look a bit peaked. Your lawn started out great this past spring and you've fed it and mowed it and were prepared for the best lawn in the neighborhood contest. Then came the rise in water bills, the worst summer on record for heat and drought, and your lawn is starting to look like it has seen better days. So much for the contest.

What are the things you can do to help your lawn when there's no water in sight? The first (here we go again) is to increase the mowing height. It's amazing how often you'll see this advice as we go through this book. Taller grass is less stressed. If you're in the middle of a heat and drought wave—mow it tall. Just for the record, taller grass can actually cool itself down by as much as 7° to 14°F. This does take some planning ahead. Start mowing a bit taller each week for several weeks before the height of the summer. By the time July rolls around, your mower deck should be on the highest setting you intend to use.

Another environmental component that you want to encourage are VAM. This acronym stands for Vesicular Arbuscular Mycorrhizae, and these are beneficial **fungi.** Good guys! They form a working partnership with the roots of your plants. They give the roots moisture and minerals, which they've mined from deeper soils, in exchange for small amounts of carbohydrate nutrients. This symbiotic relationship exists in something like 80 percent of all grass species, and these little guys can really help the grass plants survive drought and stress. You introduce VAM to your lawn by applying compost and by continually feeding the lawn with organic matter. The only negative here is that if you apply a fungicide to your lawn, one of the first victims is VAM. Remember, although they are beneficial, they are still killed by the same chemicals that kill bad fungus problems.

One of the things you can do to increase the organic matter of the lawn is easy: stop collecting lawn clippings and removing them from the lawn. This will be discussed further in other sections of the book. If you leave the clippings, you leave organic matter. If you leave organic matter, the VAM will be pleased. Grass clippings do

TIME REQUIRED TO APPLY 1 INCH OF WATER TO 1,000 SQUARE FEET

Hose Diameter	Gallons per minute	Time (minutes)
7/16	7.3	84
1/2	10.9	56
5/8	15.1	41
3/4	26.8	23

not contribute to thatch buildup, and it's a good idea to let them lie where they fall. Some researchers believe that decomposing grass clippings produce a chemical that prevents crabgrass from germinating. Although the jury is still out on this, it is one more reason to leave the clippings on the lawn.

How to Reduce the Amount of Water You Use

If you're not experiencing drought, but you want to get ready for it—or if you simply want to reduce the amount of water you use—there are several things you can do:

- Choose species of grass that are drought-tolerant. In the South, you might experiment with native grasses such as buffalo grass. In the North, Kentucky bluegrass is one of the more drought-tolerant species.
- Mow your lawn higher than normal. Taller grass blades produce more carbohydrates for the roots to use. Healthier roots grow larger and longer and can reach available water that shallow roots cannot. Do everything you can to increase the growth of the roots including fertilizing.
- Keep the grass well fed (but not excessively fed). If a grass plant is underfed, it cannot produce enough carbohydrates to feed the roots and encourage dense rooting. Overfeeding, on the other hand, increases the stress on plants that need water. It forces them to absorb nutrients and increase the shoot growth rate without adequate water to support this growth. This means that the outer layer of the grass (the cuticle) will be thinner and more prone to insect and disease attacks.
- Use antidesiccants if you are very, very serious about your lawn. These sprays coat the leaf surfaces with a waxlike substance and plug up the stomata or sweat pores of the plant. That stops the plant from losing moisture.
- Avoid excessive cultivation or cultivation at the wrong time. It can increase the plant's water usage. Time any aeration or raking for spring or fall, and not during the heat of the summer.
- Beware of excessive thatch. It can reduce the availability of water to the plants.

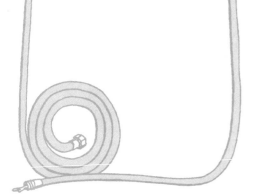

SUNSCREEN

It is a good idea to slop on some sunscreen when you venture outdoors. As a gardener, I wear a large-brimmed straw hat, old long-sleeved white shirts when the weather is really hot, and sunscreen as protection against the sun's ultra-violet rays. I'd recommend you do the same.

Thatch

Thatch is a layer of layer of dead organic matter above the soil line and below the living tissue of the green blades of grass. It is a naturally occurring phenomenon that becomes a problem only when too much builds up.

Why Is It a Problem?

When the thatch gets too thick, grass roots move out of the soil and up into the thatch layer. The result is fewer roots in the soil beneath the thatch. This thin layer of roots is easily damaged by a lack of water, excessive heat, or cold. Remember that a good healthy root system creates a good lawn.

Excessively thick thatch layers support disease spores better than healthy decomposing thatch layers. Thatch forms because there is reduced decomposition of dead grass parts. For any number of reasons, the soil micro-organisms responsible for breaking down and eating disease spores do not survive. Without these micro-organisms creating a natural defense, diseases survive and attack the grass more frequently.

Thick layers of thatch do not buffer the grass roots as does the soil. When the temperature gets very hot or very cold, these changes are passed right along to the roots rather than being buffered by the giant flywheel effect of the soil's mass. In other words, the soil stays more even in temperature because there's so much of it; changes are quite slow and gradual. These changes are not gradual in the thatch layer.

What Causes Thatch?

There are several things that create this condition, but mostly the blame can be placed squarely on the shoulders of the gardener in charge of the lawn. Thatch is a management problem. It is a symptom of an imbalance in the grass plant and soil ecology. To begin with, some decomposing organic matter is quite natural. Grass plants are dying and being reproduced, lawn clippings are left to decompose and feed the lawn again, and the normal wear and tear of thousands of growing plants in a single location leads to the accumulation of normal organic matter levels.

THATCHING TENDENCY OF TURFGRASS

High: Zoysia grass, Bermuda grass, creeping red fescue

Medium: Kentucky bluegrass, creeping bent grass, hard fescue, chewings fescue

Low: Perennial ryegrass, tall fescue, buffalo grass

KEEP OFF THE GRASS

This organic matter is normally attacked by all manner of soil organisms. Big ones such as earthworms actually eat the grass debris, turning it into super soil to feed plants and improve the soil's structure. In fact, earthworms are probably the most important thatch control system on your lawn. They eat the lawn clippings and leave behind fertilized soil. Their tunneling aerates the soil, allowing greater water infiltration and oxygen—in effect, they act as mini-decompactors. Overfeeding your lawn (particularly with nitrogen) can inhibit the growth of worms. Pesticides also kill worms. Pesticides such as chlorpyrifos, Diazinon, and trichlorfon can kill between 60 and 90 percent of the worm population in a single application. Worms will take a minimum of 30 to 60 days to recover their populations after a pesticide kill-off.

The smaller organisms, bacteria and fungi, work their magic to decompose the debris and turn it into humus to further feed the grass community and improve the soil's texture and health. There is an entire community under your feet trying to help the grass survive and thrive. If you think about it for a moment, some of the best gardening land in North America was found under the vast grasslands of the Midwest. These microscopic soil communities created that wonderful soil and they're trying to create a similar situation under your lawn.

Gardeners can create conditions in which the soil community can't do its job. Here are a few examples:

- The major culprit is overfeeding nitrogen. By feeding too much nitrogen, the grass plants are forced into excessive growth, creating more organic debris. This would not be a problem except that this excessive nitrogen also disrupts the soil organisms and kills off some of the beneficial organisms. This is a double blow; too much organic matter is being produced and not enough soil organisms are left to consume it. So, in this case, more fertilizer may make the lawn grow faster and greener, but it creates thatch and destroys the soil organisms that are working so hard to make a good lawn.

• Excessive watering is another contributor. Too much water drowns the soil micro-organisms and creates a low-oxygen environment (if water is filling the spaces between the soil particles, oxygen can't be there too). This anaerobic (without oxygen) decomposition condition also reduces the numbers of micro-organisms.

• Soil micro-organisms that eat grass debris exist in slightly acidic soil conditions. If the soil is allowed to become either too acidic or too alkaline, then the microbe population is reduced.

• Herbicides and pesticides kill earthworms and other soil microbes. A single spray can reduce the microbial population for at least a month and worm populations for even longer than that. If you have to use sprays, follow the label rates and do not increase the concentration of chemical thinking it will give you a better effect. Fungicides are particularly potent. They kill the good grass-decomposing fungi along with disease-creating fungi.

• Don't remove the grass clippings. Many lawn owners believe the gardening myth that you have to remove the grass clippings or you'll get thatch. Grass clippings are mainly composed of cellulose, a material that is easily broken down by soil microbial action. Thatch is mostly composed of lignin—a component of grass crowns, stolons, and rhizomes. Cellulose-rich grass clippings are pretty much irrelevant to the creation of thatch.

In short, the overall management of the lawn creates thatch. The management must be improved to eliminate thatch.

How Do I Control Thatch?

The first and most obvious step is to correct the management practices that lead to thatch. Do you overfeed? Do you spray too many chemicals that kill off the beneficial organisms in your lawn?

KINDS OF AERATION MACHINES

There are two kinds of aeration machines you can rent. The first is a solid-tined machine that drives spikes into the ground to create holes. No soil plug is removed with this machine. There is less damage to the turf, so the grass recovers more quickly. Unfortunately, solid tines are not as effective in loosening and aerating the soil as the core-aerification machines.

The core machines punch down into the soil (the depth is adjustable) and remove a small plug of soil. As you can imagine, this is disruptive to the grass plants, but it is quite effective for aeration and loosening the turf. The grass will take a few days to recover. Raking compost into the holes will speed up the process. The cores can be composted or left on the lawn (looking like so many goose droppings) to be absorbed by the worms and other soil critters.

Go down the list of causes and change your management practices accordingly.

The number-one cause of thatch is too much nitrogen, so this is the first place to start your remedial program. Back off on the fertilizer and allow the grass plants to get a bit hungry. Get a soil test so that your future fertility program will meet the needs of the lawn.

As soon as the beneficial micro-organism population gets back up to regular operation, the thatch will probably disappear on its own. Without high nitrogen counts producing too much grass for our small friends to handle, they will quickly expand their numbers to handle the excess organic matter.

Lime is often a good thing to add to thatch that is stubborn. Thatch tends to be on the acidic side, and a light application of lime (1 to 2 pounds per 1,000 square feet) will aid in its decomposition.

Watch your irrigation. Too much watering—especially those systems that are set to come on every day—is another prime cause of thatch. In these cases, reducing the watering reduces the thatch.

Soil compaction can also be a cause of thatch because little oxygen is available between the smashed-together soil particles. Oxygen is a prime requirement of the micro-organisms that eat thatch; they need it to thrive. Just as overwatering destroys air spaces, so does compacting the soil. The normal recommendation is to aerate the soil in the fall with a coring machine. You can rent one from the local rental store and finish the average-size lawn in an hour or so. The best time for aeration is in the early fall when the grass has recovered from the summer's heat and drought and while it still has six weeks to grow and recover before winter dormancy.

Give the grass a good stiff raking and then run the aeration machine around the lawn. If you really want to improve your lawn, rake compost into the holes created by the coring machine. Your lawn thatch will quickly become a thing of the past.

Don't Roll Your Lawn

Every spring there is a mania that hits suburban lawn owners. The lawn rollers come out to squash each and every lawn into uniform billiard table smoothness. Rollers are rented by the hundreds every

Not All Grass Is Lawn Grass

Although there are approximately ten thousand species of grass in the world, slightly fewer than fifty of them are good for lawns. Not a great percentage, but again, better than any other plant.

KEEP OFF THE GRASS

spring. To save money while searching for the perfect lawn, groups of neighbors get together to rent a lawn roller. I've even seen industrial pavement rollers used to roll the lawns to a fine smooth surface. And each gardener thinks it is helping the lawn.

Nothing could be further from the truth. Dragging several hundred pounds of lawn roller around the turf only does one thing and it does it well: *It compacts the soil.* By now, you already know that soil compaction is bad for the lawn. It wrecks drainage, lowers soil oxygen levels, increases thatch, and prevents good root growth. Soil compaction is one of the worst things you can do to your lawn and it is the only thing a lawn roller does really well. The earlier in the spring you roll your lawn (the wetter the soil), the worse the damage.

The only place a light lawn roller has is with seedling and sod establishment. Other than that, keep it off your lawn.

Mowing

It is important to understand one thing right at the beginning of this section. Grass does not like to be mown any more than any other plant. It just happens to be good at recovering from this abuse, and this is why we grow grass. If there were a better plant to act as a groundcover, to fulfill the same functions as grass, we'd use it. Grass is simply the best plant for the job.

This doesn't mean that it has to like having its head cut off each week and the other indignities we heap on it. When you mow, you cut off the growing tip of the plant. Cutting or ripping off this tip leaves open plant tissue that can be invaded by disease organisms. The removal of 30 percent of the leaf surface every time you mow also reduces the plant's ability to feed itself. Both photosynthesis and carbohydrate production are reduced, and the plant's ability to feed itself is threatened. Why would anybody think mowing was good for grass?

The turfgrass that we use for lawns does have a unique characteristic: When it is mowed, it can produce new plants from the crown and stem nodes. By cutting off the top, the plant increases the density of its growth below the cut. It retains the ability to feed itself by increasing the numbers of shoots below the cut line.

Turfgrasses do not produce new shoots by magic. They require food and water to do so, and good health depends on how the lawn gardener treats the turf. By cutting off the tops of the plants, we also restrict root growth. Without the food produced by the 30 percent we cut off, the roots are not able to expand. So you can see that our lawn management dictates success or failure.

Mowing then is an important lawncare activity. It is not just going out to hack off the tops of the grass plants. The techniques and methods used are as important in the life and health of the lawn as any other thing you'll do.

How Does Mowing Affect the Grass?

Mowing has an interesting effect on grass. A hormone referred to as an auxin concentrates in the growing points of plants. When enough of this hormone accumulates in the growing tips, growth slows down and sometimes stops altogether. Mowing grass (removing the growing ends) physically removes this concentrated auxin from the plant; once it disappears, the plant is again encouraged to grow. The plant responds to this lowered auxin level by producing new shoots and tillers.

It does so even when it is starving. Remember that we're reducing the plant's ability to produce food when we chop it back by 30 percent. These new shoots make the turf area thicken up and get more dense. We get more new grass plants in the same area of ground. The roots of a mown grass plant are not as large as those of an unmown grass plant. This means the root can't forage for food and water as effectively.

If you are going to mow, you have to feed your lawn to replace the food that the smaller root area cannot obtain. If you don't feed, the grass will not be as dense and thick. Open areas invite weeds. So mowing can be a direct cause of weed infestation.

Grasses vary in their tolerance to mowing. Kentucky bluegrass, for example, is an upright growing species. If you cut it shorter than 1½ inches, it will slowly die. Creeping bent grass, either a

HOW DEEP ARE THE ROOTS?

As a rule of thumb, multiply the height of the plant by 3 to discover how deep the roots go. If the turf is 1 inch tall, the roots will be approximately 3 inches deep. At a mowing height of 3 inches, the grass roots will be down approximately 9 inches.

RECOMMENDED MOWING HEIGHTS FOR TURFGRASS SPECIES

SPECIES	COOL WEATHER MOWING HEIGHT (INCHES)	WARM WEATHER MOWING HEIGHT (INCHES)
Colonial bent grass	0.3–0.8	0.5–0.8
Creeping bent grass	0.125–0.8	0.188–0.8
Fine fescues	0.5–2.00	1.5–3.0
Kentucky bluegrass	1.5–2.25	2.25–3.0
Perennial ryegrass	1.5–2.0	2.0–3.0
Tall fescue	1.75–3.0	2.5–3.5
Bermuda grass	0.25–1.5	Not applicable
Bahia grass	1.5–3.0	Not applicable
Buffalo grass	1.0–unmowed	Not applicable
Carpetgrass	1.0–3.0	Not applicable
Centipede grass	1.0–3.0	Not applicable
Seashore paspalum	0.45–2.0	Not applicable
St. Augustine grass	3.0–4.0	Not applicable
Zoysia grass	0.5–2.0	Not applicable

MOWER BASICS

There are two things that I learned as a kid about machines. First, it is a cardinal sin to start a small engine machine like a lawn mower without checking the oil. Running a lawn mower without checking the oil is an invitation to a blown engine. I passed along this message to my kids, and all the machines are checked for oil before work starts.

Second, there is little point doing work with a dull tool. Keeping the blades sharp is a bit of extra work, but it pays off in reducing engine wear and tear (a sharp blade cuts easier and makes the engine work less than trying to cut with a dull blade). You can either learn how to sharpen blades or how to pay for replacing engines.

Actually, I learned three things when I mowed the lawn as a kid. The third was that if I couldn't start the engine, I didn't have to mow the lawn. Engines are simpler now.

lawn weed that infests your lawn when the Kentucky bluegrass is failing or a staple grass on putting greens, can tolerate cutting to as low as an eighth of an inch under ideal conditions.

How Long Do I Leave the Grass?

The rule of thumb for mowing a lawn is to never cut more than 30 percent of the height of the grass at any given mowing. If you do, root growth will go into immediate paralysis and will remain stopped for between two weeks and a month. Heavy cutting sets back your lawn severely and is known as *scalping*. Scalping doesn't allow the grass plant time to adapt to its new low height; instead it creates a major stress on the plant. And as we've seen, stress creates an opening for disease and insects to successfully invade.

Kinds of Lawn Mowers

The first reference we have to lawns and mowing is from Pliny the Younger (A.D. 61–113) who is said to have had a small lawn at his Tuscany villa. After that, lawns—particularly including wildflowers—became part of our gardening heritage in medieval Europe. The first known reference to the word *lawn* was in 1773 when lawns were set off from the house and surrounded by fences and hedges to be used as settings for games. All this is by way of saying that mowing a lawn is not a newfound occupation. As you push the mower around your lawn, you can be pleased that you are part of a tradition stretching back almost several thousand years.

Now let's talk about the equipment. There are four kinds of grass mowing machinery that are in use today for homeowners: rotary mowers, reel mowers, sickle bar mowers, and flail or hammer knife mowers.

Rotary Mowers

Most homeowners today use rotary mowers; these are the motorized or electric-powered units with a rotating blade under a protective housing. Easy to operate, they have several advantages:

- They are adaptable to rough conditions. If your lawn isn't perfectly smooth or level, these mowers are for you.

KIDS AND MOWING

At some point in your gardening life, you may be lucky enough to have kids who are old enough to mow the lawn for you. As well they should—this is almost a rite of passage in North America—being old enough to mow the lawn means the kids have passed into another stage of life. When is a child old enough? Good question. That's a government answer, I'm afraid. It depends. It depends on the child, the machinery in question, and the kind of upbringing the child has had. If children cannot read the instruction manuals or follow safety directions, then they are too young.

The most important thing you have to teach your children is the first and most important rule of lawn mowing. Never, ever stick your fingers near the mower deck while the engine is on. I made it a point of making the kids turn off the tractor and allow the mower deck to stop spinning before I'd let them poke a stick into the discharge chute to unclog it. A mower will take fingers off so quickly and easily that those who haven't seen it happen cannot believe it. If the mower gets plugged—and they all do—the engine has to be off and the blades not moving before fingers start poking around. I use a stick to unplug the mower deck; it keeps me from making a mistake.

The second rule of saftey is *never* mow in sandals or bare feet. The blade tips are moving extremely quickly. If they pick up a pebble, a small stick, or other debris, they can whip that bit of material out from under the deck so quickly that when it strickes a bare foot, serious injury will result.

Obviously, if you have a gravel area on your property, never run the mower while crossing the gravel. The whirling blades can easily suck up gravel and shoot it out the discharge shoot. It's just like getting hit with a small load of buckshot.

All mowers come with instructions and saftey manuals. Have your children read these manuals and be able to answer questions. There is no point in me lecturing on saftey in a book when equipment-specific instructions are so clear. Read those manuals and follow the instructions! They were written for a purpose.

- They are easy to use—just push.
- Regular maintenance is easy. There are no reels to adjust or maintain.
- They are cheap to buy.

Rotary mowers are really quite useful around the garden. They can be used to chop up leaves in the fall and blow them back onto the garden as mulch. They can cut tall weeds and taller grasses after your vacation. With the easily adjustable settings, rotary mowers can be set to mow as high or low as you want. They have very low maintenance costs; sharpening the blades and gasoline are the major ones.

Rotary mowers do have some disadvantages, however. They are more expensive to run than other mowers. They operate at a high blade speed which means they demand approximately 20 to 30 percent more fuel than a reel mower. Their long wheelbase means that if your lawn is uneven and the wheel drops into a hole, scalping is inevitable. Also, if the blades aren't maintained in top condition, they very quickly begin to tear the grass rather than cut it. This tearing can open the way for diseases, which find easy entry through ragged wounds.

The perfect rotary mower would have no exit chute under the deck. I say this not because I'd want to stop the grass from coming out, but rather to stop homeowners from sticking their fingers and feet into the machine to unjam it when it is running. I cannot believe the number of people who put their hands into the discharge chute of a running lawn mower to clean out a lump of wet grass. Mind you, neither can the hospital emergency staff. Never, ever, put any part of your body near the discharge chute or the mower deck while the blade is still turning over. It *can* happen to you, and it will sooner or later if you mess around with moving mower parts.

Speaking of dumb things to do: If you have to move your mower across an area of gravel or small stones, turn off the mower deck. You'd be amazed at how fast gravel comes out the discharge chute when flicked by a fast-moving mower blade. Similarly, do not mow the grass and aim the discharge chute at your kids or allow them to play in the discharge. You never know when you'll hit a small rock, toy, or bit of debris that will spin out from that deck at

How Long Will It Take?

To mow 1,000 square feet, you can expect the following:

- A 16-inch hand mower will take 10 minutes.
- An 18-inch power mower will take five minutes.
- A 25-inch power riding mower will take three minutes.
- A 58-inch power riding mower will have you out of there in one minute!

KEEP OFF THE GRASS

an injurious rate. A word to the wise should be sufficient here. *Allow the machine to come to a full stop before putting your fingers anywhere near the mower deck.*

Reel Mowers

Reel mowers, or hand mowers, are generally used in small lawn areas where the power of a motorized unit is not needed. They are also used in turf areas where a quality cut is necessary. Here are a few particulars:

- Reel mowers are for cutting fine lawns; their scissor action cleanly and smoothly shears the lawn instead of ripping it.
- They are easy to use on small lawn areas.
- They are prone to damage from stones and require adjustment and maintenance if they are to work properly.
- Don't use reel mowers to cut tall weeds or long grass.

Reel mowers give the finest of grass cuts. To do this, however, they require an experienced hand to keep the rotating scissor-type blades sharp and well adjusted. The clean cut leaves a grass clipping that does not turn unsightly brown and heals well and quickly to prevent fungal spores from becoming established.

Running over a rock or two will quickly ruin the edge on a reel mower and it will require sharpening. Also, if the lawn gets a bit ahead of you and starts looking like Tarzan's front yard, it is a thankless task to push a reel mower around trying to bring the lawn back into some semblance of a lawn.

Sickle Bar Mowers

A sickle bar mower is a like a miniature hay-mowing machine. A long serrated knife passes back and forth over a cutting board to chop down anything in its path. These are great mowers for rough work. Here are a few reasons to use sickle bar mowers:

- They are excellent for tall grass and weeds.
- They do a good job on steep banks where regular mowing is difficult.

LOOK SHARP!

Lawn mowers need to be sharpened after every seven to eight hours of use. Doing it less often means you are mowing with dull blades.

KEEP OFF THE GRASS

- Their low speed and back-and-forth sawing motion ensures that foreign objects neither ruin the blade nor are spun out to hit bystanders.
- Because of their width, sickle bar mowers can cut a wide path in a single pass.

These machines do have a relatively low ground speed but if you need to cut pathways or rough areas, it is difficult to beat them. The rough nature of their cutting action also means they are seldom used on good turf areas. Sickle bar mowers are also excellent on rough ground, going places where reel or rotary mowers can only dream about.

Flail or Hammer Knife Mowers

A flail mower has a series of V-shaped blades hung from a central axle. When the axle starts to turn, the blades whirl around quite quickly to chop up anything they hit. This is a very useful machine for rough ground. The blades are normally attached by chains and will bounce a bit when they strike a hard object. Here are a few more facts:

- These mowers are excellent for tall or hard weeds. The whirling action traps the particles under the mowing hood until they are chopped up enough to fall out.
- They are excellent for rough ground. Their short wheelbase means that scalping is minimized.
- They are easier to power than rotary mowers.
- They do not eject foreign objects as do rotary mowers.
- Although flail mowers chop material quite finely, they do not leave a clean cut.

This is another mower for rough ground. The V-shaped blades do not leave a fine finish on a lawn. So these mowers are seldom seen in the home landscape. They are available for small home tractors. The best possible advice that I can give is: Religiously follow the safety directions in the manual and on the machine. This is one unforgiving machine if you get your fingers or clothing near the working end.

HOW TO GROW A LAWN: A SUMMARY

- A lawn requires an absolute minimum of six full hours of sunshine a day. If you don't have the sunshine, you don't have a good lawn.
- Doug's first rule of gardening and lawn care: You only have to feed your plants if you want flowers, fruit, or growth.
- You have to feed a balanced food. Lawns require higher amounts of nitrogen than they do phosphorus or potassium. They also require minor nutrients such as iron.
- Compost is great for lawns. It feeds the micro-organisms in the soil and helps them keep disease at bay.
- Set your rotary and drop spreaders properly or your lawn will become striped with irregular growth.
- If you use liquid fertilizers, pay attention to the small details such as mixing and spreading properly.
- Turf requires water to thrive. Water deeply and infrequently. The average lawn in average soil requires 1 to 1½ inches of water per week.
- Invest in a sprinkler system, even one as simple as a hose and rotary sprinkler.
- Sprinklers apply water evenly and regularly. Time the application so you apply only half the weekly watering at each application.
- Do not water too often. It is better not to water enough than to overwater too often. Grass roots will be deeper and healthier with infrequent irrigation. This means the grass will survive stress better.
- Thatch is a symptom of poor lawn management. Overfeeding nitrogen is the primary cause. It overstimulates the grass to grow and kills off the micro-organisms that decompose the grass clippings.
- Set your mower to the proper height for the time of year. Do not cut your lawn too short or you're asking for problems. Lawns that are cut too short, or scalped, can take up to a month to start growing again.
- Sharpen your mower blades. A dull tool is no tool at all. Remember this old family saying: "a dull tool is only used by another dull tool."
- When mowing, leave the clippings where they fall. They don't contribute to thatch; they improve the health of the lawn.

What About the Clippings?

Leave them on the lawn. Grass clippings do not add to the thatch problem. They are composed of cellulose and thatch is composed of lignin.

Leaving them improves the fertility of the soil. Up to 40 percent of the nitrogen that a grass plant absorbs is shunted up to the growing tip. If you remove the grass clippings, you are taking this nitrogen away from the lawn and its future growth. Leave the grass clippings alone and your lawn will absorb this nitrogen as the clippings decompose.

Removing the grass clippings and its associated nitrogen has been shown to adversely affect the color of the lawn. Lawns where the clippings have been removed have consistently poorer color than those where the clippings have been left to decompose.

Grass clippings are food for numerous soil microbes. In fact, they are a preferred food source. By leaving them, you'll be feeding your soil and preserving its underground inhabitants. Worms also love grass clippings; by encouraging worms along with the microbes, you're adding to the health of your soil and your lawn.

Grass clippings actually shade the soil when they fall between the individual grass plants. This shading reduces moisture loss so you'll use less water. The shade also stops weed seeds from germinating. Without the weeds, the grass will have fewer competitors for water and food and will be healthier. Weed reduction makes your lawn look nicer.

Clippings also act as a temperature buffer. They shade the soil in the summer, which reduces soil temperatures. This slight reduction in temperature allows the grass to grow and thrive for longer periods during high summer heat spells.

And finally, believe it or not, clippings protect the crowns of grass. By leaving clippings on the lawn, the plants' crowns are more protected from foot injury than if the clippings are removed.

So, if the question is, "What do I do with the clippings?" The short answer is, "Nothing, leave them where they fall."

CHAPTER FOUR

How to Repair or Renovate a Lawn

Repair

You've noticed that your lawn is not up to par. Now you ask yourself, "What is going on?"

Sometimes, it seems that no matter how much we work on our lawn, there is always a problem around the bend. Maybe it's the kids cutting the corner, or the mail carrier wearing a pathway during the "appointed rounds." Or perhaps some critter—from skunks to armadillos—dig up chunks of the lawn, or dogs mark their territory on your grass instead of the local fire hydrant. What's a poor homeowner to do?

One of the most useful tricks in the lawnowner's repertoire is the ability to repair damage quickly and keep the grass growing. That's what this chapter is about.

The first step, and there's always one of those in any lesson on repairing things, is to make sure the lawn is healthy. Lawns that are growing strongly are less prone to problems. A healthy lawn won't stop many of the mechanical problems from happening, but it will recover faster and won't show signs of problems as early as a stressed-out bunch of grass plants masquerading as a lawn.

The second step is to figure out what is causing the damage. Most of the time it's pretty clear. If there's a pathway across one corner of the lawn and the grass is dying in that area, then it's a pretty safe bet that someone or something is walking across it on a regular basis. Here are a few more symptoms and causes:

- If the lawn appears to be rolled back in patches, you can suspect skunks of doing the damage. See Chapter 7 for more information about these odiferous creatures of the night.
- If there are scoops of bare ground and chunks of grass lying 8 to 10 feet away, blame the local duffer and consider getting a practice mat.
- In the majority of cases, round circles of dead grass are the result of dog urine rather than diseases. This is particularly true in the early spring, but you need to repair it in either case. Chapter 6 goes into detail on how you can determine whether you have a disease or a canine problem.

- Thin grass might be the result of encroaching shade from maturing trees. You'll have to change the kind of grass you grow to a more shade-tolerant species and renovate the lawn to assist the new grass to establish itself. Or, you could cut down the tree.

- Thin or damaged grass might simply be the end result of years of neglect by the homeowner (someone else's home, of course, not yours). No matter who did the neglecting, you'll have to do the repairing and make sure the turf thickens up.

There are quite a few reasons for a lawn being in poor shape, and while these reasons are the most common, I'm sure there's somebody out there with a novel reason for a poor lawn. The important thing is to determine the cause and then stop it. Then, and only then, can you fix your lawn.

Sodding

The first step in repairing any lawn damage is to see if the grass sod that has been removed by duffers or animals is still alive. If it is, replace the sod on top of the divot holes and step firmly onto the patch. Water the area thoroughly and try to keep it damp for a few days, so the grass roots will re-establish themselves. In a way, it is very much like resodding the lawn, only in small patches. You'll have to follow all the instructions for laying sod found in Chapter 2. Remember that even though it is a small patch of lawn, it is composed of individual grass plants, and you need to carefully establish the plants—no matter how big the patch.

Adding a shovel of compost around the damaged area is a good lawn practice. The compost helps the roots re-establish themselves and reduce the stress on the plants. Having all those nutrients readily available makes the plant's job all that much easier.

Resodding is another alternative if the damage is larger than animal or golfer divot chunks. Working up the soil (digging and raking) in the former pathway and laying the sod in this area is a time-honored method of repairing damage.

STAMP OUT FOOT TRAFFIC

Grass is extremely durable. It's a tough plant. In fact, it is the toughest, most resilient plant we know, and that is exactly why we use it on our lawns. However, no plant can take the regular abuse of constant foot traffic and live. Grass pathways are not meant for daily traffic, and grass used regularly as a path (as a little experience will soon show) will not last long.

The bottom line: you have to stop the traffic if you want to grow grass. Negotiate it, fence it, dig a moat, whatever—but stop the traffic if you want a lawn.

It is a good idea to have a clean edge (a straight edge nicely cut with a shovel) and to adjust the levels of the lawn so the sod can be laid top to top and edge to edge. That is, the top of the newly laid sod will be equal in height to the top of the existing lawn. The straight edges on old and new sod will line up so no bare soil (and the resulting weed infestation) can be seen after the new sod is laid down. If you eliminate the bump where the old and new sod meet, mowing will be much easier and you won't be inclined to scalp the newly sodded area. If your mower deck is set to 2 inches in height for a good leaf survival rate, and your new sod is laid only a half inch higher, then the new grass is being mown shorter than it wants to be. Attention to the small details will go a long way in repairing a damaged lawn.

It is not too difficult to create your own sod if you have a gardening frame of mind. Take a 1020 tray—those are the plant carrying trays with no dividers garden centers and greenhouses use to hold plant packs. (They're called 1020 trays because they are 10 inches by 20 inches in size, pretty simple when you think about it.) Put a shallow layer of soil—approximately ³/₄ inch of your best artificial potting soil—into the tray and water it thoroughly. Sow your grass seed in this tray. Try to keep the seeds ¹/₄ inch apart, but as this isn't rocket science, don't worry if they are slightly closer or farther apart. Cover the seeds very lightly (no more than ¹/₁₆ inch of soil) and water with as gentle a watering can or hose-end misting nozzle as you have. Try not to dig rivulets in the soil.

Put the trays in the sun and keep the soil damp. The grass will sprout in a three to five days if the soil is kept warm (72°F is ideal). Use a regular houseplant food to feed the grass plants once they have developed two true leaves. (You can use a starter plant food if you have it; something with a higher phosphorus second number is ideal.) True leaves are the leaves produced by the plant after the seedling leaves have emerged from the seed. After several weeks, you'll find the grass is growing strongly and the roots are intertwined in the tray. Congratulations! You've produced a flat of sod. This can be cut up and applied to small areas or laid in a single block to repair your lawn. Given a few trays, you will be surprised how inexpensively you can produce small amounts of sod for repairs.

PROVIDE AN EVEN PLAYING FIELD FOR NEW SOD

If the sod is not laid top to top, scalping is a very real possibility. Most renovators get the new sod too high. This not only means the new sod gets scalped, it also means the water table is lower than the new sod roots can easily reach. Remember if the sod is higher than the surrounding sod, the roots will also be higher for a while until they establish themselves. Higher roots cannot reach the water as easily.

Scalping and reduced water levels equal two strikes against proper establishment of this repair. One more stress and this inning is expensively over.

Reseeding

Reseeding the damaged areas is an inexpensive way to garden if you have extensive areas to repair. While the main advantage is that seed is inexpensive, it is a slower way to repair a bad spot than resodding. Another advantage is that seeding is extremely easy. For small areas such as dog damage, the easiest thing to do is rake out the area to remove all grass thatch and debris. Sprinkle grass seed onto the area so the seed is just touching but not over-lapping, and then lightly cover the area with compost. Finish off by soaking the area. Keep these repaired areas damp until the grass is firmly established, and do not mow for at least six weeks.

The spring "recipe" (see sidebar) can be used either for small spots or as a general spring tonic for the entire lawn. When applied to the entire lawn, the result is a thicker, healthier lawn. After a few years of applying an annual spring recipe, your lawn will be the envy of the neighborhood.

One task that is worth emphasizing is the raking you're going to give the area to be renovated. This serves several functions. First, it removes all debris and thatch from the area. Second, it slightly roughens the ground so the seed will be in contact with the bare ground. The result of clearing away all the debris and rough-ening up the ground is that the seeds germinate in higher numbers. Many grass seeds, with the possible exception of perennial ryegrass, do not perform very well when applied on top of turf. The seeds sink down under the existing grass and the percentage that germi-nate is usually low. With a good raking, this percentage increases and the resulting repair is much better.

If raking bothers your back, you have two choices. Hire someone to do it or purchase an ergonomic rake. These new rakes are designed to be easy on the back while still performing the same garden function.

Renovation

What exactly is lawn renovation? In its simplest terms, it is killing off the grass and starting over again. The soil is usually fine, and the grading is acceptable, but the grass is in such poor condition

DOUG'S SPRING RECIPE

Every spring, for each 1,000 square feet of lawn add the following:

- 2 pounds of grass seed if the grass is thick or 3 pounds if it is thin
- A 4- to 6-cubic foot bale of peat moss. (This adds organic matter to the lawn.)
- At least a bushel of compost. (This adds nutrients plus bacteria-fighting capacity. The equivalent in purchased bags is two or three large plastic bags.
- Half a pound of nitrogen fertil-izer. (See page 77 for instruc-tions on how to calculate the amounts of nitrogen in fertilizer and how much fertilizer to add to obtain the required amounts of nitrogen.)
- *To apply:* Rake the area heavily with a steel-tined rake. This removes all dead grass and debris from the area and opens it up for seeding. Apply the seed with a seed spreader. Then apply all organic matter and fertilizer. Water the area thoroughly and heavily.

and of such poor quality that it makes more sense to start again rather than try to resuscitate the victim of previous mismanagement.

Kill the Existing Grass

The first task that has to be done is to kill existing vegetation. There are three ways to do this: chemical spray, mechanical cultivation, or solarization.

Chemical sprays such as glyphosate are nonselective, which means they kill whatever they touch. This is the kind of spray used to kill existing foliage on a lawn. The advantage of glyphosate is that you can work and reseed the lawn seven to 10 days after the initial spray. Glyphosate breaks down fairly quickly and does not damage newly developing seedlings. The disadvantage is that it is a chemical (albeit one of the safer ones), so you have to be careful around the edges of the lawn with flowering plants and shrubs.

Some homeowners prefer mechanical cultivation. They rototill the area to be renovated quite shallowly, cutting and chopping up the roots and plants of both grass and weed plants. Then they water the lawn and allow it to sit for a week to 10 days. Some of the plants will have recovered by then and will be trying to regrow. Also, existing weed seeds will see this as their golden opportunity to sprout. After 10 days, they repeat the process to chop up and kill the struggling plants and new sprouts. This tilling is normally repeated three times and will eliminate the vast majority of grass and weeds.

The advantage is that this method doesn't rely on chemicals. The disadvantage is that it takes more work and more time to kill the grass.

Solarization is a slow but effective way to eliminate all growth and weed seeds on plots of land. First thing in the spring, thoroughly water the area to be cleared, and then lay down a *clear* sheet of plastic. Secure the edges of the clear plastic so no wind or water can get underneath them. You are basically creating a solar heater. At first, the plants cannot believe their good luck; they are protected from the early spring weather and start growing unchecked. It is not unusual to see 2-foot-tall dandelions under the

RENOVATION VERSUS REBUILDING

If the soil isn't good—or the grading is poor, or the drainage needs doing—it is not renovation. It is rebuilding and starting over from the beginning. Be sure to know the difference, or you could waste a lot of time and energy.

CONTROL OF PETS AND PESTS

I get more questions about fixing lawns as a result of dog damage than I do about any other lawn problem.

The bottom line is that to control stray dogs, you need a fence.

There are sound gizmos on the market that are supposed to chase away dogs, and there are some reports of success with them. For the most part, the units that are the most successful are controlled with motion detectors. Without the detector to turn the unit on and off, animals get used to the sound. You can get these units from your local pest control business.

Speaking of motion detectors: There is a water sprinkler that is controlled with a motion detector. This device shoots a water spray onto the intruder when the electronic beam is tripped. Many dogs (and cats) do not like being hit with water. Good garden centers can obtain these units (sold as "Scarecrows" in my neighborhood).

I have had minimal to zero luck with chemicals that are supposed to discourage dogs from getting on the lawn. One of my dogs developed a liking for one product and whenever we tested it, she would go and lie down on top of the treated area. That either says something for the product or the dog—I never figured out which.

If you immediately (or within one hour) drench your lawn with water after an animal has urinated, you can eliminate the burned grass syndrome. Rain or irrigation will leach the remaining urea away from the patch. But if you are going to renovate as soon as you see dog spots, it is a good idea to soak the area (just in case there are doses of urea left) before sowing seed or placing sod.

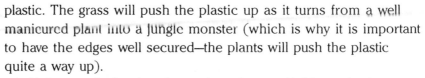

FISH AND SEAWEED TO HELP YOUR LAWN

Lawns that are under stress and need repair can benefit from an application of fish or seaweed emulsion. These products (sometimes combined) contain all the minor trace nutrients that any plant needs when it is under stress. They can be used for all plants, from roses to lawn grasses. Follow the label for application rates and watch the grass respond overnight.

Seaweed contains gibberelins, a hormone that promotes seed germination. These hormones have been used in the horticultural industry for years. Homeowners can spray or apply seaweed (it comes in either liquid or dried form) to help with the germination of new lawns.

plastic. The grass will push the plastic up as it turns from a well manicured plant into a jungle monster (which is why it is important to have the edges well secured—the plants will push the plastic quite a way up).

Unfortunately for the plants, there is no relief from the heat, and as spring turns to summer, the heat under the plastic becomes a killing force, not a gentle spring warm-up. After six weeks of summer sun, the grass and weeds will be brown and lifeless; they have been cooked. Weed seeds will also have been ruined, and will no longer germinate.

The advantages of this system are that you have a clear, weed-free area to replant and re-establish a good lawn. There are no chemicals and the only work is to lay the plastic, secure it, and clean up afterward. The obvious disadvantage is that it takes most of the summer to eliminate the weeds while your lawn is covered with plastic, not a sight for an upscale neighborhood to be sure. On the other hand, the lawn can be sown in the fall.

Mow and Sow

Once the existing grass has been killed, (no matter which system you choose), the next step is to mow the grass as short as you can. At this stage, you want to cut back all plant debris that will stop the sun from reaching the soil. You need this sunlight to encourage new seedling growth.

Remember this rule. If you want your new seeds to germinate, they must come into contact with the soil. Without this contact, germination will not occur; or if the seed does sprout, the new root will have no place to set down and the seedling will die. This means that any thatch layer will have to be removed *before* sowing grass seed if the thatch is thick enough to stop the grass seed from reaching the soil. A good raking is the simplest step here.

If the ground has been ignored and compacted over the years, rent a power aerator (it cuts out finger shaped cores from the ground) and aerate the lawn. Do not worry about all the holes or doing anything with the cores. You'll be surprised to see the grass sprouting from these holes like so many bad haircuts. The cores will disappear on their own with worm action and mowing.

The amount of seed for renovation should be increased by at least 20 to 25 percent over that of new sowing. This overseeding accounts for the difficulty the seed has with germinating in old stands of grass. If you can still see grass stems (however dead) sticking up on your lawn when you sow the new seed, rake the lawn *after* you sow the seed. This knocks the seeds off the old grass clumps and puts them into contact with the soil as well.

From this point on, the care and feeding of the lawn is pretty much the same as for a brand-new lawn. For best results, keep these tips in mind:

- Apply a starter fertilizer immediately after sowing seed to help the new seedlings get established.
- Irrigate the area as you would for any new seeding.
- Pay attention to mowing timing and do not cut the new grass plants too short.
- Clean and polish the golf clubs! It won't be long before you can practice on the lawn again.

The Organic Approach

With all the concerns being expressed about the excessive use of chemicals in our environment, you may be in favor of using organic lawncare techniques. Here's how to begin turning your lawn into an organic lawn.

- *Aerate your lawn.* Most lawns today are compacted beyond belief. They have been rolled, stomped on, played on, and simply abused more than the average soil and supporting cast can handle. Rent a corer machine that will pop the cores right out of the lawn. Next, purchase a pair of spike sandals to fit over your working boots. (You can get these through mail-order catalogs.) These sandals will (if worn) poke holes in the lawn as you mow or do yard work. Research tells us that these spike sandals actually reduce lawn grub damage because you're spearing the grubs as you walk your lawn. In addition, the spiked holes maintain the aerated lawn conditions, which will improve the health of

SOLARIZATION IN ACTION

In our experiments with solarization here on the farm, it took three years for weeds to reinvade an area that had been solarized.

the grass. Actually, wearing the sandals does three things—the third is that it gives your legs a bit of a workout because you have to lift your feet to get those long spikes out of the ground. No more shuffleguy lawn care!

- *Topdress your lawn with compost.* Spread it on at least at the rate of 2 pounds per square foot. Rake it across the lawn so that it goes down the aeration holes and leaves a covering on the surface. This will revitalize the soil in a way that has to be seen to be believed. The fungi and bacteria responsible for soil health will get this shot of food and they will start multiplying in order to bring your soil back to health.

- *Have patience.* This is not an overnight process. If you consider the length of time it took your lawn soil to be degraded and compacted, you can hardly expect the soil micro-world to recover in a single season. Experience with establishing organic systems indicates it takes between two and five years to re-establish a complete soil ecosystem.

- *Overseed.* One of the keys to success with an organic lawn is to have a thick stand of turf. The easiest way to obtain this *and* maintain it is to topdress or overseed every year with at least 2 pound of grass seed per 1,000 square feet. Another recommendation for a first step overseeding is to use your favorite grass seed mix at a rate of 1½ times the normal rate for starting a new lawn. This will thicken your lawn grass considerably.

- *Feed only with compost.* Do this twice a year—once in early spring just before the grass begins to grow and once again late in the season after the grass has stopped growing. Fifty pounds of compost per 1,000 square feet is the minimum amount needed. There is no upper limit except the strength of your back.

- *Change your maintenance to mow high, mow often.* The higher you mow your lawn, the more grass leaves will survive to collect sunshine and feed the roots. The healthier

the roots, the healthier the tops. Mow often so you never reduce the grass height by more than 30 percent at any given mowing. Remember that if you stress your grass plants in this way, you'll stop them from growing for up to a month. And weakened grass plants are prone to diseases and weed infestations.

- *Leave the grass clippings where they lie.* An incredible amount of the nitrogen absorbed by the grass plant is in the leaf ends. If you leave them on the ground, they will be absorbed by the soil micro-organisms and recycled back into your grass plants. You have to see it to believe how many grass tips the worms chew down on their nightly forays.

- *Encourage worms in your lawn.* These engines of soil fertility are the best things you've got going for aerating your lawn naturally. They leave good fertilizer behind as they eat decaying organic matter and keep you in fishing bait.

- *Use pest control biological systems only when necessary.* Your lawn doesn't have to be bug-free. There is a natural cycle out on your lawn and pests are to be expected. Yes, you'll see some grubs if you go digging around. The question really is how much damage are they doing and is this damage acceptable. For the most part, you'll find that once you have an established organic lawn, the grass will be healthier and the pest damage will be reduced. Even if you find grubs or pests, do the threshold tests for pests listed in Chapter 7. Just because they exist, doesn't mean they are a problem or have to be killed.

- *Use organic weed preventatives such as corn gluten instead of noxious chemicals.* These do the job with none of the downsides normally associated with using chemicals. And corn gluten feeds your lawn as it decomposes.

- *Consider the alternatives in Chapter 9 if you are having trouble growing grass because of environmental conditions.* There are more important things in life than trying to fight Mother Nature.

- *Spend time examining your lawn.* Every now and then, wander around the lawn examining the grass. Are the grass blades cleanly cut or are the tips dead and brown? (Does your lawn mower need sharpening?) Are there dead patches of turf where you can pull the grass away from the ground with little effort? (Roll the turf back and check for grubs—get out your turf spikes and if the grubs are above threshold limits—prepare to apply predator **nematodes** when appropriate.) The more you look, the more you'll learn about this incredibly interesting ecosystem that's right outside your front door.

The Easy System of Lawncare: Have Someone Else Do It

At some point, you may very well decide that all this lawncare and renovation stuff is something you do not want to do yourself. You'd rather hire someone to do it. After all, a well maintained lawn can add significant value to your home because of what real estate agents call "curb appeal." Plus if you're really more interested in swinging a club than mowing a lawn, hiring a lawncare company will free up those Saturday mornings. Here are a few tips to help you choose the perfect lawncare company.

- *Ask the company for a detailed listing of services and costs.* A reputable company will have all of these things listed for you to see and approve. You don't want hidden costs creeping in to inflate the price.

- *Request a written estimate for the service.* Note the length of the contract and whether it is renewable (or renews itself if you don't!). You may not want to sign a multiyear contract or tie yourself into using one service, particularly if the service is new to you.

- *Ask for references and check them*! Too many people never check references. We assume that if a company provides a name as a reference, that person will give positive feedback, but you'd be surprised what you can learn. People will tell you things they'll never tell the company. Ask about how the workers leave the property. Do they leave cigarette butts nearby? Do they show up on time in the spring before the lawn gets too long? Do they mow weekly? Do they mow neatly or is the grass scalped? How do they handle mowing around trees? Do they use a whipper snipper (string trimmer) against the trunk of the tree (a no-no) or do they employ other solutions?

- *Ask to see the appropriate state or municipal licenses or permits to do the kind of work they are contracting for.*

- *Ask to see copies of their comprehensive insurance policies.* If the company does not have business insurance, you could be liable for any damage they do to the neighbor's yard and garden. Do not think this will not happen to you. It only takes an inexperienced worker a few seconds with a whipper snipper and a lack of knowledge about where your property ends to ruin the neighbor's prize rose. And, now that pesticides are becoming a legal issue, any chemical treatment of your lawn has to be done to acceptable standards or you can become liable. For example, any spray drift of 2,4-D will destroy nearby flowers. And this does happen more than you might want to know. A word to the wise: make sure the company insurance is in force, is comprehensive, and is adequate for any claim.

- *Speaking of insurance, make sure the company has the appropriate state or provincial worker injury insurance.* If they do not have adequate insurance, you, the homeowner, can be held liable for any injury. Landscaping is often classified as construction, and this is one of the highest claims areas in worker compensation insurance. All it takes is one worker to twist a back spreading peat moss on your lawn and without adequate company insurance, you may be paying that injured person's wages and rehabilitation expenses.

- *Ask if the company is a member of a professional association.* Most of the better companies are. The associations often have ethics statements that members must agree to follow. The associations also often have problem resolution lawyers or groups on retainer to help homeowners and members with conflicts without the expense of going to court. If a company is going to the trouble and expense of belonging to an association, it will tend to be a better, more committed company.

CHAPTER FIVE

Weeds

Don't you just love weeds? Think about them for a moment. A weed is simply a plant growing where you don't want it to grow. And to do that, it has developed a particular growth habit and skill at exploiting your gardening weaknesses to ensure its survival. A weed is a survivor. And while I may not enjoy its ability to survive, I have to admire its tenacity.

I have to examine what it is that I'm doing on my lawn that enables those weeds to survive and grow from year to year. Why don't they die? A wag would suggest that the grass dies—why won't the weeds?

Let's examine the nature of lawn weeds for the answers to these questions. The first thing to remember is that most weeds will not survive on the lawn. The constant mowing cuts them off and without a special ability to regrow, they cannot persist in that environment.

So, what then are those special abilities? The first one is shared with the grass plant itself, and that is the ability to regenerate themselves from their crowns in some way. Grass plants survive constant mowing because they are able to regenerate new leaves; some weeds are able to do the same thing. The largest group of lawn weeds that regenerate are other grasses—and we don't want these weed grasses in our lawn.

Another thing that weeds do to tolerate the constant mowing is to grow from a low growing rosette. Dandelions are the perfect example. The crown and leaves radiate out from a low-growing central source. Only the flower head and odd adventurous leaf poke their way up over the height of the mower deck. Plantain is another example of a plant that grows from a central rosette and whose flower stalks can sometimes rise above the level of the cut grass.

Some plants such as clover or creeping charlie (ground ivy) produce runners that root and move along the ground under the height of a mower deck. They gladly exchange their height for a secure existence where you can't kill them by mowing.

These plants have moved into our lawns because we provide a good secure home for them. We feed them, we water them, and we provide lots of sunlight by keeping the grass cut short enough for them to reach the sunlight as well. If you think about it from a weed's perspective, we take good care of our weeds.

So what's a poor homeowner to do? Get out the chemicals and nuke the lawn? Well, before we consider the use of chemicals to control weeds, there are quite a few other steps we can, and should, take. You see, chemicals are the last solution in a gardener's toolbox; they are the Band-Aids of the gardening world. It is easier, cheaper, and better to fix the problem causing the weeds than it is to hammer the lawn with chemicals that simply kill the weeds and don't resolve the underlying problem.

So then, what things can a homeowner do to create a better lawn?

Cultural Controls

Mowing

Mowing properly is the single most important task you'll do with your lawn; it has the greatest impact on weed survival. As mentioned earlier, many farm weeds never appear in your lawn because they can't tolerate being mowed regularly. Mowing does control some weeds.

Every turfgrass has a specific height that is best for its growth. Any turfgrass that is mowed at its proper height is healthier than one that is mown too short. Short mowing is an invitation for crabgrass and annual bluegrass to invade and become well established. Annual bluegrass is rarely a problem in a home lawn that is mowed at the proper height. If you persist in trying to make your home lawn appear to be a golf green, weeds will invade.

Fertilization

It is mostly the timing of fertilizer programs that influences the growth of weeds. The basic premise is that we want to feed the grass, but we do not want to feed the weeds. This means that in northern grass areas, the main fertilizer applications take place in late fall and early spring, not during the summer. Grass roots absorb the fertilizers in these late and early spring applications when the annual weeds are not around to benefit. If fertilizer is applied during the summer, annual weeds such as crabgrass will get a full feeding as well.

WEEDS: SYMPTOMS, NOT PROBLEMS

I invite you to turn your gardening thinking upside-down. In any gardening situation, weeds, diseases, and insect pests are not problems. They are symptoms.

Let me give you an example. If you cut your lawn too short, the grass will not have enough leaves to produce energy. This lack of energy will create a weakened, thin grass stand or lawn. Lawns with thinning grass patches (where the sun can reach the ground) are invitations for weeds to colonize.

Remember that nature abhors a vacuum. Old Mother Nature will send plants to cover any bare stretch of ground she can find—that's one of her rules. If your grass is thin because you cut it too short, Mother Nature will fill the bare spot with weeds.

Now, what is the problem? The weeds or the too-short mowing?

You can (repeatedly) spray and kill the weeds or you can simply set your mower deck to a higher setting and make your lawn healthier and more weed-free in the process.

A weed is not a problem. It is a symptom telling you to garden better on your home lawn.

WEED IDENTIFICATION

The first item of business on any weed control agenda must be: Know the weed you are trying to control.

There is no sense applying some chemical to your lawn if you don't know what it is you are trying to kill. It would be like taking a prescription medication to treat an ailment without even getting a doctor's diagnosis.

Once you identify the weed, you can identify whether mowing or feeding or any other of the cultural controls will work on your lawn.

This sounds pretty obvious, but more times than I'd want to tell you, I've had customers come into the nursery for "stuff to kill some weeds." What weeds? "I dunno— just weeds."

A word to the wise: Your local extension or agricultural office will have a good book on local weed identification. Get it. It will save you time, effort, and money. Also, check the Web resources at the back of this book for some useful information.

In southern areas, exactly the opposite holds true. Feed the lawn during the summer months when the grass is growing strongly. Avoid the cooler months when the weeds are more likely to appear.

So, if you know what weed you want to avoid, then you can design a fertility program to feed your lawn and not your weed.

Fertilizer Analysis

The analysis of the fertilizer and the amount you apply are also factors in weed establishment. For example, we use phosphorus mostly as a starter food for young seedlings by putting it on the surface for these small tender roots to absorb and use. In the average soil there is enough phosphorus for normal grass growth a few inches below the soil line where mature grass roots live. In most cases, we don't have to apply phosphorus to our home lawns. Applying phosphorus on a regular basis (remember that phosphorus does not move easily in the soil) to the top of the lawn doesn't feed the grass roots—it feeds the weed seedlings. So, if you want to feed the weed seedlings, apply lots of phosphorus. If you want to feed the grass, hold back on phosphorus on mature lawns.

Irrigation

In the chapter on starting lawns, we talked about the need for frequent and light watering when establishing a lawn from seed. This indicates that young seedlings like to be kept damp. Well, if you water frequently and lightly with a mature lawn, you're encouraging the growth of weed seeds and not the growth of the mature grass. Mature grass needs deep watering—and only when it needs it.

Seed

It isn't a nice thing to say about some grass seed companies, but there is a difference between good seed and bad seed in the nursery business. You get what you pay for, and if you don't pay a lot for the grass seed because it's a discount brand—you might very well be paying for weed seed. There's no way to tell beforehand what you have in the package, so the cheapest insurance is to purchase only good seed with the appropriate labeling for weed seed content.

Cultivation

Broadleaf weeds are easily controlled on the home lawn using either of these old-fashioned tools: weed spuds or rakes.

Weed Spuds

A weed spud is an old-fashioned tool that is making a come-back on home lawns. It is a flat strap of steel with a V-shaped gouge cut into one end. The other end is attached to a long handle. You put the V-shape against the root of a weed and lean or push on the handle so the steel strap cuts through the root. It is not hard work. On average-size urban and suburban lawns, it is amazing how quickly an entire patch of dandelions can be cut in half. The dandelion plant regrows in a week or two and the operation needs to be repeated. It only takes a few such cuttings to deplete the energy sources of the dandelion and the plant will die. It's easy work, doesn't require fancy clothes or equipment, and leaves the lawn weed-free and healthy. It does however require patience and commitment to the process.

Rakes

There are special weed rakes with tines that are quite close together. Pulling them through the grass will remove creeping charlie or ground ivy. These rakes are ideal for removing runners and vine-type weeds from home lawns. Again, more than one raking is going to be required to control the problem.

Chemical Controls

Pre-Emergence Herbicides

Pre-emergent herbicides kill weed seeds as they try to germinate, but have very little impact on mature grass plants. In most cases, if the pre-emergent agent is applied after the seed has germinated, it will not influence the developing plant.

Pre-emergent chemicals work in a variety of ways. Generally speaking, they destroy the emerging root or prevent it from growing, so the top of the plant either does not develop or, as it develops, it outgrows the root growth and dies of starvation. There

---

IN PRAISE OF THE WEED SPUD

I own my grandfather's weed spud. It's a simple tool and one I quite enjoy using. There is a savage satisfaction in chopping dandelions in half in search of that perfect lawn. I never quite get there of course, but the spud is a favorite tool.

I prefer the part lean–part push working technique and I'm always surprised at how many weeds I leave wilting behind me in the course of a few minutes' work. You'll develop your own system. The nice thing is that once you become proficient (and it doesn't take long), you can use it one-handed. That leaves the other hand free for a cool drink.

They're making spuds again and I highly recommend them.

are both organic and chemical pre-emergent controls listed in the table later in this chapter.

The interesting thing about pre-emergents is that their use varies across the continent. The nature of the springtime weather will determine which works (or conversely does not work) in your area. Cool temperatures or wet weather influence the growth rates and effectiveness of any pre-emergent control. Be sure to check with local gardening experts about regional variations.

Post-Emergence Herbicides

Post-emergent chemical control influences the growth of plants after they have germinated and are growing strongly. This can sometimes be difficult in turfgrasses because most of the chemicals that are selective in their action (they don't kill everything they touch) are pre-emergent types.

Nonselective Controls

Nonselective controls are not fussy about what they kill. Apply the material to grass or weeds and it makes no distinction. I remember seeing a lawn where the owner had been using spot sprays of glyphosate to kill dandelions. He was wearing rubber boots to do this chore (a good idea) and had obviously sprayed his boots. In his wanderings, he had left his footprints in dead grass tracks. The leftovers on his boots had killed the grass wherever he walked.

Obviously we can't spray these kinds of products over our lawns to kill the weeds. We can use them as spot sprays (with a little more care than my friend) to kill weeds such as thistles or dandelions.

Chemical Mixes

Chemical mixes are quite common on the garden center shelves. In fact, when you start investigating the labels, it will be quite difficult to avoid having to purchase a mix. The most common mix is a combination of 2,4-D (to control grass) and dicamba (to control broadleaf weeds), although there are often others added for extra killing punch. These mixes certainly do the

HERBICIDE TIP

Although it is very tricky to give exact dates for applying pre-emergent herbicides, the best markers are the other plants in the garden. In zone 4 and warmer, when the forsythia bloom, it is the time to apply pre-emergents to the lawns and gardens.

KEEP OFF THE GRASS

HERBICIDE SAFETY

There are enough concerns listed with herbicides that it is important for homeowners to follow, at the very minimum, the most basic of personal safety rules. Here they are:

- Wear rubber boots when applying any lawn chemical. Wash them thoroughly before going into the house. Do not under any circumstances wear them onto the porch or any area where a child plays until they have been thoroughly washed. Running shoes or leather boots are not appropriate footwear because they absorb chemicals rather than repel them. And we won't even consider the idiots who wear sandals to do this job.

- Wear long pants and a long-sleeved shirt. Take these off immediately after spraying and wash them separately. I guarantee they will have chemical product on them. Do not wear them to do further work or sweat in them. The sweat will move the chemical product to your skin.

- Wear impermeable gloves to mix and spread the product. DO NOT TOUCH YOUR FACE with these gloves. Do not wipe the sweat off your face with these gloves. The face and head are the most sensitive skin areas (right up there with the back of the hands) for chemical absorption. Wash these gloves immediately after use with a hose. Wash them before taking them off. Do not handle them with bare hands before they have been washed.

- Keep a special "spray hat" that can be worn and washed along with the clothes. Use your rattiest looking hat to give you a certain panache while doing the job.

- Remember that this is your life and the lives of your children we're talking about. You might feel foolish wearing safety gear, but you'd feel a lot more foolish (or worse) if you made a mistake.

Use, Don't Abuse

I've probably said this before but I'll say it again.

If you want to kill weeds using a chemical, then use the appropriate chemical to do the job and use it at the recommended rate. If you want to feed your lawn, then use the appropriate product and use it at the recommended rate.

Using a weed-and-feed compound as a matter of routine is simply an abuse of chemicals not to mention an abuse of your wallet or purse. Try all the things mentioned in this chapter to control weeds before you use sprays. Weed-and-feed (a mixture of fertilizer and herbicide) is an expensive product when compared to comparable compounds sold separately.

"Twofers" (two for the price of one) don't exist in the gardening world and you'll pay—one way or the other—for the overuse or abuse of feed or weed killers.

job if applied correctly and at label rates. It is far better to purchase a ready-made mix than to mix the products yourself because the combination rates will be correct in the packaged products. (We call doing it yourself a "tank mix" because you use two products in the same spray tank.) It is quite easy to confuse spray rates when trying to combine two or more products yourself.

Organic Controls

The upcoming table lists many sophisticated organic controls for weeds in turf. But here are a couple of very easy solutions you can use. Pour boiling water on your patio stones to rid yourself easily and quickly of any weed. Slowly pour the boiling water onto the weed and within a few minutes, it will wither and die. The key is to make sure the water is boiling, and to pour it quite slowly over the weed. It will take you a few tries to find out how much water it takes to kill each weed. In my garden it takes about a pint poured slowly over a full-grown dandelion to cook and kill it. This is a safe and effective control mechanism with no negative environmental side effects.

Another quick and easy solution is to use sulfur as a grass preventative. Sulfur is quite acidic. If you sprinkle it around in areas where you don't want grass (or anything else to grow), you'll create a very acidic soil that will not support vegetation. You'll have to experiment to get the correct amount to stop specific plants from growing, but it does work. The only caution here is that sulfur is yellow and can stain concrete and brick products.

How to Control Moss

Moss, that green carpety stuff, sometimes becomes a problem in lawns. If moss starts to grow, it is because the conditions are right for moss and not for grass. To convince grass to grow instead of moss, you have to reverse those conditions. What are they? Well, moss likes the following:

- *Shade.* You'll rarely see moss growing in full-sun gardens in most parts of North America. It is difficult to tell any homeowner to cut down a tree to increase the light as a method of eliminating moss. I would much rather use other techniques or give up trying to grow grass in deep shade.

- *Acidic soils.* Most soils that moss thrives on have pH of less than 6.0. Acidic soils with pH levels lower than 6.0 can easily be corrected by adding lime to the lawn. Two pounds of lime per 1,000 square feet will move the pH up (on average soils) by .01. How much to add to the soil depends on the original soil acidity. It is best to get a soil test and then add the amount of lime the test recommends. Otherwise, you're just guessing, and you won't know how much to add—whether your're doing a good job or not. Do a soil test.
- *Moisture.* Damp areas are perfect havens for moss. The only long-term solution is to hire a landscaper or drainage contractor to solve the problem. You have to get rid of the water.
- *Low fertility.* Moss does not thrive in areas with good fertility. Low fertility is similarly easily solved. Feed your lawn. An oft-recommended application is to add superphosphate at 1 pound per 1,000 square feet. Although I wouldn't guarantee this without a soil test, it would be a good place to start.
- *Thatch.* Often moss will thrive in lawns where thatch is present. Thatch is covered in Chapter 3. If you get rid of the thatch, you'll likely get rid of the moss. The conditions that help keep the thatch accumulating will also work in favor of keeping moss alive.

A 50:50 solution of vinegar and water will kill most moss and algae spores quite quickly without harming the grass. There are fatty acid (soap-based) products available such as Safer's De-Moss that also do the trick. Dilute copper sulfate is also packaged as a moss killer, as is ammonium and iron sulfate.

Commonly Available Herbicides

The table on pages 126–127 lists the most widely available and used herbicides for homeowners. Not all the commercial names are listed; they change as fast as the companies can dream up new

CLASSES OF WEEDS

There are annual weeds and perennial weeds.

Annual weeds grow and set seed in a single growing season. To complicate life, these can be summer annuals (they start growing in the spring and complete it in the fall), or winter annuals (they start in the fall, overwinter, and then finish growing in the spring and early summer).

Perennial weeds live for two or more years and do not need to reseed themselves every year.

combinations. Learn the active ingredient name because that is what will be on the label.

Note also that many products are combination products. These products combine two or more chemical agents to obtain a wider spectrum of control. Dicamba and 2,4-D are two very popular mixes: one for broadleaf and the other for grasses.

Read the label and know what you are trying to control. In some cases, some of these products are not recommended for certain types of grasses. This is mostly a problem in the South with grass such as Bermuda grass, but it is useful to read the label to find out what the product concerns are.

Application rates and methods of application are listed on the label as well.

The Lawn Weed Hall of Fame

If you don't agree that a weed is simply a plant in the wrong place, you'll have to agree that some plants seem to always appear where we least want them. The following plants deserve to be recognized as the best of the best, or, perhaps more appropriately, the worst of the worst.

White Clover

This familiar low-growing perennial is characterized by three-leaflet leaves and numerous white flowers resembling pompoms. It spreads by creeping stems that root where nodes touch the soil. Often included in grass mixtures in the past, white clover is still added to some of the cheaper mixtures. Although it looks pleasant initially, clover soon suffocates desirable lawn grasses, then fades in hot weather and leaves large dead patches.

Clover

The other species of clover are often considered to be the equal of white clover for weediness. Clovers attract bees, which can be a threat to those who suffer from allergies to bee stings. If you are prone to rolling on your lawn with the kids, clover will stain your clothing much faster than ordinary grass will. Clover also tends

DROUGHT WON'T KILL MOSS

Moss can tolerate very long periods of drought. If you see the moss and the grass on your lawn turning brown without water during the summer, rest assured that both will come storming back with the fall rains.

LAWN CHEMICALS
AND THE ENVIRONMENT

In the broad context of things, anything that we put on our lawns to control weeds, insects, or pests comes with a cost. Some of these costs are small and some are quite large, depending on the chemical we choose to use and the way we apply it. The evidence is mounting that there are serious costs to using garden chemicals to create something as nonessential as a perfect lawn. We can create a quite-good lawn without the use of chemicals.

Rachel Carson brought the dangers of some chemicals to our attention with her groundbreaking book *Silent Spring*. You might say this was the wake-up call of the 1900s. Sad to say, *Our Stolen Future* by Colborn, Dumanoski, and Myers is the similar book of the 2000s. Rachel Carson spoke to us of cancers and environmental problems, Colborn's book speaks to us of the new yard chemicals mimicking hormones (they don't cause cancer) and creating increased numbers of birth defects, lowered sperm counts, and childhood problems such as Attention Deficit Disorder. This data (and more) comes from medical epidemiology studies from worldwide sources.

There is increasing evidence that children who live in homes where garden chemicals are used have higher rates of childhood cancers than in nonchemical homes.

Use of lawn and garden chemicals is responsible for the likelihood that there will be chemical residues around the inside of the house at doorways. Residues on shoes and clothing are deposited when people are exposed to the products and then remove their clothing or shoes at the doorway. The average North American carries approximately 250 chemicals in his or her body.

The question that has to be answered by every reader is whether the use of chemicals is worth the price they may have to pay. The second question is whether children and neighbors should have to pay the price as well.

In this book, I've tried to give both environmentally friendly and chemical approaches to lawn care so readers can make informed decisions.

I've made my choices, and they fall squarely into the environmentally sound camp. No lawn is worth the potential problems created by chemicals.

COMMONLY AVAILABLE HERBICIDES

Chemical Name	Name Sold Under	Weed Control	Characteristics	Concerns
Acetic acid (Common name of Ethanoic acid)	Burnout	Annual broadleaf and annual grasses.	• Nonselective. • Burns the tops so it is excellent for annual weeds. • Does not kill roots of perennial weeds, although it will burn their tops.	• This is essentially vinegar and lemon juice (plus other spreaders). • As natural as they come. • Do not inhale. • Those with skin sensitivities should not come in contact with the concentrate.
Atrazine	Aatrex Atranex	Broadleaf and grassy weeds.	• Post-emergent, but with residual action. • Effective for 3 months.	• One of the most widely used of farm herbicides. Studies have shown up to 13% of rural wells contaminated with this product (below EPA danger levels). • Long-sleeved shirts and long pants (or equivalent), chemical-resistant gloves, and waterproofed boots are necessary. • Do not use within 50 feet of any water or well.
Benefin	Balan	Annual grasses and broadleaf weeds in established turf.	• Pre-emergent.	• Persistent—at least one full season. • No leaching.
Benuslide	Betasan Prefar	Annual grasses and broadleaf weeds in established turf.	• Pre-emergent.	• Moderately to highly toxic to aquatic life. • Moderately toxic to bird life. • Persistent—season-long control.
Corn gluten	WeedBan	Broadleaf and small grasses.	• Pre-emergent. • Best applied in the spring and fall. • Breaks down into nitrogen to feed the lawn.	• Applied before germination, this food-grade product inhibits the growth of small weed seeds such as crabgrass and dandelion. • Completely safe.
2,4-D	2,4-D	Broadleaf and some grassy weeds.	• Post-emergent. • Widely used, selective herbicide.	• Volatile—it has a gaseous component that can travel to nontarget garden areas.
DCPA	Dacthal DAC 893 Dacthalor	Annual grasses and some broadleaf weeds.	Pre-emergent.	• Low mammal toxicity. • Some concerns about dioxin being in product in small doses. • Low to moderate toxicity in birds. • Low toxicity in aquatic life. • Very persistent in soil—up to 100 days.

COMMONLY AVAILABLE HERBICIDES *(continued)*

Chemical Name	Name Sold Under	Weed Control	Characteristics	Concerns
Dicamba	Metambane Dianat Banfel Banvel Banvel CST Banvel D Banvel XG Mediben	Annual and perennial broadleaf weeds. Brush and bracken.	• Pre-emergent. • Post-emergent. • Will kill broadleaf weeds before and after they sprout.	• Highly mobile in soil—may easily contaminate groundwater. • Moderately toxic by skin exposure. • Corrosive—do not splash into eyes! • Slightly toxic to birds. • Low toxicity to aquatic animals.
DSMA	Weed-E-rad DSMA	Selected plants and crabgrass. *Do not use on St. Augustine grass, bent grasses, or fine fescues.*	• Contact herbicide. • Do not use when temperature over 80°F.	• Avoid skin contact. • Wear protective clothing. • Toxic to fish.
Endothall	Aquathol	Annual grass Broadleaf weeds in grass Weed species and algae Aquatic environments	• Contact—must hit to kill.	• The lethal dose rating earns a product "warning" label. • Highly mobile in soil, but with a 21-day breakdown with or without soil moisture.
Glufosinate-Ammonium	Finale Rely	Broad spectrum, kills what it hits.	• Nonselective. • *Do not use in any food crop area.*	• Rapidly degraded biologically. • This active ingredient was originally discovered as a metabolic compound of a soil-inhabiting bacteria. • Moderately toxic to aquatic life. • Mobile in the soil and persistent 3 to 72 days before breakdown.
Glyphosate	Roundup Rodeo Blot-out	Broad spectrum, kills what it hits.	• Nonselective.	• Moderately toxic—can cause eye irritation. • Slightly toxic to birds. • Nontoxic to aquatic life. • Nonleaching. • Breaks down within 6 months.
MCPP	Agritox Agroxone Chiptox Rhonox Weed-Raph	Creeping broadleaf weeds.	• Post-emergent.	• Nontoxic to birds and aquatic life. • During in soil is about 2 months.
Oxadiazon	Ronstar	Annual grass and broadleaf weeds.	• Pre-emergent. • Early post-emergent.	• Little impact on birds or aquatic life. • Tightly held by soil so leaching is not significant.
Siduron	Tupersan	Annual grass.	• Pre-emergent.	• Long-term residual—at least 4 to 5 months. • Does not leach.

Nick Christians, *Fundamentals of Turfgrass Management* (Chelsea, Mich: Ann Arbor Press, 1998).

to grow in patches, so after it starts smothering the grass, it will make the lawn appear patchy. The advantage to clover is that it stays green during the heat of the summer when lawn grasses start to fade and wither. Sometimes after a severe pest infestation, clover is the only plant left alive. In fact, there are many gardeners who enjoy a clover lawn for its low maintenance and constant color.

Plantains

The two species of *Plantago* called buckhorn (*P. lanceolata*) and blackseed *plantain (P. rugelii)* are common perennial weeds in lawns. They have thick fleshy roots with multiple smaller roots, making them tough plants to hand-weed. Every chunk of root left in the soil will produce a new plant. To add insult to injury, plaintains are one of the heaviest seed producers in the lawn. The seedheads occur in late spring and early summer and are low enough that the mower passes them by.

Sorrels

There are several sorrels (sorrel signifies "sour") in our lawns and herb gardens. All have bitter-tasting leaves. Sheep sorrel is one of the major lawn weeds because it has a perennial rootstock that runs underground, enabling it to spread rapidly. It is particularly a problem in acidic soils or soils that are depleted of nutrients.

Spurges

The spurges are the opposite of sorrels; they love well fed lawns. The easiest way to identify a spurge is to rip off a leaf or stem. The plant will bleed a milky white juice. Most spurges are heavy seeding annual weeds.

Chickweed

Annual chickweed is a talented little lawn weed. It is properly classified as an annual, mostly a winter annual. However, it also roots at the nodes of stems, so it can spread quite quickly. Chickweed thrives in cool weather. You'll normally see it growing quickly in the spring and fall. It does not grow during the heat of the summer, except in shade or damp conditions. The appearance

COMMON WEEDS IN NORTH AMERICAN LAWNS

SPECIES NAME	COMMON NAME
Annual Grasses	
Cenchrus echinatus	Southern sandbur
Cenchrus pauciflorus	Sandbur
Digitaria bicornis	Tropical crabgrass
Digitaria ciliaris	Southern crabgrass
Digitaria ischaemum	Smooth crabgrass
Digitaria longiflora	India crabgrass
Digitaria sanguinalis	Large crabgrass
Echinochloa crusgalli	Barnyard grass
Eleusine indica	Goose grass
Panicum capillare	Witch grass
Panicum dichotomiflorum	Fall panicum
Poa annua	Annual bluegrass
Seteria lutescens	Yellow foxtail
Perennial Grass	
Agropyron repens	Quack grass
Bromus inermis	Smooth brome
Dactylis glomerata	Orchard grass
Mehlenbergia schreberi	Nimblewell
Paspalum dilatatum	Dallis grass
Phleum pratense	Timothy
Sorghum halepense	Johnsongrass
Sporobolus indicus	Smutgrass
Sedges	
Cyperus compressus	Annual sedge
Cyperus esculentus	Yellow nut sedge
Cyperus rotundus	Purple nut sedge
Cyperus spathacea	Hurricanegrass
Summer Annual Broadleaf	
Amaranthus blitoides	Prostrate pigweed
Amaranthus viridus	Slender amaranth
Euphorbia maculata	Prostrate spurge
Lactuca scariola	Prickly lettuce
Malva rotundifolia	Common mallow
Matricaria matricariodes	Pineapple weed

SPECIES NAME	COMMON NAME
Medicago lupulina	Black medic
Mollugo verticillata	Carpetweed
Oxalis stricta	Yellow woodsorrel (perennial in the South)
Polygonum aviculare	Prostrate knotweed
Portulaca oleracea	Purslane
Richardia scabra	Florida pusley
Winter Annual	
Erodium cicutarium	Redstem filaree
Descurainia pinnata	Pinnate tansymustard
Lamium amplexicaule	Henbit
Lepidium virginicum	Virginia pepperweed
Plantago virginica	Southern plantain
Stellaria media	Common chickweed
Tifolium dubium	Small hop clover
Veronica arvensis	Corn speedwell
Perennial Broadleaf	
Achillea millefolium	Yarrow
Artemesia vulgaris	Mugwort
Aster dumosus	Bushy aster
Cerastium vulgatum	Mouse ear chickweed
Chicorium intybus	Chicory
Cirsium arvense	Canada thistle (biennial)
Daucus carota	Wild carrot (biennial)
Dichondra carolinensis	Dichondra
Erigeron quercifolius	Southern fleabane
Eupatorium capillifolium	Dogfennel
Glecoma hederacea	Ground ivy/creeping charlie
Hypochoeris radicata	Catsear dandelion
Plantago lanceolata	Buckhorn plantain
Plantago rugelii	Blackseed plantain
Rumex acetolsella	Red sorrel
Rumex crispus	Curly dock
Sonchus asper	Spiny sowthistle
Taraxacum officinale	Dandelion
Trifolium repens	White clover
Viola papilionacea	Wild violet

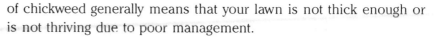

of chickweed generally means that your lawn is not thick enough or is not thriving due to poor management.

Mouse-eared chickweed is a low growing perennial plant that has hairy leaves shaped like—surprise—a mouse's ear. It is a darker green than common chickweed. This plant has creeping stems that run along the soil surface and form a dense mat that can easily smother weak stands of grass.

Knotweed

This is an annual plant that germinates in late winter or early spring—just about the same time as the grass starts to green up. It grows quite close to the ground so mowing doesn't affect it much. You'll know knotweed is a problem by the reddish brown patches that appear in your lawn as soon as frost kills the grass top growth or your southern lawn goes dormant. It thrives in areas of high compaction.

Bunch-Type Grasses

You'll recognize bunch grasses on your lawn. They're the clumps of grass that stick up like a sore thumb on an otherwise fine carpet of grass. There are several species that are responsible for this. Even though tall fescues are often used as a turfgrass, when they are in single clumps in another species, they look like a weed. Orchard grass is another bunch-type grass that is normally a contaminant in seed mixes.

The easiest thing to do when you have a low infestation of these bunch grasses is simply to dig them out. Make sure you get all their roots by cutting down into the soil at least 3 to 5 inches. Immediately fill the holes with good soil and repair the hole.

Alternately, a nonselective herbicide such as glyphosate can be used. The easiest way to apply this on bunch grass is to use a weed-wiper type of tool. This is a sponge fitted onto the end of a hollow tube. You simply fill the tube with the herbicide, which slowly releases into the sponge. Then, wipe the sponge across the leaf surface to leave a thin film of herbicide. With the weed-wiper, there is no spray drift and application is much safer. These are available in good garden centers or agricultural supply stores. After seven to 10 days, the area should be repaired.

Spreading Grasses

There are several of spreading grasses that make life difficult for homeowners. While creeping bent grass is a desirable grass species for golf courses, it is a weed on a home lawn. It is often found in circular patches trying to crowd out the desired grass. It has a fine texture and spreading habit.

Another spreading pest that resembles creeping bent grass is called nimblewell. This weed has thin, flat leaves with four veins on the upper surface. It turns brown at the first hint of frost in the fall and is late to green up in the spring. So, if you have brown patches in early fall and early summer, you may have nimblewell infestation.

Quack grass is one of the most invasive of the spreading grasses. Its underground rhizomes with their pointy, white, sharp-tipped ends are well known in the gardening world.

Bermuda grass is a weed grass in some gardens. It will outcompete almost all other grass species during the hot summer months. It is classed as a weed because it is very slow to green up in the spring and turns a classic dead-brown shade after the first frost. When mixed into other species, this ruins the look of the fall and spring lawn. It is very aggressive. Zoysia is another of the southern grasses that has exactly the same growth habit and weed factor as Bermuda grass. Note that these southern grasses are mostly a weed species in the overlap area where both Northern and Southern grasses thrive.

The best way to control these weedy grasses is mostly by nonselective herbicides such as glyphosate with a wick wiper. Read the label for timing; normally, the best time to use a nonselective spray is when the plant is actively growing. Because of the aggressive root action, two applications may be needed for some grasses. Spot spraying works best when the problem is just becoming established. Once a severe infestation exists, it may be necessary to kill off the entire grass population and start fresh

with good seed. There is no doubt that controlling perennial grasses in an established lawn is one of the most difficult parts of lawn management.

Nut Sedge

This weed can drive a person nuts (if you'll excuse the pun). Nut sedge usually establishes itself in waterlogged soils, and its presence often indicates that drainage is poor or there is too much irrigation. Just to make life interesting, once established, nut sedge will tolerate drought or normal watering conditions. You'll be able to identify this weed because, while a normal grass plant sets its leaves in opposite sets of two, the nut sedge sets its leaves in sets of three. The stems of nut sedge are also triangular when compared to a rounded grass stem. The nut sedge produces "nuts" on the end of rhizomes (more botanically correct, they are tubers) underground to sprout and form new plants. Each individual plant can set off "nuts" and continue spreading until they easily occupy 10 to 15 feet across. Difficult to dig out, the tubers are eight to 14 inches deep.

The key to management of nut sedge is to get it while it is young and before it has started producing tubers. Remove the plants before they have five to six leaves; generally it will take a plant two to three weeks of active growing time to reach this stage. Up until this leaf stage, tubers have not formed and if you remove the plant, it will have to regrow before setting tubers. So, every two to three weeks, go out and take as much of the plant out of the ground as possible. A weed spud is a decent tool for this job. Remember that approximately 60 percent of the plant's root energy reserves go into making the first spring plant. Cut that off and the plant is weakened. Each succeeding plant takes up 20 percent of the remaining root reserves. This means that a fully mature tuber can sprout up to 10 times.

Do not take a rototiller to nut sedge. You'll only spread the nuts around. Also, many homeowners believe that spraying with glyphosate on the mature plant will eliminate this pest. It will not. There is remarkably little translocation of the chemical once the leaves are mature. If you intend to use a systemic, nonselective

SOMETIMES YOU FEEL LIKE A NUT

If you want to know whether you have yellow or purple nut sedge, you can taste a nut. The tubers of yellow nut sedge have an almond taste while purple nut sedge tubers are quite bitter.

Although nut sedges are not poisonous, purple nut sedge is not recommended for fine dining. Yellow nut sedge, on the other hand, has a long tradition in cuisine, ranging from a coffee substitute when dried and roasted to fresh eating in salads. I'm told their original introduction to North America was as a gardening food source and that they escaped to become the noxious weed they are.

WHAT HAPPENS WHEN YOU CUT THE LEAVES OFF PLANTS

To clarify the way a plant uses its energy reserves, let us assume the plant starts with 100 units of energy.

- The first plant produced in the spring takes up to 60 percent of those energy units, or 60 units.
- You cut off the top growth and the plant regrows.

The second plant takes up 20 percent of the remaining energy.

$$100 - 60 = 40.$$
$$20\% \text{ of } 40 = 8, \text{ leaving } 32 \text{ energy units.}$$

- The third plant takes up to 20 percent of the remaining energy.

$$20\% \text{ of } 32 = 6.4, \text{ leaving } 25.6 \text{ energy units.}$$

This decreasing percentage of energy units is primarily because as soon as the first leaves are exposed to sunlight, they start feeding back into the root to reduce the draw on the reserves. So the earlier you chop up a developing plant, the more energy it takes from its root reserves to produce leaves capable of feeding itself. Nobody said getting rid of perennial weeds such as nut sedge or dandelions was all that easy.

herbicide, use it when the leaves are young and actively growing. Be prepared to repeat the treatment at least twice.

If you have nut sedge in a small patch of turf, it is probably best to dig the soil out of that patch along with the nuts (to a depth of 10 to 12 inches). Refill with good soil and then renovate.

In vegetable or flower gardens, nut sedge can be controlled by laying down layers of newspapers and then mulching on top of the papers to prevent the paper from blowing away. The paper decomposes in a few years, but blocks the sunlight to the plant in the meantime, eventually killing it. This is not possible on a lawn. The normal black polyethylene landscape fabrics do not control nut sedge, because the sharp ends penetrate the fabric. Solarization over an entire summer also destroys nut sedge, but it is not possible on an actively growing lawn.

CHAPTER SIX

Lawn Diseases and Their Cures

Lawn diseases are a tricky problem for any gardener. The "disease triangle" is an excellent way to understand how diseases get established in any gardening adventure.

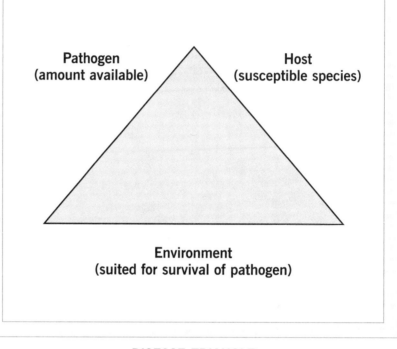

DISEASE TRIANGLE

All three sides of the triangle must be present to create a disease condition in a lawn. To get a solution, you have to modify one of the sides. In most cases, the environmental side must be modified for effective long-term control. Short-term control can be effected by attacking the pathogen itself. Pathogens normally live in all soils and gardens, and it is only when the environment is suitable that they grow into a problem. This means that your job as a gardener is to grow your grass in the healthiest way possible—to care for the soil that supports it and to mow it properly. Doing these two things will go a long way toward creating a healthy lawn environment that will reduce your lawn problems.

FUNGUS FIGHTER

An effective technique to fight any fungus problem is to sprinkle cornmeal (yes, the kind you eat) onto your lawn at the rate of 20 pounds per 1,000 square feet. While soil scientists don't know exactly how it works, they do know that many fungal problems disappear after cornmeal is applied. One effect is that the cornmeal feeds the good guys that eat the bad fungus spores.

Diagnosis: The First Step

To begin with, it is important to diagnose properly the problems on the lawn. It doesn't make a lot of sense to use a spray if it's the wrong spray and doesn't help the problem. Try to keep the following points in mind before you bring out the spray gun and work down this list to help with the diagnosis. As with insect attacks, the spray gun is always the last alternative in having a good lawn. With a bit of experience, you will find that the vast majority of so-called lawn disease problems are not diseases but a direct result of poor management practices. Fix the way you take care of your lawn first, and the problems will likely take care of themselves.

The second reason that it is so important to change management practices first is that correctly identifying lawn disease problems is not easy, even for the experts. Richard Duble, a turfgrass specialist in Identification and Control of Turfgrass Disease, with the Texas Agricultural Extension Service, wrote, "Identifying turf problems requires expertise, experience and, sometimes, good detective work. A homeowner may correctly identify a turf problem 30 to 50% of the time and an experienced turf manager might correctly identify a turf problem 70 or 80% of the time, but neither will be correct 100% of the time. The problems and their interactions are often too numerous and complex to correctly identify." (See *http://aggie/ horticulture.tamu.edu/plantanswers/turf/publications/disease1.html.*)

This means that if you change your management practices and grow a healthy lawn, the problems will largely go away. It also means that if you follow a few basic recommendations for repairing the damage that does occur, most of the time it won't matter which specific species of fungus is doing the damage—your management practices will prevent or cure the problem.

This is not to say that you shouldn't spray fungicides when appropriate to knock down problems. But a spray is a Band-Aid, and it is better in the long run to solve the underlying problem rather than keep applying short-term fixes. Fix your lawn environment and most of your disease problems will disappear.

Many problems are caused by nondisease events such as drought or too much fertilizer. They are not diseases; rather, they

NONLIVING CAUSES OF DISEASE

Nonliving causes of disease include:

- Improper fertilization practices
- Pesticide and fertilizer "burn," (the scientific term is **phytotoxicity**)
- Drought
- Freezing or low-temperature damage
- Poor air circulation
- Root injury (e.g., dog feces)
- Poor rootzone conditions (e.g., excessive moisture, compacted soil)
- Sun scald and shock

are the physical results of mismanagement. Is this a problem on your lawn? Consider the following:

- *What are the current growing conditions on your lawn and how do they influence the disease?* In other words, the disease has been dormant for some time on your lawn, why is it emerging now? Can you change the environmental conditions (e.g., leaf wetness, fertility, soil pH, soil moisture, soil texture, humidity, wind, drainage, compaction, thatch) that created the problem?
- *Look carefully at the problem.* Does it have a pattern, such as round circles or irregularly shaped blotches? What color is the grass? Where is the problem happening? Is it evenly spaced over the lawn or next to garden areas?
- *Try to identify the species of turfgrass being affected.* Is it the weed grass (crabgrass) or the good grass?
- *Examine individual grass plants.* Look at the leaves, the crowns, and the roots. Are there lesions on the leaves? Is the crown soft? Are the roots long and healthy or does the grass pull out of the lawn easily?
- *Look for signs of disease.* Are there spores on the leaves? Are there black threads on the roots?
- *If you cannot identify the problem, get help.* Take a sample and put it into a clear plastic bag. Then, take the bag to a good garden center or local extension office along with a description of the problem, using the identifiers discussed here.

Do Not Mistake These Problems for Diseases:

Improper Fertilization. If you apply unbalanced amounts of fertilizer—say, too much nitrogen—then the grass will respond with quick, lush growth. This lush growth is a clarion lunch invitation to every pest and disease in the area. It is far better to feed at the recommended levels than to try to push the lawn along with a bit more food just because you want to finish the bag.

KEEP OFF FROZEN GRASS

In the early fall, before the grass has totally stopped growing, never walk on a lawn that is frosty and covered with ice crystals. If you walk on frozen turf, you will break and wound the grass plants, opening them up to fungus damage. Allow the sun to melt the frost and thaw out the grass plants. Once they are thawed, it is safe to walk on them. This warning does not apply later in the fall after several hard frosts have caused fungus spores and the grass to go dormant with no aboveground growth.

Nutritional Imbalance–Fertilizer Burn. Fertilizers are basically forms of salt. If you apply too much of them to a lawn, you'll kill the roots of the plants. We call this burning the plant. You'll most often see this problem where you fill the fertilizer spreader and that little bit extra bounces out of the spreader. This is why most garden centers recommend filling the spreader on a driveway or other nonlawn area where the spills won't do any damage.

Drought. Grass that is allowed to become too dry may in fact become dead. Even though grass may go dormant in the heat of the summer, it still requires some moisture around the root zone. Sometimes when the top layers of the soil become very dry, the soil compacts and rain will have a hard time penetrating the compacted layer. Some of the rain will run off and not be absorbed and used by the grass plants. Some grass experts refer to this excessive drought condition as "permanent wilt."

Freezing and Low-Temperature Injury. There is a wide geographic zone that will never see this particular problem, but sometimes when the weather conditions are just right, grass will be winterkilled. Normally, this occurs in late winter when the snow begins to melt and then refreezes and stays frozen as an ice layer on top of the turf. If the temperatures drop quite low under these conditions, grass death can occur due to temperature stress. This is most often seen in cases where the grass plants are already stressed by other disease or environmental conditions.

Shade and Poor Air Circulation. Grass is undeniably a sun-loving plant. If you try to grow it under evergreen trees or dense shade trees such as maples, the grass simply does not getting enough light; it is under stress. Combine that with poor air circulation caused by city fences and it is no wonder that you have grass problems. It's a wonder that you have any grass at all.

QUICK TIPS

If you have a camera light meter, you can check out the level of shade under trees. If the shade level is 600 foot-candles or less, forget about growing grass. It's too shady.

• • •

You might think slowing down the grass growth by cutting too much off sounds like a good idea. You know, "If it doesn't grow, then I don't have to mow it." Let me point out, however, that if the grass isn't growing (and it won't for upward of a month with a severe scalping), then the only thing that will grow is weeds. Mother Nature abhors a vacuum, and she'll fill it with weeds if you don't fill it with grass.

• • •

The best cure for dog damage is prevention. However, if you do see a dog squatting or lifting a leg, you have one hour to solve the problem before it creates damage. After an hour, the urine has started to break down into urea and will begin to burn the grass roots. If you water before an hour is up, you'll drive the urine or urea products (they're water soluble) below the level of the roots or dilute them so they won't hurt the roots.

Root Injury–Dog Urine. This is the number one cause of small 8 to 12-inch circles of dead grass on the lawn. By the time you see the problem, it is too late. See Chapter 4 for instructions on how to fix the dead grass patches. If you see a dog urinating on the lawn, soak the area with water. This dissolves the excessive urea (which is another form of nitrogen) and drives it out of the rootzone.

Soil Compaction. This can be a problem with heavier soils or soils with larger amounts of clay. It is particularly a problem where there is a lot of foot traffic (like kids who cut across your corner lot or the mail carrier's path). Compaction prevents oxygen from getting to the roots. It can also stop water from entering the soil, or, once it gets in, it slows its drainage. Compaction really stops tender young roots from growing strongly. The cure here is to aerate your lawn with a machine that removes a core of soil. Rental companies usually stock these.

Sun Scald and Shock. If you mow the grass too short, you remove foliage that is necessary for making food. On some species of grass, you also expose the growing stolons to sunlight. These stolons then get sunburned; if you look closely, you'll see burned brown areas. This burning causes grass stress and as should be clear by now—stress is something we want to avoid on our lawns. The grass will also go into physiological shock if you remove more than one-third of its growing surface at any given time. Mow off too much and your grass will simply stop growing under its stress. During this stress period, it is open to attack from disease and pests.

Usually It's Fungi

Most of the diseases that plague lawns are caused by fungi. This a mixed blessing because most of these fungi are just doing their job, trying to follow nature's assigned task of breaking down organic matter to be recycled and used by future generations of plants. When fungi cause disease, it means that for some reason—mostly cultural—the fungi have attacked the stressed grass plants, which becomes a problem for the homeowner.

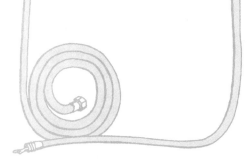

Fungi are themselves plants. Not that you'd recognize them as such because they have no roots, no stems, and no leaves. But, biologically, they are plants. A single strand of fungus is called a **hypha**. When you get a bunch of hypha together, they are usually referred to as **mycelium**. If you see a chunk of fungus (like the stuff on moldy bread), you are seeing mycelium, not the individual fungal strands or hypha (those are microscopic).

Identifying Diseases

It isn't easy to give overly general advice about lawn diseases because they tend to be geographically based. A problem in a wet coastal region is not going to have the same impact a few miles farther inland, and away from the constant humidity. A problem of high clay and damp soils will seldom be a problem on sandier soils. Trickier still, different grass species are predisposed to certain diseases while others are immune. It's very much like a horse race. You just have to go with the odds.

That's the long way of saying there are no hard-and-fast rules for identifying which diseases are going to be problems for all gardeners. It really depends on your area and your garden management. The following descriptions, however, should get you started on figuring out how to identify and treat these major lawn diseases.

These are the major lawn diseases that a homeowner might face. Keep in mind, of course, that there are many more lawn diseases than the ones we list here. Some diseases are so specialized that it takes a laboratory to differentiate between them and the ones listed here. Realize, however, that the following is a thorough overview of what you'll need to know. The vast majority of lawn diseases will never grace your yard. Most of them are found on golf courses where the grass plants are forced to grow and are stressed more than your lawns will ever be.

So read about these diseases, but relax. If you grow your lawn properly, you'll never get to meet them.

KNOW YOUR SIGNS AND SYMPTOMS

A **symptom** is a visible expression of disease on a grass plant. For example, yellowing grass plants are symptoms.

A **sign** of a disease is the visible expression of the pathogen. For example, visible mycelium masses are signs and not symptoms.

Looking at it another way, symptoms are the visible results of the effects of the signs. Sometimes you can't see the signs, but you can see the symptoms.

You'll get the best results in diagnosing a problem when you have both symptoms and signs. Unfortunately, in the real world this is hard to obtain. See the instructions on pages 137–138 and try to obtain both signs and symptoms. Your choice of treatment will depend on proper identification.

Anthracnose

This fungus overwinters In the plant debris and sheaths of grass plants. When the temperatures rise above 78°F and the relative humidity is high, spores germinate and infect grass leaves. If this problem is going to happen, it will happen after a period of high temperatures and high humidity. Anthracnose discolors the grass (yellowing) in patches that range from an inch or two to several yards. You can recognize anthracnose by the marks on individual grass leaves. Small yellow **lesions** will have black centers. As the disease progresses, the grass will yellow and then bronze. As it dies, it becomes a lovely shade of khaki tan. In advanced stages, the fruiting body of the fungus, a small black moldlike circle, grows out through the grass cuticle. These fruiting bodies are about the size of a pinhead but are clearly visible with a 10x lens.

Annual bluegrass is the most severely affected; it can be killed in a single season. Anthracnose targets Kentucky bluegrass and red fescue, but not as severely. Other grasses may get the problem but will not die from it.

If the lawn is prone to this problem, syringe the lawn mid-morning and midafternoon with your sprinkler system. This cools the turf area and prevents the spores from developing. Note this is not watering to get the soil damp, but just a light misting to reduce the temperature around the grass leaves. Ensure adequate fertility, aerate the soil, and raise the mower height. Do not water during the evening to minimize water staying on the leaves. In general, reduce the stress on the lawn as much as feasible.

Bermuda Grass Decline

Up until recently, this problem was thought to be one of those complex multidisease problems specific to Bermuda grass. None of the labs had been able to identify a specific species of fungus causing the grass to thin out and have yellowing patches 12 to 24 inches in diameter. The roots go brown and die because the feeder roots rot off. As with many fungal diseases, most of the badly infected lawns were also under stress from other causes. Removing the stress sometimes helped the lawn to recover and slowly regain its health. It is interesting to note that the number-one stress agent was too low a mowing height.

Now, researchers have found that a specific fungus is responsible for this problem. Although its name is too long for any tongue to get around, it is related to the take-all patch problem (page 160). and while its name is too long for any tongue to get around, it is related to the take-all patch problem.

Get the management right and this fungus is not going to be a problem on most home lawns. If you have a severe case, there are fungicides registered for this problem. Apply them in the fall. Most of the fungicides have to be used at the beginning of the problem. Once this fungus is established, control is normally less-than-satisfactory with fungicides. See the tables on pages 164-165 for general fungicide recommendations.

Brown Patch

This is a fungus that survives on thatch and one that the average homeowner will never see. It is primarily a disease of low-cut grass (low as in golf green low). Brown patch creates a ring of quite distinctively purple grass. This ring appears first thing in the morning and disappears by noon in most cases. On home lawns, there may be a round circle of brown grass and some healthy grass will still be growing within these small circles. The circles can expand to 1 yard in width and may appear dead or simply as thinned-out, weak-growing grass.

Brown patch attacks all turfgrasses, particularly the bent grasses used on golf greens. Annual bluegrass and perennial ryegrass are also particularly susceptible.

In terms of cultural controls, avoid excessive nitrogen and water. Eliminate the overwintering protection of thatch. Do not water during the evening to minimize water staying on the leaves. If this is a constant problem, increasing the soil pH to 7.0 will provide some relief. Spray fungicide when day temperatures reach approximately 65°F.

TOPDRESSING TIPS

Generally speaking, a topdressing is used to repair damaged areas of lawn. I've found using three things in combination works quite well. The first is good-quality grass seed. Sprinkle it onto damaged areas so that the seeds almost touch each other. You don't want them piling up on top of each other, but neither do you want much space between them on the ground. It takes a small bit of practice but it's not rocket science, you'll get it pretty quickly.

The second is cornmeal. Sprinkle it on any damaged area to help the fungus predators destroy fungus spores. If you control the fungus where it breeds, you'll have less of a problem.

The third is good compost. I always recommend sprinkling a quarter inch of compost over the damaged area on top of the seed and then watering the area until it is well soaked. The compost feeds the soil and knocks back fungus. The seed will have no problem germinating and growing through the compost. You'll have to keep the seed damp until it germinates, so a daily soaking is part of the routine.

Centipede Decline

With this disease, circular dead areas appear in the spring and continue to enlarge all summer long. The grass at the edges of the dead areas continues to yellow and die, particularly if the grass is under stress. This is strictly a problem on centipede grass.

With this southern turf, maintain the soil pH between 5.0 and 5.5 (quite acidic) and do not fertilize excessively. Do follow the 1 pound per 1,000 square feet of nitrogen feeding rule for southern lawn grasses. Avoid drought stress and do not mow too low. Chelated iron sprays help green up the foliage. Treat for nematodes. If the problem persists, choose another grass variety.

Cercospora Leaf Spot

This fungus causes a small brown spot on the leaves of St. Augustine grass; sometimes the spots are brown ranging to purplish brown. As the spots get older, the center of the spot may turn a tan brown. Where the fungus is well established, the entire grass leaf may get the problem and then the leaf simply turns yellow, withers away, and dies. This dying causes what appears to be a "melting" of irregular spots on the lawn as more and more individual plants are infected.

While St. Augustine grass is most susceptible to the problem, the common or yellow green-leafed forms are more likely to be infected than the newer bluer hybrids and selections. Warm, humid weather favors the incidence of this disease.

Proper feeding with nitrogen lowers the outbreaks; stressed lawns are more likely to see this problem. Try to keep the grass blades as dry as possible; irrigation should be deep and infrequent. Fungicides that control leaf spot diseases will control this problem.

Crown and Root Rot

This fungus affects the crowns and roots of the plant leading to plant death. Initial symptoms are a leaf spotting with purplish brown lesions, and then the turf takes on a purplish tinge. The turfgrass starts to thin out and then finally the crowns and roots are infected and the grass begins to die. The experience of many turf experts is that this disease can infect a lawn and is often not recognized until the grass starts to die off in irregularly shaped patches on the lawn.

LAWN LINGO

If you read much technical horticultural writing, sooner or later you'll come across these terms. I don't use them in this book, but they make great cocktail-party conversation starters.

Abiotic plant disease: Caused by unfavorable growing conditions.

Biotic plant disease: Caused by plant pathogens.

So, most of our lawn problems are abiotic, even though this particular section is discussing biotic problems.

RESISTANCE TO FUNGICIDES

Just as insect pests develop **resistance** to chemicals used to kill them, infectious fungi are equally capable of developing resistance to fungicides. This happens most often when a product is used repeatedly instead of alternating its use with another unrelated chemical. The problem of resistance is made worse when lawnowners rely on chemicals to control problems rather than fixing the underlying causes. Without the environmental pressures to reduce their growth, the fungi grow and mutate quite quickly to develop chemical resistance. There are now many fungicides, particularly the **systemic** fungicides, that are useless for disease control.

There are two strategies that homeowners should adopt to reduce the risk of fungicide resistance building up in your area. First, don't rely on fungicides alone when faced with a problem. Fix the underlying cause so the fungus is not given a free ride. By fixing the underlying causes, fungus propagation will be reduced. Second, use different fungicides if repeat sprays have to be done. Do not spray with the same chemical product time and time again. The best system is to use at least two sprays on alternate application dates. Another recommended practice is to tank-mix (use two products in the same spray tank) two different products. Be sure the two products are registered as being compatible. Read the label for this information. If you tank-mix incompatible sprays, you run the risk of harming not only your lawn but also yourself.

This problem can attack a wide range of plants; no species is particularly vulnerable. You can control crown and root rot by following good cultural practices, in particular, ensuring that nitrogen and potassium levels are adequate for good growth. The problem is more developed on compacted soils, so aeration is indicated if the problem exists. Do not use a herbicide. It will weaken the grass further. Mowing at the proper height is also important in the management of this problem. Fungicides will help; however, without improving cultural practices, the problem will return. If the problem is particularly bad, it may be worth considering a preventative spray program as well as a remedial one.

Curvularia Blight

Irregular patches and streaking are the first sign of this fungus disease. Then the leaves yellow and brown from the leaf tips down to the sheath. The fungus invades the grass through the cut tips of the leaves.

Bent grasses, annual bluegrass, and fescues are the most susceptible, particularly during the high heat of the summer when poor cultural conditions weaken the plants.

Control is mainly to improve the growing conditions by avoiding overwatering and to ensure moderate growth through proper fertilizer application. If this is a problem on your lawn, increase the mower height immediately and reduce the thatch layer by raking. You can use fungicides, but the damage is rarely so bad as to warrant the expense.

Dollar Spot

This fungus produces small spots (2 to 6 inches in diameter) in lawns. It usually occurs later in the spring, so you know it is not a winter-caused injury. The spots on the leaves are shaped like an hourglass and extend across the blade. They have a lighter center with darker border and the border appears to be a shade of brown, purple, or black. Early in the morning before the sun hits the grass you'll often be able to see a cottony fungus growth on the infected blades, but it disappears with the hot sunshine.

THE MANY FORMS OF PESTICIDES

Plant scientists now refer to all chemical sprays as **pesticides**. Anything you don't want on your lawn is a pest. So we have:

- **Insecticides:** Pesticides used to kill insects.
- **Herbicides:** Pesticides used to kill weed pests.
- **Fungicides:** Pesticides used to control fungi.
- **Bactericides:** Pesticides used to kill bacteria.
- **Bacteriostats:** Pesticides used to stop bacterial growth and reproduction. I thought I'd throw this one in even though it isn't a "cide." These sprays don't kill bacteria, they simply stop them in their tracks. You won't often see them on the garden center shelves.

Centipede grass, Bermuda grass, zoysia grass, bluegrass, rye-grass, and fine fescues are hosts. This occurs especially on poorly nourished lawns.

The easiest control for this problem is to feed your lawn adequately. Reduce any water stress by irrigation. The grass plants are very rarely killed. They are simply knocked back, but they will regrow new leaves with feeding and care.

Adequate fertilizer will help the turf overcome this disease. Irrigate turf as needed to avoid drought stress. Do not mow too low and avoid excessive leaf wetness.

Fairy Ring

Fairy ring occurs in three different stages: a killing ring, a stimulated ring, and a ring of mushrooms. The killing ring starts as a ring of wilted, purple-tinged turf. This ring then dies off leaving brown dead grass in a circular form. The circles can be anywhere from one yard across to several yards. The area in the middle of the ring appears normal. The stimulated ring is slightly more common in northern areas. It is a circle of dark green, fast-growing grass that is darker and taller than the surrounding lawn. These circles are usually smaller, with the largest only reaching several yards across. The last ring—a ring of mushrooms—is exactly that, a ring of mushrooms in the lawn. Gardeners will normally see only one of these conditions when the problem strikes.

This mushroom fungus grows throughout the soil, forming a white network of mycelium up to 12 inches deep. Untreated, the circles will get larger every year as the fungus grows.

The most drastic option is to remove the infected soil and replace it with good soil. Otherwise, ensure good nutrition because the disease more often strikes soil with low fertility. Adding iron in a spray formula will often mask the damage. Adding compost will increase the soil micro-organisms that fight fairy ring fungus. Drenching with an organosilicone wetting agent may alleviate symptoms. The problem will eventually go away on its own regardless of gardener activity.

RAKES

Rakes are one of the lawn managers' most useful tools. Weed rakes, leaf rakes, and small-tined rakes all have their place in the management of the lawn. Invest in good rakes because you will use them more than any other tool on the lawn. Ergonomically designed rakes are a good investment and a good idea. Although a little more expensive than common discount-store tools, they'll help your back and make it easier to do the job.

KEEP OFF THE GRASS

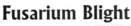

Fusarium Blight

Once thought to be a separate disease, Fusarium blight is now recognized as a complex mix of several similar diseases: necrotic ring spot, yellow patch, and summer patch. Treat it as you would those problems.

Fusarium Patch or Pink Snow Mold

The pink snow mold fungus grows over the summer. In the fall, spores germinate to grow and attack grass blades over the winter. Although it prefers snow cover, this mold lives and grows without it. The typical reddish brown patch when the snow melts is the prime symptom; if you look closely the pink mycelium are visible on the edges of the dead spot for a few days immediately after the snow melts. If the fungus continues to live in a cool, damp spring, it can create secondary symptoms known as Fusarium patch, which are small dead areas with the typical reddish brown color. Sometimes, you can see both at the same time—the new growth of reddish brown Fusarium patch growing on the edges of the dead turf killed by pink snow mold.

The primary management technique is to reduce thatch because this is where the fungus lives during the summer. Prevent succulent growth that is a good food source late in the fall by regular mowing right up until the grass stops growing. If you don't give the succulent food, it doesn't grow well. Do not apply any nitrogen within six weeks of dormancy. Good potassium levels will help the grass fight off this problem, so make sure that your potassium feeding is adequate. In the fall, rake the lawn to remove leaves and dead and decaying grass (this stops spores from hiding and germi-nating in the debris), and do not topdress. If the problem is severe and consistent, apply fungicides in the fall.

Gray Leaf Spot

This fungus causes small brown spots to grow on the grass leaves. These spots then enlarge into oval or elongated oval spots on the leaves, sheaths, and stems. The color is a dark ash-brown with purplish margins. During wet or humid conditions, the spots are covered with a gray velvety fungus mycelium. Severely infected

COMPOST, THE WONDER DRUG

Cornell University has done research into the disease-suppressing components of compost. In general, they found that many different disease organisms are suppressed by compost. The current recommendation is for two applications of 50 pounds of compost per 1,000 square foot of home lawn. Apply compost first thing in the spring and again late in the fall.

The most effective composts are those that are at least two years old and are composted on a natural soil base or under trees. Compost works on the lawn in several ways.

1. It produces chemical compounds that actually kill bacteria and fungi. So, by applying compost, you are actively killing the bad fungi that attack your lawn.
2. It acts as a food source for those micro-organisms that eat fungi. If you feed the good guys, they'll eat the bad guys for you.
3. In the process of breaking down into humic acids (to feed your plants), compost uses the same food sources as the bad fungi. So, it competes with them for food.

By applying compost, you are actively killing some fungi, feeding the good guys that eat fungi, and competing with the survivors for the remaining food. Oh yes—and you're feeding your plants at the same time.

Compost is the closest thing to a wonder drug that Mother Nature has produced for gardeners.

leaves wither and die, lending a scorched look to the lawn. Note that the dead grass is brownish in color, not yellowish.

Bahia grass, Bermuda grass, centipede grass, ryegrass and St. Augustinegrass are the worst hit, particularly the St. Augustine grass blue cultivars.

As with most fungal problems, warm humid summer months are the optimal time for this problem to become firmly established. Prolonged wet spells or extended periods of wet leaves through improper irrigation techniques also help establish this problem. Excessive nitrogen feeding has been implicated as well in creating conditions right for gray leaf spot establishment.

It only makes sense then that the initial control methods would include proper watering and fertilizing. Also look for disease-resistant cultivars as a primary line of defense.

Leaf Blotch

Leaf **blotch** is not quite a blotch at first, it appears as tiny purplish to reddish spots on the leaf blades and sheaths. It is mostly a disease of seedlings. The infected seedlings normally wither away and die, turning brown in the process. In fact, there will be so much seedling death that patches, ranging in size from 2 inches to 3 feet in diameter, are developed. Interestingly enough, older grass plants develop an immunity to this problem.

It is a disease of Bermuda grass and as older plants are not bothered, it is normally only recommended that thatch be removed, adequate nitrogen be applied, and good cultural practices be used. No sprays are indicated.

If you are reading the fine print in many of these diseases, you'll often see that excessive nitrogen is implicated in many of the problems. Excessive nitrogen creates lush growth that is tender and has thin cell walls. The thin cell walls are more easily damaged by physical injury and invaded and colonized by fungus. Overfeeding is something you can control. And you should if you want to avoid the problems discussed in this chapter.

Landscaped backyard with impatiens and climbers

Chewing Fescue

Kentucky Bluegrass

Buffalo grass

Zoysia grass

Stepping stones in lawn

Fine Fescue lawn

Lawn with landscaped area

Lawn with bench and garden

©1999 Alan & Linda Detrick

Manicured lawn and beds

©1997 Alan & Linda Detrick

Meadow lawn

Tiered landscaped lawn

Garden of Reflections

©2000 judywhite/GardenPhotos.com

Medium-maintenance lawn

©1993 judywhite/GardenPhotos.com

Laying down sod

©1999 TPI

Lawn between garden borders

Cottage-style lawn and garden

Secret garden atop Rockefeller Center

Leaf Spot

Leaf spot is one of the more easily recognized grass problems. Occurring mostly in warm weather, the leaves develop small brown to tan spots with purplish red (sometimes fading to purplish brown) borders. The spots may be as wide as the grass leaf and are almost always longer than they are wide. The tips of the grass leaf often die, giving a brown look to the lawn. If the leaf sheath is infected, the plant will often die, leaving a thinned-out section of turf. This fungus is very similar to the melting out fungus, and sometimes leaf spot can create similar large patches of "melted" grass. The grass appears withered, slimy, and dead—rather like it has been melted under a hot sun.

It is very important to avoid the excessive use of nitrogen fertilizers with leaf spot fungus problems. Lush growth is particularly sensitive to leaf spotting. Remove excessive thatch; this is where the fungus overwinters. Never water in the evening; it is important to keep the leaves as dry as possible and keep the fungus dry. If you use fungicides, apply them as soon as the problem is seen at the "spot" stage. If you delay treatment until patches start to brown, the results of spraying will be less than satisfactory. Topdress to repair any damage.

Melting Out

Melting out is very similar to leaf spot. The melting out spots start as purple to brown with a lighter center. They grow by moving down the leaf sheath to the crown to eventually kill the plant. When this fungus disease gets to an advanced stage, irregularly shaped patches (from a few inches to several yards across) are created. As in leaf spot, the dead grass appears to be wilted and "melted." It's not a pretty sight. Although many different grasses are susceptible, Kentucky bluegrass and Bermuda grass are the most susceptible.

The control for melting out is the same as for leaf spot.

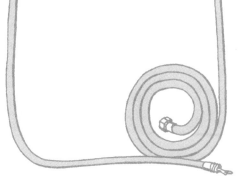

LEAF SPOTTING DISEASE

The older Kentucky bluegrass varieties are more prone to leaf spotting than the newer ones. Check with your garden center to obtain new varieties if you are having a problem. Bermuda grass is also prone to leaf spot diseases.

Necrotic Ring Spot

The initial symptoms of this fungal problem are dead patches 6 to 24 inches in diameter. Surrounding the patch is a mix of normal, yellow straw-colored, and sometimes reddish blades. It is said to resemble a "frog's eye" pattern where a circle of dead grass surrounds green growing turf. Black strands of the fungus cover the roots and crowns of individual plants. Sometimes, existing thatch will decompose quickly in these patches, and the patch will appear sunken or lower than the rest of the lawn. This problem normally appears in spring or fall, but in warm weather, the red blades are seldom seen. The infected plants (either infected in spring or fall) are very susceptible to summer heat and drought stress. In fact, under summer stress, weakened plants are quite likely to die.

Once necrotic ring spot is established, it is difficult to control and damage may remain or reappear yearly for two to four years. Fine fescues and bluegrass are affected; it can be a serious disease of Kentucky bluegrass in some areas.

To control this problem, avoid high nitrogen feeding and drought stress. Topdress with a grass/compost mix, using a tall fescue or ryegrass varieties that are resistant to the problem. Adequate control requires a combination of practices including: thatch control, adjustment of fertilizer practices, relieving soil compaction, changing watering practices, and possibly using a fungicide. Keep the thatch to as low a level as possible to reduce the over-wintering home of the fungus. Avoid excessive nitrogen feeding, particularly in the spring when the grass doesn't need it. Rent a core-aerator machine (one that takes little cores out of the grass) to improve aeration and compaction. Mow a bit higher to reduce the stress on the grass plant and irrigate a bit more often than normal. More frequent waterings reduce any water stress by keeping the top inch or two of soil moist most of the time. This reduces both water and heat stress on the plants.

You'll need to adopt all of these management practices, and you'll find a fungicide a useful tool here. Remember that the fungicide alone will not solve the problem, you'll need to change your management practices to keep the grass healthy and the fungus from reappearing.

TO STOP OR REDUCE
SNOW MOLD PROBLEMS

Fertilize cool season grasses in late fall (after the last mowing) with a slow-release nitrogen carrier. This feeds the roots and enables them to store lots of carbohydrates. This food storage means they'll survive the winter in good shape and start growing strongly in the spring.

Keep mowing in the fall until all leaf growth stops. Do not leave long grass to overwinter. It will decay over the winter and become a food source for fungi.

Reduce thatch with aeration, vertical mowing, power raking, or a combination of these practices. Again, thatch decomposes and provides a ready food source for these snow molds.

Prevent large drifts of snow on important turf areas by proper placement of snow fences or landscape plantings. Deep snow provides exactly the right conditions of temperature and humidity that these particular fungi enjoy.

Prevent snow compaction by restricting walking, snowmobiling, skiing, or sledding on important turfs. This is not as much of a problem on the home lawn as it is on golf course greens. The intensively managed turf on golf courses is more easily damaged than a healthy home lawn. So, don't worry about the kids playing on the lawn and making snow forts. As a father of four, I would suggest the snow forts are more important than a bit of snow mold anyway.

Repair snow mold damage by raking the affected patches in early spring to disrupt the encrusted mat and by lightly fertilizing to encourage new growth.

Use a preventative fungicide program on high-value turf and on areas where snow molds cause injury year after year. Make the initial fungicide application in early- to mid-November and repeat applications during mid-winter thaws, as needed.

Nigrospora Blight

This fungus girdles the stolons of St. Augustine grass, and the girdling prevents the stolon from getting water and nutrients. The leaves and stolons are under severe moisture stress and dry out turning a yellowy brown color. The problem is particularly bad during a dry spring followed by a dry, hot summer. In many ways, the symptoms appear to be exactly like chinch bugs— patches of yellowing grass. The key difference is the brown lesions on the stolons.

The good news is that this fungus is a particularly weak one and only picks on weak plants. Grow your lawn properly and you'll never see it. If you do, immediately improve your management practices and spray with a fungicide to stop the problem in its tracks. Grass will recover nicely with improved management without the need for fungicides.

Pink Patch

Pink patch and red thread are quite similar problems with nearly identical symptoms—irregularly shaped patches of dying grass, and from a distance the grass appears to be ever so slightly pink tinged. The fungus usually restricts itself to the leaves, sheaths, and stems; but in severe cases, it will kill the plant. Both pink patch and red thread develop well when the temperatures are 65° to 75°F. The major difference is an obvious one. The fungus on pink patch tends to create pinkish fungal growth, while red thread has reddish fungal growth. Prolonged humid or rainy weather is also blamed for high incidences of this fungus.

In general, if pink patch is a problem, increasing the level of nitrogen to the lawn will help the grass plants outgrow the problem. Focus on reducing the stress by increasing the level of management to get a good control. For the most part, this disease is not severe enough to warrant using a fungicide. Sometimes a pure stand of ryegrass or fine fescue may be severely hit, which may warrant fungicide use.

Powdery mildew

Powdery **mildew** is a relatively minor fungus problem of turfgrass. The primary symptom is a whitish or grayish powdery covering on the grass leaves. It looks as if the leaves have been dusted with white flour. Badly infected leaves may yellow and die. In very severe cases, the plant may die. Powdery mildew is normally found only in shady sections of the lawn under conditions of high humidity and temperatures of 60° to 72°F.

It is a problem on almost all lawn grasses, bluegrass may be marginally more susceptible to it than other species.

To control powdery mildew, avoid high nitrogen feeding and low mowing. Both activities stress grass more in shady situations than in the full sunlight. If powdery mildew is a problem on shady bluegrass, replace it with a shade-tolerant grass species. Fungicides can treat the primary symptoms, but once established, it will return unless the underlying causes are corrected.

Pythium Blight

The early signs of this fungus are small spots (about 2 inches across) that are dark and slimy looking. They will continue to increase in size. In the early dew-soaked morning or other wet period, the water-soaked leaves collapse and mat together. The white mycelium of the fungus will be visible at these times. As the weather dries, the mycelium disappears and the grass turns a dead shade of brown. The shape of the dead patches often streaks along the direction of the lawn mowing because the mower will spread the fungus spores. This fungus does kill the plant crown, so the grass won't recover and you'll need topdressing.

The fungi grow most rapidly in hot, humid weather and are not a problem in cooler temperatures. Creeping bent grass, annual bluegrass, and perennial ryegrass are the most susceptible to Pythium blight.

This is a difficult problem to control once established because it explodes so quickly. Use infrequent and deep watering with good drainage to keep the humidity levels around the grass crowns low. No nighttime waterings. If Pythium is a problem on your lawn, avoid mowing and watering the lawn when the temperatures go above 82°F, if at all possible. Fungicides are recommended—follow label directions.

Red Thread

This fungus overwinters as a dormant mycelium in diseased or dead tissue. In the spring, while the turfgrasses are still growing slowly, it invades the leaves. High summer temperatures slow its growth. In the fall, when the temperature drops and normal moist conditions prevail, it can explode into growth just as the turf is going dormant.

The primary symptom is a reddish brown irregular patch on the lawn. While initial symptoms look like dollar spot, later symptoms are like those of melting out—oval spots on the leaves that eventually girdle and kill the leaf. The grass appears to wilt, turn a yellow straw color, and, if the crowns rot with severe cases—disappear. Under advanced infections, a pinkish red gelatinous mass grows from the cut ends of the grass leaves.

This fungus infects nearly all northern lawn grasses. Perennial ryegrass and fine-leaf fescues are the most commonly infected.

This disease is most commonly found on poorly fertilized lawns where the grass cannot outgrow the initial infection. As with most fungus problems, try to minimize evening waterings to keep the grass leaves as dry as possible. The good news is that most of the time, damage from this problem is insignificant unless you have perennial ryegrass. Fungicides will knock it back if the problem persists.

Rusts

Rust-infected grass blades start with a small yellow-orange pinhead-size fleck on individual grass blades. These flecks enlarge and develop into brick red pustules. If you rub the pustule, the spores will easily come away on your finger. Severely infested rust grass starts to look reddish brown or yellow as it dies. Severe infestations can thin out the grass stand but rarely kill the lawn area. A severe rust infestation may weaken the lawn, making it more likely to be thinned out and killed by other stress or winter's cold. The development of rust is greater with night temperatures of 70° to 75°F, day temperatures of 85° to 95°F, and wetness from dew lasting many hours after sunrise. Homeowners who water lightly and frequently have more rust problems than those who water deeply and less often.

Although any grass plant can get rust (even zoysia), perennial ryegrass and bluegrasses are the most susceptible. Bluegrass varieties Merion and Touchdown are more susceptible than other varieties.

To stop rust from becoming a major problem, avoid low nitrogen conditions and leaf wetness. Plant resistant cultivars available from good garden centers. There are fungicides registered for rust, but most are not all that effective. Sulfur-based fungicides are your best bet in severe infestations. Minor infestations are not worth spraying; feed to help your grass outgrow the problem. Be prepared to topdress thinned out areas. Rust is easily controlled on the home lawn by maintaining good lawn growth with adequate fertilization and adequate watering.

St. Augustine Decline

A nonfungus problem, St. Augustine decline (SAD) is a **virus** that causes a yellowing and stippling on the grass leaves. As the disease progresses, the leaves turn mostly yellow. The grass becomes weak and the stands thin, enabling other weeds or grasses to invade. This is particularly true with grass growing in the shade. An important diagnostic tool is that infected grass is slower than healthy grass to recover in the spring. So, if your St. Augustine lawn is still brown when your neighbor's is greening up, get suspicious. The virus is widespread in Texas and has been reported in Louisiana and Arkansas. It can also infect centipede grass.

The decline can be slowed by the proper use of fertilizer, and an extra application of iron in the summer will help the grass maintain its green color. Do not confuse SAD with iron deficiency, however. Iron-deficient leaves are uniformly yellow, or their veins are still green, particularly on new and younger leaves. SAD, on the other hand, produces the mottling in both young and old leaves, and it is a mottling, not a consistent yellow color. Iron deficiency is also easily and quickly corrected with a single iron spray—SAD is not.

Because SAD is a virus, there is no use spraying anything on the lawn. Fungicides do not work on viral problems. Instead obtain some SAD-resistant cultivars of the grass and plug them into the lawn at 2- to 3-foot centers across the lawn. They will spread in the weakened lawn. Within a few years the problem will be eliminated as the strong grass crowds out the weaker.

WHERE DO THE FUNGI COME FROM?

Most fungi start from spores–tiny reproductive cells. Spores commonly are blown around by the force of wind. If they land where conditions are right, they start to thrive and reproduce.

KEEP OFF THE GRASS

Sclerotium Blight (or Southern Blight)

This fungus kills rather large patches of grass plants in circles up to 3 yards in diameter. The grass turns a reddish brown as it dies and the odd plant will survive within the dying fungal circle. In advanced cases, the mycelium mass is quite visible as a whitish growth on the lawn. Look for tiny mustard seed–size bits of fungus resting bodies (resting bodies are called sclerotia and function like seeds) at the base of grass stems.

Bent grass, bluegrass, fescues, and ryegrasses (along with many different nongrass plants) are susceptible to this problem. The disease is spread by the sclerotia and infected plant parts. As with many fungal problems, warm to hot weather, high moisture, and heavy thatch layers all contribute to this blight.

To control the problem with cultural methods, reduce the thatch and fertilize regularly. Fungicides are extremely useful at the first sign of the disease.

Slime Mold

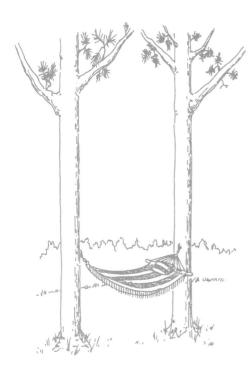

Slime mold is one of those opportunistic fungus problems that can hit any grass if the conditions are right. The mold looks like a white or grayish powdery covering that affects the grass leaves in a 6- to 12-inch circle. It normally develops during warm, wet, or humid weather, and the fungus will leave by its own accord during hot dry weather. You can remove these white fungus bodies by washing, mowing, or brushing the leaves. This does not require a fungicide treatment.

Spring Dead Spot

This fungus primarily attacks the well-managed Bermuda grass and zoysia grass lawn and is rarely seen on low-maintenance lawns. As the grass starts to green up in the spring, circular dead patches of 3 to 4 feet across appear. The problem usually appears in the same area year after year and the grass can take upward of two to three months to regrow into this area.

To control this problem, keep nitrogen levels at a moderate level throughout the growing season to keep the grass growing steadily. Annual dethatching is important to remove the overwintering site for the fungus. Potash applications seem to help, so a fall application of a fertilizer should focus on potash (potassium) and not nitrogen. This is one problem where fall fertilizing with nitrogen is not recommended. Control with a fungicide in the fall.

Stripe Smut and Flag Smut

This fungus problem is a cool weather disease that sometimes shows up when there is a long period of cool weather either in the early spring or fall. Temperatures of 50° to 60°F are favorable for its development. It disappears in the heat of the summer. Leaves of infected plants have long yellow-green streaks that turn gray and then black. When the streaks turn black, they break open to release fungus spores. Because of this rupturing, the leaves look tattered and split into ribbons. The tips of the leaves curl downward, and then the leaves turn brown and die. Infected plants can die, resulting in a thin patch of lawn. The fungus hits irregularly across the lawn so the lawn is uneven, generally thin, and in poor health.

Stripe smut attacks some varieties of bluegrass, as well as creeping bent grass. Damage is seldom severe with stripe smut, so control is not usually required. If the damage is severe, apply nitrogen and water deeply early in the day. Topdress to fill the lawn holes. Avoid watering late in the day or with light applications. If disease is severe, there are fungicides registered for this problem. Apply them either in early spring or in late fall.

Flag smut has almost exactly the same symptoms and controls. It attacks bluegrass as well and is best controlled by sowing resistant varieties.

Summer Patch

This fungus attacks the roots and crown of grass plants, especially during the high summer when the temperatures rise and drought is likely. So when it is hot and dry, look for spots about 6 to 12 inches in diameter. The grass in the spots starts turning light green and then it fades quite quickly to a straw brown color because the tips of the grass leaves are all bronzed and straw colored. The dead patches may have tufts of sickly grass or weeds may colonize those areas. Summer patch kills bluegrass and fine fescues.

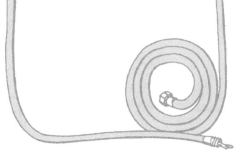

SAFETY CHECK

When choosing fungicides to treat your lawn or garden, be sure to choose one that presents the fewest health risks to you and your family. You also want a fungicide that will be friendly to the enviornment.

To prevent the lawn from losing patches to this problem, avoid high nitrogen feeding, overly wet soils, compaction, and the stress caused by low mowing. If the problem occurs, replant with a tall fescue or resistant cultivar of bluegrass.

Take-All Patch

This fungus attacks the roots of grass plants, rotting them and creating dark strands of mycelium (quite visible) on the roots. The dying grass creates circular or ring-shaped dead areas ranging from a few inches to 3 or more feet in diameter.

Bent grasses are the most susceptible to the problem, although fescues and ryegrass are also susceptible.

The fungus overwinters in grass debris. Conditions that encourage take-all patch include a sandy soil, low organic matter in the soil, low or unbalanced fertility, high pH, and high moisture conditions.

Reverse these conditions to reduce the problem; improve the soil and organic matter through the use of compost applications, improve drainage, lower the soil pH using sulfur if it is above 7.0. Replant with grass varieties that are resistant to this problem. Apply fungicides in the fall.

Take-All Root Rot

This fungus is responsible for Bermuda grass decline, yet take-all root rot is mostly a disease of St. Augustine grass. Centipede grass is also known to be affected. Generally, all cultivars of St. Augustine grass are susceptible, particularly if they are grown under stress.

The initial symptom is a patchy yellowing of the grass and as the roots decay, the turf thins out. As the fungus stops the plant from transporting water from the roots, the plant dies. If you dig up the plants, you'll find that the roots are rotted.

The susceptible times for this fungus are the summer and fall seasons when temperatures and moisture levels are both high. Poor management practices such as low mowing (scalping) or insect injury such as nematodes will stress the plant making it susceptible.

The solution to this problem is deceptively simple. Avoid stressing the plant by providing good cultural conditions. If a

problem strikes, mow St. Augustine grass at 4 inches in height to further reduce plant stress.

Typhula Blight (Gray Snow Mold) Typhula Species

Also known as snow scald and winter scald, this fungus attacks all cool season turfgrass varieties; creeping bent grass, annual bluegrass, and perennial ryegrass. (Note that the first two grasses mentioned are weed species in home lawns.) Kentucky bluegrass, red fescue, and tall fescues are less susceptible.

Visible in the spring immediately after snowmelt, Typhula blight appears as an overall blighting rather than as distinct dead patches. The turf appears to be bleached in irregular patches. These patches can range from a few inches in size upward as patches overlap to contain large areas.

The fungus is active over the winter. It takes snow cover of at least three months to create conditions for the survival of this fungus.

To control this fungus, minimize thatch. Prevent succulent growth in the late fall by stopping or reducing summer feeding. In other words, no nitrogen within six weeks of the last frost date in your area. Mow the grass right up until growth stops, so there are no long, succulent grass leaves for infection. In the spring, the infected areas can be raked and cleared of debris to encourage drying out, which reduces the fungus spread. Lightly fertilize the damaged areas to encourage new top growth and apply light topdressing to severely damaged areas. To be effective in stopping the overwinter life of the fungus, apply any fungicide before the first snowfall.

White Patch

This is an interesting disease of grass plants planted in recently wooded areas. The symptom is a circular white patch between 6 inches and 1 foot in diameter. Sometimes small tan colored mushrooms will ring the circles.

Fescues seem to be more susceptible to this than other grass plants, but usually enough plants survive to start filling in the lawn again.

Ensuring proper soil pH and nutrient levels (particularly phosphorus) will eliminate or reduce white patch on new lawns. The problem rarely requires fungicides.

RAISE THE MOWER DECK

You'll see this advice in other parts of the book, but it bears repeating here. Raise the mower deck as a first line of fungus prevention. For every eighth of an inch that you raise your deck, you increase the remaining working surface of the grass leaf by approximately 30 percent. Research at the University of Maryland showed that rhizome development increased just over 10 times when the mowing height was raised from 2¾ inches to 3½ inches.

There is also evidence that mowing high in the spring reduces the incidence of weeds later in the summer. For example, if the grass is mown higher, crabgrass is less likely to receive enough light to germinate.

Mowing at taller heights is the most effective form of weed control we have.

Yellow Patch

The early symptoms of this fungus are small patches (2 to 3 inches) of light green to a sick yellow-green grass color. These small areas turn a light brown and grow in size up to 2 feet across. A "frog's eye" pattern is common; this is where a circle of dead grass surrounds green growing turf. These patches may appear sunken because of the decomposition of the thatch layer. The leaves near the margin of the brown patch may have a reddish tinge, which starts at the tip and progresses down the leaf. There may also be some mid-brown darker spots on the leaves below the red discolorations.

The difficulty in identifying yellow patch is compounded by its overlap with necrotic ring spot. The key difference is that the roots and crowns of yellow patch–infected grass do not have the black fungus strands on them that characterize necrotic ring spot.

This fungus is a particular problem on Kentucky bluegrass lawns, although others can be infected. New sod lawns laid on clay soils are quite susceptible because of the constant moisture needed to establish the sod.

Control is the same as for necrotic ring spot (see page 152). Emphasize reducing the wet conditions for the lawn and aerate the lawn if it is on clay soils. There are no effective fungicide sprays for this problem.

Zonate Leaf Spot

This fungal problem tends to attack Bermuda grass and St. Augustine grass particularly during hot, humid temperatures when the thermometer climbs over 85°F. Two types of symptoms are displayed when grass starts to succumb to this problem. One is a large irregular area of chlorotic (yellowing) turf. The grass just starts turning yellow.

The second is **necrotic** (dying) rings of grass, full circles as well as half and quarter circles that enlarge quite rapidly. The fungus causes the individual grass leaves to be spotted and die.

Make sure the turf has a balanced fertilizer program, perhaps by using slow-release fertilizers instead of the more normal fertilizers. This avoids excessive applications of root-ready nitrogen that seems to promote the disease. Irrigate only to keep the plants alive—do not overwater. Apply the water early in the morning when dew is already present. Do not wet leaves more than necessary. To reduce the spread of the fungus, limit the movement of people and objects across the grass.

Pesticide and Spray Injury

Sometimes pesticides and herbicides can burn the lawn or cause chlorosis. This is particularly true when applied at higher doses than recommended on the label. The common symptom of this is a yellowing or chlorosis for a week or more and then a gradual recovery as the grass outgrows the problem. Remember that a check in growth caused by poor management can easily set the grass growth back by a month or more.

Another problem that sometimes happens on lawns after a nonselective herbicide such as glyphosate is used is that dead patches will appear across the lawn. If you've spot-sprayed weeds in gardens bordering the lawn or within the lawn itself, your boots will also be sprayed by the spray-drift. Walking across the lawn will leave spray "footprints" and the grass will die in those areas. You'll need to apply topdressing with seed and compost to restore the grass to its normal green state.

WHO REALLY GETS LAWN DISEASE?

By now, you've probably become somewhat dizzy with all the diseases listed here. As I said earlier, most home lawns will never see these diseases. The majority of them will only appear where turf is managed intensively like a golf course.

This means that golf courses are one of the single biggest users of fertilizers and chemical sprays on the continent. Golf greens are the most intensively managed turf areas on a golf course and are the highest users of chemicals.

This is why your golf glove should never be used to wipe your face and why you should never hold your tee in your mouth. Putting your ball against your face or other tender skin areas is not recommended.

After your game, thoroughly wash your hands before eating or drinking on the 19th hole.

COMMONLY USED FUNGICIDES ON LAWNS

Chemical Name	Name Sold Under	Controls	Mode of Action	Concerns
Benomyl	Benlate	Wide range of fungal diseases in turf. See label for list.	Systemic mode of action	• Very low toxicity data. Inconclusive mutagen data. • Very toxic to soil organisms, especially earthworms. • Persistent up to 22 weeks. • Does not leach in ground water.
Bordeaux	Bordeaux	Wide range of fungi.	Contact	• Mixture of hydrated lime and copper sulphate. • Nontoxic to bees. • Extremely corrosive—do not expose skin. • Not compatible with other fungicides—do not tank mix. • May injure plants if mixed too strongly.
Chlorothalonil	Bravo Daconil	Broad spectrum control.	• Organochlorine (same class as DDT) • Contact	• Slightly toxic to mammals. • Can cause eye irritation in low doses. • In high doses see a doctor immediately. • Carcinogenic. • Nontoxic to birds. Highly toxic to fish. • Persistent in soil (half-life is 1 to 3 months in organic soils) but does not leach.
Maneb	Maneb Dithane Manzate	Controls one of the widest range of fungi of any chemical.	Contact	• Moderately toxic to humans. Byproducts of decomposition are unstable, carcinogenic, and of concern to pregnant women. • Not toxic to birds but highly toxic to fish. • Persistent to 60 days in soil but does not leach into groundwater.

COMMONLY USED FUNGICIDES ON LAWNS *(continued)*

Chemical Name	Name Sold Under	Controls	Mode of Action	Concerns
Metalaxyl	Subdue Ridomil	Use on ornamentals, fungi, and powdery mildew.	Systemic	• Nontoxic to birds, freshwater fish, and bees. • Medium-acute toxicity.
Sulfur	Sulfur In many products	Broad spectrum.	Contact and protectant	• Low toxicity—little or no human effect. May cause some dermatitis in those with skin sensitivities. • Nontoxic to birds, aquatic life, and bees. • Natural substance— no environmental impact.
Triadimefon	Bayleton	Powdery mildews, rusts, and a wide range of fungi.	Systemic	• Moderately toxic. • Slightly toxic to aquatic life and birds. • Nontoxic to bees. • Breaks down in 18 days in sandy loam soils. • Carcinogenic tests inconclusive.
Ziram	Milban AAProtect	Wide range of fungi.	• Contact • Used mainly as a seed protector	• Toxic labeling—major irritant to eyes and skin. • Mutagenic and carcinogenic. • Toxic to soil bacteria.

Identifying Problems Other than Diseases

Is the problem caused by mowing your grass too short?

This is a major cause of problems and visible damage. The most used grass species—Kentucky bluegrass and the fine leaf fescues—should not be cut lower than 1 to 1½ inches. Short mowing reduces the leaf surface and creates a huge amount of stress on the plant. If the plant can't make new energy because you cut off too much leaf, it will have to take its food needs from the root reserves. This depletes the energy needed for health and winter survival.

How often do you cut the grass?

It is necessary to cut the grass regularly. Infrequent mowing leads to removing more than a third of the grass blade at a time, which sets back the grass by at least a month's growth. Again, the grass will draw on its root energy reserves to live. Excessive clippings left on the lawn tend to smother out the existing turf, leaving weakened grass behind after it has decomposed. If excessive clippings are left on the lawn and hot, humid conditions occur, it is an invitation for fungus to come, have lunch, and become established.

Are your lawn mower blades sharp?

If your turf looks a little peaked—dull gray or light brown—after mowing, it would be a good idea to pull the blades and sharpen them. This is mostly a "disease" of rotary mowers and lazy gardeners. When the grass tips are torn, split, and shredded by the dull blade, the grass tips die. The browning is caused by the deteriorating grass blades and is not a disease. However, all this shredded grass tissue is another invitation to the fungus family.

Do you scalp your lawn?

Most of the time, scalping occurs when you try to cut an uneven lawn and drop a wheel into a small hollow that is lower than the small hill the blades are cutting. The solution is pretty simple: level the lawn to avoid the dead spots. Also, when cutting steep hillsides, cutting crossways leads to more scalping than going up and down the hill. You'll find sections of grass across the hill that are doing poorly because of this scalping. It has absolutely nothing to do with a disease.

Do you washboard your lawn?

If you always cut your lawn in the same direction and on the same pattern, you may find that the grass compensates for this by giving you a ridged look. The solution is as simple as cutting the lawn in different directions and different patterns. This also partially controls the runners of creeping grasses and reduces thatch.

Have you applied fertilizers equally?

When you apply fertilizers, there are two potential problems. The first is that you overapply the fertilizer in an area because you spill it or simply put too much on. This will burn and kill the grass in these areas. The more common problem is that you apply the fertilizer unevenly. There are areas that don't get quite enough and are a paler green or slow growing, and there are other areas that get too much and grow like gangbusters. The lawn looks patchy and yellowing in some areas. This is not a disease other than one we might call homeowners' disease. Remember that fertilizer doesn't move sideways very much, so where you drop it is where it will do its work.

Is your lawn pale green?

In the vast majority of cases, a lawn that is pale green is suffering from a lack of nitrogen, not from disease. If nitrogen doesn't fix the problem, try applying an iron feed. If the iron feed doesn't solve the problem within a few hours, you do not have a feeding problem.

Did you just apply weed killer?

Let's face it, there are two problems here. The first is that some homeowners think that if the label says to put a certain amount of chemical onto 1,000 square feet of lawn, then putting on two times the recommended amount will work faster and better. This isn't so. Read and follow the label directions on all chemical products or you're inviting grass problems. The second error is more of a human kind. That is making a mistake in the

math or the measuring while mixing a chemical (is that 2 table-spoons or 2 teaspoons per gallon of water?) or in recognizing how many square feet have to be sprayed. How big is your lawn anyway? Needless to say, the cure for this disease is right on the label and on the tape measure.

How do you water your lawn?

If you apply more water than is necessary, you not only waste water; on some heavier (more clay) soil types, you'll actually compact the soil at the surface. This compaction slows subsequent water and fertilizer from reaching the roots and creates conditions where water runoff is more likely. Moss and algae thrive on overwatered lawns. Watering deeply when the plants are almost at the wilting point is the best watering method to ensure plant health.

Do you have localized dry or dead spots where the grass has trouble growing?

Sometimes construction debris is buried in a dead zone (often mushrooms grow from this discarded material), and the soil drainage is poor to nonexistent in these areas. The buried debris changes the drainage pattern and the soil itself so the grass roots have trouble in this area. If the same problem exists in the same area for several years, suspect a physical cause.

Sometimes excess thatch will build up in overfed areas, creating localized problems on the lawn.

When you walk across your lawn do you leave footprints?

This isn't a disease. It's an indication that the grass needs water. Apply water heavily to reduce wilting. This is particularly a good clue for bluegrass species. If you live in an area where late spring and early fall frosts freeze the grass blades, remember that walking on grass while it is frozen will damage the turf and may leave footprints behind. Avoid walking on turf while it is frozen at these times of year.

Does your lawn have dead patches in the spring?

This might not be a fungus problem—particularly if you can't see any mycelium. Think about your winter weather. Winterkill is most likely to happen in areas where snowfall is nonexistent and a few bright sunny days with high winds occur at the same time. This mostly happens in late spring. The ground will thaw out for a few inches and the winds will dry the soil out. The roots cannot replace the water—it's still frozen a few more inches down—and they dry out and die. Sometimes winterkill happens when the grass plants are under stress from a variety of summer lawncare practices. Without adequate food reserves in the roots, the plants simply die. In areas where late springs can melt the snow and then refreeze it into a layer of ice, grass can suffocate under the ice.

Think about your winter. Was there something that could have killed the grass?

Do you have a septic tank?

If you do, the grass over the tank is a candidate for browning during the summer, particularly during dry spells. The clue here is that the dead spot tends to take on the shape of the top of the tank. Big *square* patches of dead grass are not a disease, although I have had more than one gardener come to my garden center and try to tell me it is.

Have you compacted your soil?

Grass will often die in areas of high compaction. Heavy traffic (particularly when the ground is wet) squashes the soil structure and stops water, air, and nutrients from reaching the roots. Do not walk or play on grass when the ground is quite wet.

Do you have standing water on your lawn?

In winter, this may create winter scald: heat shines through the ice, warms the soil, and starts the plants growing. With no oxygen exchange possible through the ice, the turf is likely to be damaged. In the summer, water-ponding created during rainstorms creates conditions of oxygen deprivation, which causes the roots to die. The only real solution to this problem is to improve the drainage in these areas.

Do you have enough light to grow grass?

Grass loves full sunlight. As you reduce the light, you reduce your ability to grow good grass. The more shade on your lawn, the more problems you have with disease because the grass isn't strong enough to fight it off. If you have a very shady area, there comes a point when you have to admit that you can't grow grass and need to consider alternatives.

Do you have trees on your lawn area or close to your lawn area?

A mature deciduous tree (like a big maple) will use upward of 200 to 300 gallons of water every day during the summer. The roots of these big plants reach far beyond their drip line (the edge of the branches). In fact, the average root spread is twice the distance from the trunk to the drip line. If the distance from the trunk to the edge of the growing tree is 20 feet, then the roots go out another 20 feet. A tree in a neighbor's yard is likely to be feeding over in yours.

If you want to grow good grass in competition with trees, you have to water and feed both the trees and the grass. The trees are more competitive and will get their share first. Tree leaves (particularly maple) can smother out grass in the fall when they drop their leaves and the leaves mat up. It is a good idea to compost the leaves and return the compost to the grass and trees the following year. Alternatively, the leaves can be finely chopped and left to compost under the trees. Just don't leave thick mats of leaves and expect the grass to grow through them. That's how trees eliminate their competition.

Grass that is in shade or that is in competition with trees needs to be mowed higher than grass that is growing in sunny areas.

Did you use the right seed mix for your lawn, your management, and geography?

Kentucky bluegrass is probably the most famous grass, but it takes a higher management level to keep it looking good than a grass such as ryegrass. If you are a low-management lawn person, don't even consider Kentucky bluegrass. If you have shade, don't consider Kentucky bluegrass. Pick the seed that does best in your climate.

Did you spill the gas?

Often when you're filling the mower, there will be a small gas or oil overflow. Gas and oil cause severe damage to grass plants. There is not immediate damage. It takes some time for the plant to die, but grass will not grow in this area until the petroleum product disintegrates or is removed. Always fill power equipment away from turf areas.

Peat moss is an excellent material to use on petroleum spills. It supports bacteria that also use petroleum as a food source.

How did you keep your walkways clear of ice this past winter?

Salt damage is often found in areas that are either next to walkways or get the spring runoff from areas that have been salted to remove ice. A similar problem exists if high-nitrogen fertilizers are used in place of salt. Heavy applications of water will dissolve and remove the salt.

COMMON DISEASES AND THEIR SYMPTOMS

SIGN	SYMPTOM ON GRASS	SUSPECT
Distinct patch—2 to 3 inches in diameter	• Leaf lesions present. • Lesions are light tan or straw color.	Dollar spot
	• Start as 2- to 3-inch patches of dead grass, can grow to 2 to 3 feet. • Frog's eye pattern—green grass growing inside circle of dead grass.	Yellow patch Necrotic ring spot
Distinct patch larger than 2 to 3 inches	• No leaf lesions. • Circular or ring pattern where grass appears normal in center of ring, or ring of mushrooms.	Fairy ring
	• Distinct patches from 2 inches to 2 yards. • Small yellow lesions on leaves with black centers.	Anthracnose
	• Initial symptoms look like dollar spot. • Later symptoms look like melting out. • Oval lesions on leaves. • Pinkish mycelium for pink patch. • Reddish mycelium for red thread.	Red thread Pink patch
	• Patches up to 3 yards across. • Grass turns reddish brown as it dies. • Presence of sclerotia (mustard seed–size resting bodies).	Sclerotium blight
	• Six to 12-inch distinct circles. • Circles are light green and then brown tips on grass give brown appearance. • Grass dies.	Summer patch
	• Leaf spotting with purplish brown lesions. • Turf takes on a purplish tinge. • Grass dies in irregular patches.	Crown and root rot
	• No leaf lesions. • No ring pattern. • No mushrooms. • Grass blades matted together. • Fading to light tan brown.	Pythium blight

COMMON DISEASES AND THEIR SYMPTOMS *(continued)*

SIGN	SYMPTOM ON GRASS	SUSPECT
Distinct patch larger than 2 to 3 inches *(continued)*	• Grass blades on edge of dead circle can be pulled from stolon. • Outer edge of patch is yellowy brown.	Brown patch
	• Bermuda grass—outer edge of patch is yellow, chlorotic.	Take-all patch
	• Leaves not easily pulled from stolons.	Bermuda grass decline
	• Patches smaller than 3 feet, green grass in center. • Grass in ring is chlorotic, or straw colored.	Fusarium blight
	• Patches of dead grass immediately upon snowmelt. • Pinkish mycelium are visible immediately after snow melt.	Fusarium patch (pink snow mold)
	• Bermuda grass and zoysia grass brown patches appear in spring. • Grass does not recover.	Spring dead spot
	• Distinct dead patches with grass growing vigorously on edges.	Dog damage, appears immediately after snowmelt or during summer.
Distinct circular patches and/or streaks of dead grass	• Alternate patches of yellow and dark green grass.	Poor fertilizer distribution
	• Grass stems and crown exposed. • Browning and ground visible.	Poor mowing
	• Irregular shapes, from inches to yards. • Grass appears wilted or melted. • Individual leaves start with purplish spots enlarging to kill crown.	Melting out
	• Similar to melting out, only leaf spots are tan to red spots with purplish borders. • Spots are always longer than wide.	Leaf spot
	• Tips of leaves burned.	Minor fertilizer burn
	• Leaves rolled up. • Brown grass in spots or streaks.	Gas, oil, or fertilizer spill
No distinct patches—variable amounts of chlorosis	• Rusty spots or bumps on leaves.	Rust

COMMON DISEASES AND THEIR SYMPTOMS *(continued)*

SIGN	SYMPTOM ON GRASS	SUSPECT
No distinct patches—variable amounts of chlorois *(continued)*	• Mottled green coloring on St. Augustine grass or centipede grass.	St. Augustine decline
	• Oval spots with tan or gray centers. • Spots surrounded by chlorotic yellow. • Spots easily seen.	Gray leaf spot
	• White or light gray spotting on leaves. • Under the gray cover, leaf turning brown.	Powdery mildew
	• The spots are not distinct and easily seen. • Grass is chlorotic.	Curvularia, Nigrospora, Centipede grass decline
	• Large areas of chlorotic turf on Bermuda grass and zoysia grass. • Full, half, or quarter rings of dying grass. • Individual grass leaves spotted.	Zonate leaf spot
	• Irregular shapes—dead grass immediately after snowmelt. • Grass chlorotic.	Typhula blight
	• Seedstalks abundant. • Growth is slow. • Root normal. • No pattern to problem.	Nitrogen or iron deficiency
Spots not distinct and the grass is not chlorotic	• Leaf tips frayed. • Grass not wilting. • Brown after mowing.	Dull mower blades
	• Grass wilting in spots not overall.	Water stress
	• Leaves rolled.	Compaction
	• Soil is wet. • Leaves are rolled and wilting.	Poor drainage
	• Leaf blades turn yellow and brown right after fertilizer application or pesticide spray.	Fertilizer burn Pesticide burn
	• Thin turf. • Grass grows very rapidly, wilts quickly.	Too much nitrogen

*Duble, Richard L. Turfgrass Specialist, Identification and Control of Turfgrass Disease, Texas Agricultural Extension Service
http://aggie-horticulture.tamu.edu/plantanswers/turf/publications/disease1.html

CHAPTER SEVEN

Lawn Pests and Cures

Lawn pests driving you buggy? Before you run out and buy a can of pesticide, there are two very important things you need to understand about insects and lawn pests.

- Pests in lawns are a symptom of an underlying problem. The pest is not the main problem; the reason the pest is able to thrive is the problem.
- The existence of small numbers of insects is not a problem.

Let's look at these points in a little more detail. In my experience in gardening and lawn care, insect pests arrive when there is an imbalance in the growing conditions that weaken the plants. For example, if a lawn is fed too much nitrogen, the grass grows very green and lush. This very lushness is a signal to some insects: "Lunch time!" The sugar content of the plant changes in response to the extra nitrogen and makes the plant that much more delicious to eat.

Some researchers believe that plants give off hormones and electronic vibrations that either attract or repel insects. When the plant is weakened, it sends a different signal than when it is growing strongly. Insects are able to interpret these changes and attack the weakened plants. How often have you seen a plant growing in your garden and blamed the insects for making it grow poorly? In reality, it was likely growing poorly and the insects were attracted to it. It is the same for the lawn. The lawn is simply a lot of individual grass plants growing together, and when they get sick, they send out different signals and the bugs come running.

To have a healthy pest-free lawn, you have to solve the underlying problems that are stopping the grass plants from achieving optimum health. Fix them and the pest population will decrease accordingly. Constant spraying with garden chemicals does not fix the underlying cause; it only puts a temporary bandage on the problem. Also, as we'll see, garden chemicals can create more problems than they cure.

Should a homeowner become upset when insects are roaming freely over the lawn? Not necessarily. As we all understand, there is a balance in nature, and the vast majority of insects are harmless to grass plants. In fact, many of the insects out on the lawn are just waiting to pounce on and eat the odd insect that likes to eat grass. We call these good guys *beneficial predators* or simply **beneficials**. The term used in the turf industry to determine whether pests are causing problems is **threshold**. For example, what is the threshold number of grubs on a lawn before spraying is necessary?

Please understand that to have the beneficials out there eating and protecting your lawn, you have to have something for them to eat. You have to create a balance in which the good guys can keep the bad guys in check (and the subsequent damage to your lawn minimal). If you spray a lawn to kill the odd bad bug, you'll be killing the beneficials as well. It is an unfortunate fact that the grass-eating pests can usually reproduce faster than the beneficials. When you kill off the beneficials, the first population to regrow to its former level is the pests. And there are no beneficials around to stop them from munching on your grass plants.

I once encountered a homeowner who wanted my advice. He stated quite clearly that he didn't want insects of any kind in his backyard and asked what spray he could use to kill everything. He and his wife didn't want worms, ladybugs, ants, beetles, or flies—nothing. They wanted to get rid of them all so they could sit out without being bothered by the wildlife. Hmmmm. My first suggestion was pavement, but he demurred. With my tongue firmly in my cheek, I suggested that he explode a personal nuclear device and that he could likely get one at his nearest discount store. Gardening is about creating balances with nature, and lawns are simply one thing that we homeowners do outside where we have to find that balance.

In human medicine, doctors refer to a **disease cycle**. This means that there are five separate things that have to occur in a progressive order that leads to disease. In both diagnosis and treatment, you have to start at the bottom of the cycle and work toward the top, you just can't start at the top. Turfgrass management has exactly the same cycle when a pest becomes a problem for our lawn. This is the *lawn pest cycle*.

What Is a Pest?

A **pest** is an organism that creates a problem for a lawn. Weeds, insects, nematodes, bacteria, fungi, and viruses that interfere with the normal growth of grass are considered pests. Some insects, nematodes, bacteria, and fungi are beneficial. They do not interfere with the normal growth of grass and are not considered pests. Proper identification is necessary to determine the pest status of any problem.

KEEP OFF THE GRASS

The Five Stages of the Disease Cycle

1. *Inoculation*: The weed seed, pathogen, or insect egg has to come into the lawn area. Scientists call anything that carries a pest problem a **vector**. It could be the wind, a bird carrying weed seeds in its crop, or adult insects arriving from the neighbor's yard. The wind could be a vector if it shares dandelion seed from yard to yard or blows small, weak-flying insects from yard to yard.

2. *Prepenetration*: Where specific conditions exist that are beneficial for the pest to become established, the pest has to start to grow before it can influence the grass plants. For example, some bacteria can start to grow in the soil that will attack the grass plant. If conditions exist to allow the bacteria to grow, they will survive and prosper. However, if conditions are not good—if there is competition for the food source or soil chemicals (compost provides both of these things) that kill the bacteria are present—the bacteria will not survive. Insect pests need a place to grow and develop. For example, if the soil population of beneficial nematodes is low because of chemical sprays, then flea beetles will be able to lay eggs.

3. *Penetration*: This is the stage when the pests physically attack the grass plants. The bacteria gain entrance through a wound like a ragged mowing cut (from dull blades) or the insect pests start to have lunch.

4. *Infection*: This stage is immediately after penetration when the pest population starts to feed off the individual plants or successfully compete with them for nutrients.

   Some infections are immediate and the effects will show for all to see, while others are latent. Latent infections exist in the lawn but are partially suppressed by the lawn's natural defenses. It takes a bit of stress on the grass plants (such as drought or overfeeding) for the infection to explode fully and make its presence felt to the homeowner. For example, if Diazinon is sprayed to eliminate lawn grubs, it will kill off most of the spider

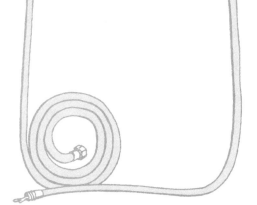

THINK AHEAD

Prepenetration work is the preventive work in the garden that hinders pests. It is here that average gardeners can stop the majority of problems they are ever likely to see. In simple terms, keep the grass healthy and the pests can't become established.

CHEMICAL TOXICITY

You'll often see the term LD50 in technical literature about gardening chemicals. This stands for Lethal Dose 50 percent. In short, it is the amount of a chemical it takes to kill 50 percent of the test population of animals. These tests are most often done on rats. Although the chemical is measured based on the ratio of the chemical to the weight of the rat, the bottom line is still when half the rats are dead, that's the LD50.

"LD" is a good relative measurement in that we can see how one chemical stacks up against another. We know that there are ranges above which garden chemicals are relatively safe and below which they are considered quite dangerous to use.

Toxicity of Chemicals

Toxicity Level	Range	Example
High toxicity—dangerous	Oral: less than 50	CleanCrop PMA LD50 = 22
	Fatal at 1 drop to ½ teaspoon	Diazinon LD50 = 108
	Dermal (skin): less than 200	Dursban LD50 = 135
Medium toxicity—medium	Oral 50 to 500	Sevin LD50 = 400–850
	Fatal at ½ teaspoon to 2 tablespoons	Banner LD50 = 1310
	Dermal (skin): 200–2,000	
Low toxicity—low	Oral: greater than 500	Insecticidal soap LD50 = greater than 10,000
	Not fatal unless over 1 ounce ingested and then variable	Roundup LD50 = 4320
	Dermal (skin): greater than 2,000	

So, while there are potential problems using any garden chemical, the LD50 rating is a good general guideline to immediate dangers. Most home gardening product labels do not list the LD50 rating. However, they do categorize themselves in the following manner:

- If the LD50 rating is high toxicity, the label will say, "Danger—Poison."
- If the LD50 is medium toxicity, the label will say, "Warning."
- If the LD50 is of low toxicity, the label will say, "Caution."

mites and their predators as well. Spider mites rebound much quicker than their predators, so experienced lawnowners check for an explosion of spider mites after they have sprayed Diazinon for grub control.

5. *Propagation*: Once the pest has established itself and started to feed, the next step is to reproduce, find a vector to take it on a journey, and replicate its success in some other yard or area of your yard.

The important point about lawn or grass plant health is that the homeowner can stop or attack plant pests at any one of these five stages. Remember pests are insects, diseases, or anything that negatively influences grass. Once you know the pest, you can figure out the easiest way to control it for the long term.

Monitoring Techniques

Before you go out to spray and control any insect, there are two things you have to do. First, you need to identify the insect pest correctly. Second, you need to make sure that it is damaging the lawn and that natural predators cannot handle the problem.

Correctly identifying the pest is extremely important: it will determine exactly what control steps to take. If you spray for insects when it is really a fungus decimating your lawn, you'll be spraying chemicals that unnecessarily degrade the environment, don't have any positive effect, and cost you money. Not only that, but the fungus will continue to grow and wreak its havoc on your lawn.

You'll find that wandering around the lawn once a month is usually sufficient to catch most problems before they reach the critical stage. This is not onerous duty. Wandering around with a cool drink in one hand, a hand-magnifying lens in a pocket, and full license to lie about on the lawn looking for problems is just good lawn management.

It is tough to figure out how to control insects in turf. One day you can't see a problem or a pest, and the next, you've got dead turf patches scattered around your lawn. The obvious goal is to find and identify pests *before* they become a problem. Here are

FIRST THINGS FIRST

Most problems on the lawn are the result of cultural decisions, not insects. Correct the underlying problem and the insects will become less of a problem.

KEEP OFF THE GRASS

several techniques that will work to help you identify potential garden pest problems.

The Famous Coffee Can Technique

This trick works best with chinch bugs (see page 209) because they live on the grass blades and not under the soil. When you fill the can with water, they just float to the surface. And no, they can't swim very well.

1. Take an old coffee can (8 to 9 inches long) and remove both the top and bottom, leaving a pipe length of metal.
2. Insert the can into the soil so the bottom of the can penetrates approximately 2 inches.
3. Fill the can with water.
4. Wait 10 to 15 minutes. (You may have to continue filling the can with water if it all leaks out because you want to keep the can filled.)
5. After 15 minutes, count the number of chinch bugs floating on the water. If 20 or more chinch bugs are present, you need to apply a control. If there are fewer than 20 pests, no control is needed.

The Soap Solution Technique

To find sod webworms and cutworms, use this trick. The webworms don't like the soap solution and come to the upper surface to avoid it.

1. Make up a soap solution using 2 tablespoons of liquid dishwashing soap to 2 gallons of water.
2. Pour this solution over an area approximately 1 square yard (3 feet by 3 feet).
3. Within five minutes, all webworms will come to the surface of the grass. If there are more than six caterpillars per square foot, then control is necessary.

> **BE A DETECTIVE**
>
> If you're really interested in examining your lawn insects (and this makes a great science project if you have school-age children) purchase a simple 10X or 20X hand magnification lens. This inexpensive tool will go a long way in helping you positively identify the problems (or nonproblems) crawling around on your turf.

The Cup Changer Trick

To do this one, you need a cup changer. This is a small tool that golf courses use to cut a cup hole (the hole that everybody swears at when the ball doesn't go in) in the green so they can move the cup around. A local golf course will probably get one for you if you ask the pro. You can substitute anything that will cut a 4-inch hole and remove the plug of soil; a small shovel or hand trowel works equally well.

Grubs are only in the top few inches of soil during the summer months, so if you dig 6 inches deep, you'll find every grub in that area.

1. Dig a 4-inch core (4 inches around and 4 to 6 inches deep).
2. Count the number of grubs you find in the soil core.
3. Multiply this number by 10.5 to give you the number of grubs per square foot.
4. Repeat this several times per 1,000 square feet of lawn and average the results.

June beetles have a threshold of five per square foot. In other words, if you count less than five, don't spray. European chafers have a threshold of five to 10 on nonirrigated lawns and slightly higher (10 to 20) if the lawn is irrigated. Japanese beetles have a threshold of five.

An Important Pest Control Point

Before we go charging off to investigate specific insect pests and their controls, let's look at the products we use to control them and how these products work. This is important to understand because the safe use of insect control is vital to your family's health and the health of your environment.

We use two methods of controlling insect pests on the lawn. The first method is biological controls that will naturally control or kill pests and the second is foliar or drenching sprays that kill pests.

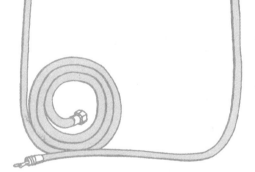

LAWN LINGO

foliar spray: A spray that is applied to the leaves or foliage of a plant.

drench spray: A spray that is applied to soak into or drench the soil underneath the plant.

A SHORT SAFETY STORY

Let me tell you a short story. As a commercial nurseryman and greenhouse operator, I have passed examinations and am registered to use agricultural chemicals safely. I have a full spray suit with a forced-air helmet to protect me from any chemical I use.

In my greenhouses, I use a lot of insecticidal soap to control pests. Insecticidal soap is effective, clean, and easy to use. It doesn't create worries about cleaning up or residual action when my children and I are working in the greenhouse. Now, one day I was in a hurry and decided to do a bit of spraying without going to the trouble of putting on the full spray suit. Heck, it was only safe, organic, insecticidal soap.

I did a quick spraying without my mask using the air-blast sprayer. For a full week afterward, I felt as if I were breathing underwater; my lungs were congested and I hacked and coughed my way around the farm. The insecticidal soap had done its thing on my lungs.

The moral of this story is that even the safest chemical can have an effect on the human body. In the case of the soap, there was no long-term effect and I'm quite thankful it was such an easy lesson for me to learn. Other chemicals (organic or not) are not as forgiving and can have much more serious consequences.

I had never before gone without wearing my face mask when spraying anything on the farm and I have never forgotten to take the time since. Indoors or out, if I spray, I wear a mask and appropriate clothing.

Biological Controls

Biological controls are in a very active development stage right now. There is a tremendous level of ongoing research to identify natural controls and to set up systems to use them to our advantage. I mention this because by the time this book comes out, the situation will have changed from the time it was written—things are moving that fast in the lawn and garden industry.

The basic thinking behind the use of biological controls on lawns is to encourage natural populations or augment the level of insect predators on the lawn area. For example, if we add extra beneficial nematodes to the lawn, they'll eat up the grubs and eggs of some two hundred different lawn pests. Once the lawn pests have been destroyed and eaten, there will be no food source and the beneficial nematode population will crash back to normal levels. (They aren't fast and mobile, so if food isn't really close—a few inches—they'll starve.)

Researchers are also discovering new bacteria and fungi that attack and kill insect pests. One of the most widely known is *Bacillus thuringiensis*, and it has been used to control a variety of caterpillar species. There are even subspecies of *Bacillus thuringiensis*—for example, *B. thuringiensis*, subspecies *bubui* (who makes up these names?)—that control other noncaterpillar species. *Bacillus thuringiensis bubui* controls scarab beetles.

Natural controls are also being developed from plant products. One of the best known of these is azadiractin, a product derived from the neem tree. This product is extremely toxic to a wide range of insect pests.

Other natural controls are discussed later in this chapter.

Foliar or Drenching Sprays: Insecticides

An insecticide is any product that kills an insect. It can be a safe insecticide such as soap or one that is much more deadly such as Cygon (dimethoate). There are several things you should know about any insecticide before using it because the effectiveness of that chemical depends on how it is used and stored. There is little sense using any chemical (organic or otherwise) improperly. It

A Spoonful of Sugar

The U.S. Department of Agriculture (USDA) research folks have released some findings that suggest that sugar esters are quite potent insecticides. Now, for any insect that has a sweet tooth, it will also have a sweet death. Nature controls her own if we let her.

KEEP OFF THE GRASS

is only a waste of time, the chemical, and its costs, as well as the fact that you still haven't solved the problem.

Insecticides are made in different ways to have different effects. This is important to understand when trying to decide which product you want to use. For example, you wouldn't want to use a low-solubility material if you want the insecticide to penetrate the soil. Without the ability to be soluble in water, the product will not get down into the soil to do the job. Here are three things to consider when choosing and using pest control chemicals: persistence, solubility, and resistance.

Persistence is the ability of a chemical to stay in the soil and continue its work. Organochlorine insecticides have tremendous persistence, remaining in the soil from year to year. This is why they are now banned from use. We simply don't want products like DDT to become part of our food chain. Insecticidal soaps, on the other hand, have almost zero persistence; they either hit the pest directly or they are degraded into their constituent fatty acids.

Solubility is the ease with which a product dissolves in water. Most chemicals are treated with additives to be more soluble. Powders are not as soluble as liquids and require extra steps to make sure they completely dissolve. (An old kitchen blender is great for properly dissolving powders in water, although once used for garden chemicals it must never be allowed back into the kitchen.) It is clear that highly soluble chemicals penetrate lawn thatch layers better than insoluble chemicals. This is why you'll see the recommendation to water the lawn thoroughly before and after applying a chemical. Watering before spraying moistens the soil and helps keep the spray soluble. Watering after spraying drives the spray down into the soil to hit the target population.

Resistance to a chemical means that the pest is no longer killed or deterred by that chemical. The chemical is ineffective. This happens to both insect and weed pests, especially if the chemical is used to the exclusion of all others. If one chemical, such as Diazinon, is used, the first time it is applied, it will kill almost all the pests on the lawn. Those that survive will be genetically immune to this chemical control. Some of their offspring will also be immune because they will pass along this genetic inheritance.

THE BUGS THAT GET AWAY

I understand that there is no chemical currently in use in agriculture that does not have a target population already resistant to it. It doesn't matter whether it is a common insecticide such as Diazinon or a herbicide such as glyphosate (Roundup), there is an insect or weed that will not be killed by the product.

I have to confess that we had a big problem for a while in our greenhouse. By using insecticidal soap too often in the propagation greenhouse and not freezing the greenhouse out in the winter to kill residual populations, we created a population of aphids that were resistant to insecticidal soap. We had a bunch of very clean aphids. I had to substitute other products for a while, freeze out the greenhouse, and re-establish a spray rotation to bring this pest back under control. Creating a resistant population is more easily done than most people realize.

(Remember Gregor Mendel and his peas? Theoretically, you can expect at least 25 percent of the offspring to be resistant to the Diazinon.) Now, if you spray again and you kill off a bunch of pests, you can't kill them all. All you're doing is killing the ones that are not resistant to Diazinon. After a few such sprays, the only pests left alive are the ones that have Diazinon resistance built into their genetic makeup. Your spray no longer works.

This resistance is built up quickly in insects, fungi, and bacterial diseases but more slowly in weeds. This is why using several different chemicals in rotation is a recommended practice in controlling lawn pests. It is also why biological practices are becoming more and more common as lawnowners use nature to keep pests and weeds within acceptable limits. We now see resistance to all control agents, including organic sprays, if a single chemical is used in exclusion.

Pests That Hurt Grass: Chemical and Organic Controls

As you're reading the following insect table, please remember that you may never see any of these insects nor should you imagine that every one of them will automatically infest your lawn. They are included so you know what to do *if and when* they become a problem for you.

Also it is useful to note that the insects are grouped according to family and that the controls for each family are generally the same regardless of slight differences in the insects' biological names. Any major differences, for example, Japanese beetle, will be outlined under the specific pest. This means when you use a control for one kind of grub, you are likely controlling for all grubs. Similarly a control for cutworms will get all the cutworms. Isn't it nice that some things are simple?

It is very difficult if not impossible—given the differing legislation from state to state and between Canada and the United States—to recommend a pest control product that is available and legal in all states and provinces. What we have done is recommend certain kinds of controls for each pest and then provide descriptions of the

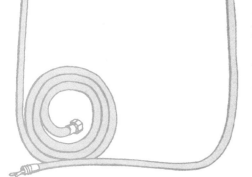

SAFE STORAGE

The safe storage of pesticides is an important gardening technique. For example, never store liquid pesticides where they can freeze. Freezing will degrade the ability of the product to do its job. Also, do not store pesticides in direct sunlight. Plastic containers degrade in sunlight and may fall apart, allowing a dangerous spill. Follow all label directions for proper storage.

most commonly used chemicals at the end of the chapter. In this way, you'll be able to see exactly what products are available at garden centers in your area and make reasonable, informed choices.

Grubs

Black Turfgrass Ataenius *(Ataenius spretulus)*

This is a beetle and like all beetles the main problem is with the **larvae** that eat grass roots. Larvae simply cut off the roots to eat them and if there is enough damage, the grass will wither and die in irregularly shaped patches. You'll know there are grubs down there because the grass can easily be pulled loose from the soil. Less severe infestations will cause a yellowing of the grass (due to stress on the plant) during the heat of summer. The yellow or dead patches will continue to increase in size until the larvae stop feeding and **molt** into the **pupal** stage.

You'll have to use a golf course cup changer to identify this pest. Threshold limits are difficult to establish, but if there are more than 10 per square foot, there is likely to be visible damage. Control is indicated when the grub population goes slightly over this figure.

Adults are active by late May and fly into grass areas to lay their eggs. This is about the time annual crabgrass starts to set seed. Lush, overly moist lawns seem to be the biggest targets. Larvae hatch quite quickly and feed continually right through until the end of July when they pupate. Adults hatch fairly quickly and lay a second generation of eggs in areas where the temperatures do not decrease in the fall (just about the time when the Rose of Sharon plants begin to bloom). In colder areas, the adults will start looking for winter hiding places, usually under debris, rather than lay a second generation of eggs.

Identification: Adult beetles are very small ($^3/_{16}$ inch), very black, and shiny. The wing covers are not smooth but have shallow grooves parallel to the length of the body. The hind legs have several rows of small spines. These adults overwinter on garden debris or under the leaf litter from trees.

Larvae are typical white grub, but they are small when compared to normal white grubs ($^3/_{16}$ inch at the largest). They are normally C-shaped with a brown head capsule and three pairs of legs.

HOW DOES GRASS RESPOND TO BEING EATEN

I don't imagine that any of us would appreciate being the main course at lunch. Quite frankly, grass is no happier about it than we are. Plants as a whole have four different adaptive responses to pests.

1. They manufacture toxins that affect the biology of the pest; in effect, they poison the pest that is trying to eat them.
2. They make themselves less attractive by changing their smell, taste, or nutritional value, thus encouraging the pest to eat elsewhere.
3. They develop a tolerance to pest damage. In other words, they develop a way to continue growing and propagating in spite of being eaten.
4. They change their physical properties such as developing a thicker cuticle of both stems and leaves to make it more difficult for a pest to influence them.

PESTS THAT HURT TURF

COMMON NAME	SPECIES NAME
White Grubs	
Black turfgrass ataenius	*Ataenius spretulus*
Asiatic garden beetle	*Maladera castanea*
European chafer	*Rhizotrogus majalis*
Green June beetle	*Cotinus nitida*
Japanese beetle	*Popillia japonica*
Northern masked chafer	*Cyclocephala borealis*
Southern masked chafer	*Cyclocephala lurida*
Oriental beetle	*Anomala orientalis*
June beetles	*Phyllophaga sp.*
Chewing Insects	
Annual bluegrass weevil	*Hyperodes maculicollis*
Bluegrass billbug	*Sphenophorus parvulus*
Hunting billbug	*Sphenophorus veratus vestitus*
Webworms	
Sod webworm	*Crambus teterrellus and species*
Bluegrass sod webworm	*Parapediasia teterrella*
Tropical sod webworm	*Herpetogramma phaeopteralis*
Cutworms	
Black cutworm	*Agrostis ipsilon*
Bronzed cutworm	*Nepholodes minians*
Variegated cutworm	*Peridroma saucia*
Armyworms	
Common armyworm	*Pseudaletia unipuncta*
Fall armyworm	*Spodoptera frugiperda*

PESTS THAT HURT TURF (*continued*)

COMMON NAME	SPECIES NAME
Mole Crickets	
Mole cricket	*Gryllotalpa hexadactyla*
Short-winged mole cricket	*Scapteriscus abbreviatus*
Southern mole cricket	*Scapteriscus borellii*
Tawny mole cricket	*Scapteriscus vicinus*
Aphids	
Greenbug aphid	*Schizaphis graminum*
Chinch Bugs	
Chinch bug	*Blissus leucopterus leucopterus*
Hairy chinch bug	*Blissus leucopterus hirtus*
Southern chinch bug	*Blissus insularis*
Mites	
Bermuda grass mite	*Eriophyes cynodoniensis*
Clover mite	*Bryobia praetiosa*
Banks grass mite	*Oligonychus pratensis*
Winter grain mite	*Penthaleus major*
Scale	
Bermuda grass scale	*Odonaspis ruthae*
Turfgrass scale	*Lecanopsis formicarum*
Other	
Ground pearls	*Margarodes meridionalis*

Control Measures: The easiest time to control this pest is at the larval stage. Biological controls such as predator nematodes are extremely effective in controlling white grubs. There are other products that must be watered in to ensure they penetrate the soil. See the table on current control agents later in this chapter.

Asiatic Garden Beetle *(Maladera castanea)*

The larva of this pest is a typical C-shaped white grub with brown head capsule, and it does the typical amount of damage expected by any ¾-inch-long grub. It eats grass roots. Lawnowners will also notice typical symptoms of wilting, even though the grass is not under water stress; then, irregular brown patches will show up in late summer where the grass has died from lack of roots. Asiatic beetles are not particular about which grass species they eat—they eat them all. They are most often found in sunny locations near flowering shrubs and particularly around areas where night-lights are left on. The adults are attracted by these lights and lay eggs in these areas.

Identification: The larvae is typical but the adult is a light brown beetle (a chestnut to medium brown) with slightly iridescent wing covers. The adult beetle is approximately ½ inch long.

Control Measures: Use regular controls for grubs during early to midsummer. Threshold is five grubs per square foot.

European Chafer *(Rhizotrogus majalis)*

The larvae of this pest are not particular when it comes to food. Give them grass roots, or the roots of any corn, potato, bean, or other legume, and they'll be delighted. Luckily the adults don't do a lot of feeding and cannot be blamed for any serious plant damage. They do congregate on trees at night and beginning gardeners will assume they're consuming the tree—after all, there are a lot of them in one small space. The reality is that they're congregating, not munching, so relax about congregating beetles unless you see a lot of damage. If you see a lot of damage, then you know you don't have European chafers, you have another beetle.

Most of the time, there is one generation of chafers every year. In late June and early July, the beetles emerge from the lawn and

LIFE CYCLES OF INSECT PESTS

All insects start life as an egg. Then they undergo **metamorphosis**, or a series of changes that lead to the adult stage. Once the egg hatches, the insect takes one of two methods to turn into an adult. Control methods will depend on which method the insect takes and are described under specific insects. The importance of this fact is that you can recognize that there is more than one way to control most insect pests: You can get them as adults or you can get them as larvae.

- If the egg hatches into a nymph (a smaller but similar shape to the adult form), then it goes through several development stages to reach the adult shape and form. At each of these stages, however, the nymph generally resembles the adult. *This gradual or incomplete metamorphosis* is found in insects that eat the same food throughout their life and stay in that same environment. To control these pests, we have to apply a control where they live.

- If the egg hatches into a larva (most common) that has to form a hard-shelled pupa before it can develop into an adult, we call it *complete metamorphosis*. The larva stage eats different food than the adult stage and lives in a different environment. This means we can control this pest by using alternative methods depending on the current life stage of the pest. Larval control will be different than adult control.

fly to trees where they congregate. Just for the record, this congregating has more to do with mating than it does anything else. (Now, you know why they aren't eating!) The beetles fly around just at dusk and the fertilized females lay between 25 and 50 eggs a season in the lawn. The larvae hatch out two to three weeks later in late July and mature within seven to eight weeks (September). These larvae feed on the grass roots and crown until late fall when the mature grubs move down 6 to 12 inches below the frost line to overwinter. In the spring, the warming soil brings the grubs to the surface where they begin feeding on roots for the next four to six weeks. The grubs begin to pupate by early May and hatch out as adults in late June to early July again. A very small percentage of this insect population may remain as grubs for a second season, overwintering again to emerge as adults after two years.

Identification: Adults are very similar to June beetles except that they are slightly smaller and most are tan. A distinguishing feature is that the chafer does not have the hook or tooth on the end of the feet that the June beetle possesses. (It's that hook that enables the June beetles to cling to things.) Larvae are very similar to June beetle larvae as well. The have the same C-shape, the same brown head capsule—in fact there are only two distinct differences—and the anal slit is Y-shaped. The June Beetle is Y-shaped too, but the base of the Y is as long as the arms of the Y on the chafer's anal slit; on the June beetle, the Y base is much shorter than the Y arms. Not that you need to know this because a white grub is a white grub is a white grub when it comes to grub control methods. I mention it because you never know when that kind of information will be useful—just think how impressive it would sound at your next cocktail party.

Control Measures: They are the same for June beetles and Black turfgrass ataenius.

Green June Beetle *(Cotinus nitida)*

The bad news is that this is one of the largest grubs. The good news is that it usually doesn't eat grass roots, preferring instead the decaying organic matter in the soil. The adults are the problem; their burrowing activity can create minor damage. You'll normally

find them near compost piles or under trees—anywhere there are high levels of organic matter. Adult activity can be spotted by the very small piles of soil around the entrances to their tunnels.

Identification: The grubs are larger than June beetles but the identification is primarily of the adults. The adult beetle is approximately an inch in length with a rich, velvety green topside and a shiny, metallic green bottom side coloring. They fly during the day and usually feed on overripe fruit.

Control Measures: They are the same as for other beetles. As the grubs are not a problem, control is not recommended unless the adult population is seriously disfiguring the lawn surface. If you control other grubs, you'll knock back this population as well.

Japanese Beetle *(Popillia japonica)*

Adult Japanese beetles differ from other beetles in that they are voracious eaters of most things leafy and green. They love fruits and vegetables as well as foliage plants such as grass. The larvae are not any more discriminating, eating the tender feeder roots of many plant families. If you have Japanese beetle damage, expect to see the typical yellowing patchy lawn in August and September followed by dead turf shortly afterward.

This is an introduced pest in North America and is not a major pest in its native Japan, where predators restrict its population. Much of the northeastern United States and Canada is a target for this pest because of climate similarities. The adult beetles usually emerge just as the heat of the summer starts, normally the first two weeks of July in our zone 4 gardens. The adults live for 30 to 45 days and feed voraciously while the females lay between 40 and 60 eggs in the soil. The larvae hatch after two weeks and begin feeding. In the fall when the soil temperatures begin to drop, the larvae move deeper into the soil to avoid the frost. The following spring, they return to the surface where they start feeding again. Pupation is in June for this second-year grub. The adults hatch out in early July to start the cycle once again.

Identification: This is a beautiful and physically distinctive beetle. The thorax (main body) is a bright, metallic green while the wing covers are a coppery color. There are also six tufts of white hairs

KNOW YOUR ENEMY— OR LACK THEREOF

In an interesting research project at Cornell University, three hundred lawns were monitored in upstate New York for lawn grubs. This research found that even in a bad year for grubs, only 18 percent of the surveyed lawns actually passed the threshold for lawn grubs and required treatment. The vast majority (82 percent) did not require treatment at all. Any treatment would have been a waste of time and money.

This is why threshold testing is so important. Know what you're trying to kill before you actually go out and waste your time and money on sprays.

along both sides of the abdomen. This is a small beetle—just over a half inch long. The grubs, on the other hand, get to about an inch long with the same characteristics of other white grubs: a brown head capsule, C-shaped, three pairs of legs. The distinguishing feature of this grub are two short rows of spines in a V-shape on the raster and a crescent-shaped anal opening.

Control Measures: They are the same as for June beetles with the following additions. Scented lure traps specifically for Japanese beetles catch quite a few adults. The bait is a substance called geraniol, which turns on the adult beetles and they fly to the lure and are trapped there. Also, a product that creates milky spore disease in grubs (*Bacillus popilliae*, sometimes sold as Doom) is available in the United States. This naturally occurring product is spread onto the lawn and colonizes it, providing a natural, effective grub control. Follow the label directions to ensure a high population of natural control. This product is not as effective in the South as it is in the North.

Masked Chafers: Northern Masked Chafer (*Cyclocephala borealis*) and Southern Masked Chafer (*Cyclocephala lurida*)

We'll deal with both of these pests under one heading because they are really quite similar in appearance and action, if not always location. The damage to grass is from the larval or grub stage and not the adults. Because this grub eats decaying organic matter as well as grass roots, lawns can tolerate higher concentrations of chafers than of other grub species (a threshold of 10 versus normal threshold of five). In some parts of the continent, particularly the Northeast, masked chafers are the primary grub problem and the damage can be significant. The adults fly at night and, unlike Japanese beetles, do not cause plant damage.

Identification: The adults are reddish brown and approximately a half inch long. The term "masked" refers to a darker red-brown area around their eyes and head. You can distinguish between the southern and northern chafer by the hair on their front wing. Northern masked chafers have short hairs on the front wing, while southern masked chafers are hairless. The grubs are typical lawn

GRUB IDENTIFICATION

The bottom line in grub control is that the easiest way to distinguish between the different grubs is by the shape of their anal opening and hairs on their raster (rear end). The reality is that not many of us are going to go looking at the back end of grubs to see who they are. For all practical purposes, unless you're dealing with Japanese beetles (the adults will be the tip-off), a grub is a grub and you control them when you hit the threshold. As you'll recall, the threshold limit for most grubs is five per square foot of lawn.

So, regardless of whether it is a Japanese beetle, a June beetle, or whatever—if the combination of all these grubs averages more than five per square foot—control is appropriate. As the control systems are pretty much the same for all grubs (with the exception of Japanese beetles) it's hard to go wrong.

You'll identify Japanese beetles more easily when you see the gorgeous adults eating your garden. Once you identify the adult Japanese beetle, then control for them and their grubs.

GRUBS—NORTHERN OR SOUTHERN PROBLEM?

Both!

The major grub pests in the South are the June beetle and the southern masked chafer. They readily attack warm season grasses (Bermuda grass, zoysia grass, St. Augustine grass, and buffalo grass).

In the South, the cool season grasses such as Kentucky bluegrass are usually attacked by another June beetle called the May beetle. If that's confusing, it's because June beetles are all scientifically named *Phyllophaga*, and so is the related May beetle. They're kissing cousins so to speak. It's known as the May beetle because it gets off to a faster start (in May obviously) than its cousins.

In northern climates June beetles normally require several years to complete their life cycle. In the South, however, they can complete their normal cycle in one year or at most two years. Most of the damage from grubs occurs in the midsummer to late fall period when the larger grubs are actively feeding.

The best time to control white grubs in the South depends on your location. Northern lawns are heavily weather dependent, and the temperatures and rainfall the grubs need to start feeding are usually quite predictable. Southern temperatures, rainfall, and insect responses are not as dependable. Control is best achieved five to six weeks after the June beetles have started flying in your region. So, when you hear them thwacking off the screen doors, wait five to six weeks to control them.

grubs: white, C-shaped, and varying in size from a quarter inch when in their first instar stage to an inch long when fully developed as grubs.

Northern masked chafers tend to fly from midnight or slightly later (2:00 A.M.) until sunup, while southern masked chafers tend to start flying at sundown and stop around midnight. Both will be highly attracted to irrigated lawns in dry periods and will fly more immediately after a rainstorm.

The eggs are laid in July and by mid-August the first instar grubs are feeding away. They'll overwinter in the soil to start feeding when the soil warms up. Pupation occurs in late May to early June, with the adults appearing in July to start the cycle anew. They have only one egg-laying period per year.

As can be expected, the distribution of these pests is concentrated along geographic lines. The South for the southern masked chafer and the North for the northern masked chafer. There is considerable overlap however along the demarcation lines particularly in the Mid-Atlantic states. Maryland, for example, is home to both species and as a result this pest is one of the most serious pests in this state. Chafers are quite indiscriminate about the grass species they eat—they like them all, warm or cool season grasses.

On lawns where effective Japanese beetle control has been established, the chafer is becoming a major pest. In areas where the Japanese beetle is still the major pest, the chafer is not dominant. This is one of those we-don't-know-why things in insect interaction. Once you control one, you'll likely see the other move in.

Control Measures: They are the same as for other grubs. Avoiding irrigating during the egg-laying period in July will deter adults from your lawn area.

Oriental Beetle *(Anomala orientalis)*

Once established, this grub can be quite a problem for lawns. Introduced from the Philippines around 1920, it feeds quite close to the soil's surface and chews off the roots at that level. As you can imagine, this is pretty devastating for the individual grass plant and browning and death is much quicker than with other beetle species.

LAWN SPIKES

If you want to use a totally organic approach to your lawn grub problem and get some exercise at the same time, use lawn spikes. At specialty garden stores and through catalogs, you can purchase spiked sandals that slip on over your shoes. Research studies have shown that by wearing these spiked sandals while you are mowing your lawn, you can reduce grub populations by as much as 50 percent. As you walk, you spear the grubs. The more you walk, the more grubs you kill.

Adults feed on most garden plants but are not nearly as destructive as Japanese beetles.

Identification: The adult beetles are typical oval-shaped, about an inch long, and straw colored. The back has a variety of black markings that are not consistent over the species. The fully-grown grub reaches 2 inches in length and is a typical C-shaped, white grub with brown head capsule. It will take an expert to identify this grub because it resembles the Japanese beetle grub. The life cycle is also quite similar. The eggs are laid in July and early August, and the young larvae eat until winter drives them lower into the soil. In the spring, they start eating right away and hatch out in June.

As this book goes to press, the Oriental beetle is only found in the Northeast and North Carolina. It will undoubtedly spread past these boundaries. Oriental beetle grubs are usually found next to flower beds and on the edges of lawn areas.

Control Measures: Even though this grub resembles the Japanese beetle, it is not controlled using Japanese beetle techniques; rather, normal grub controls work best.

June Beetles *(Phyllophaga* sp.*)*

Besides thwacking off screen doors and windows in early summer, the main problem with June beetles is the same as other beetles—their larvae eat grass roots. June beetles also have the distinction of not being fussy about their food. They'll eat the roots of any small seedling they come across. Once the roots are gone, the grass plants will wilt and die—normally in patches due to the concentration of hatching grubs. Remember, the grub or larval stage is not very mobile in the soil.

If the grass is yellow and dying, the grub population will be at least three to five per square foot. You can evaluate this by peeling back the sod. Adults also consume the foliage of many trees. This is usually not a problem; there would have to be an extremely large population to pass the threshold for an established tree. However, watch your young plantings when the adults start flying.

June beetles take three years from egg to adult. The females lay eggs in June in grassy areas, usually next to houses. They are attracted by the lights at night. The eggs hatch in a few weeks and

DIAZINON CAUTION

One of the most common of grub control insecticides is Diazinon. *This product is extremely toxic to birds and fish*. If you choose to use this product, pay special attention to the label directions and *never* flush leftover spray product down storm drains or sewers where it can come into contact with wildlife from the effluent discharge.

Measure the amount you need to use very carefully so you do not have excess product when you are finished with your spraying.

KEEP OFF THE GRASS

the young larvae feed for the remainder of the summer. They retreat deeper into the soil to overwinter. The second season is when the serious lawn damage is done by the sophomore grub. It eats constantly from early spring right through until late fall when it once again heads for deeper ground to overwinter. The third year, the grub rises to the rootzone, replenishes its energy by snacking on some tasty grass roots, and then forms a hard shell to pupate. The adult hatches from the pupa in late summer but remains underground for the rest of the year and over the winter. The following May or early June, it emerges to start the cycle once again.

Identification: Adults are black or brown and around an inch in length. They have long spiny legs that seem to attach themselves to anything they land on. There are seven species distributed around eastern North America so there is some variation in color and size. Larvae, or the grubs, are quite small when first hatched but quickly grow to 1 to 1½ inches. They are C-shaped with a large brown head capsule as well as the typical three pairs of legs.

Control Measures: It is much easier when the grubs are small than when they are fully grown. For this reason, any controls—biological or chemical—should be applied approximately three to five weeks after the adults are seen flying. Control agents are the same as for black turfgrass ataenius.

Chewing Insects
Annual Bluegrass Weevil *(Hyperodes maculicollis)*

These weevils are found in the Northeast as far south as southern Pennsylvania. For the most part, homeowners won't see this pest; it seems to confine itself to the lush grass and vast expanses of golf courses. Now, if you treat your lawn like a golf course, you may indeed run into it. Although it can feed on many plants, its first choice is short mown bluegrass species, just like you see on golf courses. The larvae sever stems from the grass plant and this creates small brown patches on the lawn. The newly hatched small larva is the hungriest, so expect early damage in May and June. As the larva matures, it reduces its feeding so the grass generally has the ability to outgrow any damage inflicted by losing the odd stem or two. The adult usually overwinters under trees where the leaf litter is deepest. In a good year, the adults can lay two sets of eggs, so there may be a second crop of young larvae in late August.

Identification: The weevil is small (¹/₈ to ¹/₄ inch long) and varies from dark brown to black. The snout projects forward and slightly downward from the front of the head. The most conspicuous identifying characteristic is the knobby **antenna** attached to each side of the snout near the tip of the snout. The larvae are quite small (about ¹/₄ inch to ¹/₂ inch when mature), creamy white, with no legs, and a somewhat pointed end.

Control Measures: Sometimes birds will attack the larvae, but there are no known natural predators. Contact insecticides will kill the adults. **Endophyte** enhanced grass varieties are the easiest method of control.

Bluegrass Billbug *(Sphenophorus parvulus)*

The major symptom of billbug infestation is that the grass appears to wilt and does not respond to watering. In severe infestations, large areas of the lawn may turn yellow and die. Individual grass blades may be shredded from adult feeding, while the crowns and roots are destroyed by the larvae. You may even find **frass**, or excrement from the adult billbugs, on the grass stalks.

Adults overwinter in protected areas or under leaf litter and become active just after spring thaw. They are often seen wandering around on the lawn before the grass has started to grow or around the foundation of buildings where they've overwintered next to the heat of the building. By late June they are feeding in earnest, and the females start laying eggs under the leaf sheaths. After egg hatch, the larvae feed on the leaf sheath for a short time but soon outgrow this sanctuary and move on to feed on the crowns and grass roots. By the end of August, all feeding has stopped for the year and the new adults emerge shortly afterward. The adults then search out a place to overwinter and begin the cycle again the following season.

Identification: Adult billbugs have the distinctive, long curved snout of the rest of the weevil family. They also have a distinctive antenna with an "elbow" in it. Bluegrass billbugs are one of the

SUMMARY STEPS TO GRUB CONTROL

1. Did you see significant numbers of adult beetles flying and bouncing off house screens and outdoor lighting?
2. Wait for five weeks.
3. Peel back lawn sod areas.
4. Check for white grubs—if there are more than five per square foot, treat. If five or fewer per square foot, do not treat.

larger weevils, approximately a quarter inch in length. Larvae are quite difficult to differentiate from other weevil larvae, so you'll have to figure it out from the adult phase.

Control Measures: The easiest is to grow endophyte-enhanced grass varieties. Typically, these have good billbug protection built right in. Other than that, try contact insecticides.

Hunting Billbug *(Sphenophorus veratus vestitus)*

The hunting billbug is a pest of warmer lawns, naturally occurring along the eastern seaboard from Maryland into Florida. There have been reports in other warm areas such as California and Hawaii; but for the most part, it is only a problem in its more northerly ranges. These pests prefer warm season grasses such as zoysia and Bermuda grass. Both the larvae and adults munch away on the grass. The larvae feed on the roots, while the adult beetles eat leaves and burrow into the stems near the soil line. The damage is typical of root damage; that is, irregularly shaped yellowing or dead patches on the lawn. Fortunately, this pest only produces one generation per year with the adults overwintering in leaf litter and garden debris. In the South, billbugs may overwinter at any stage of life, from egg to adult while in the North, adults seem to overwinter best.

The damage is similar to the bluegrass billbug in that it will be early in the year. Even though the larvae are growing, the grass can usually survive and outgrow problems later in the season.

Identification: Black to brown with the typical snout of the weevil, this billbug is about $1/8$ to $1/4$ inch long. The hunting billbug resembles the bluegrass billbug, but is slightly larger and has parenthesis-like markings on the back of the thorax.

Control Measures: Billbug populations may be managed by using resistant turfgrass variations. Some perennial ryegrasses and fine fescues with fungal endophytes are resistant to billbugs.

Webworms
Sod Webworm *(Crambus teterrellus)*

The sod webworm family is a large one with much overlapping of species in their geographic areas. In other words, you probably

won't know for sure which webworm is eating your lawn. The larvae have a neat trick of cutting off the grass blades just above the thatch line and pulling them into their tunnels to eat. The identifying problem then is a small circle or patch of closely cropped grass with some of the remaining grass turning brown. It looks as if a miniature lawnmower were operating in a small part of the lawn. If there are numerous larvae eating, then the small patches will turn into a bigger patch or section of the lawn. These patches are irregular in shape. Sod webworms generally are more of a problem on Kentucky bluegrass and Bermuda grass lawns, but they will attack other grasses as well as some farm crops.

Beginning in May, adult webworm moths start to fly and this continues right through the summer. They are not great flyers and they only live a few days while feeding on dew. Their most active time is dusk and they hide in the grass during the daytime.

Identification: The moth is 1 to 1½ inches long with wingspans ranging from 1 to 3 inches. The forewings are brown or dull gray, with a whitish streak from the base of the wing to the outer edge. The hind wings are midbrown. When resting, the moths fold their wings in a tentlike manner over their body. This is not a particularly pretty moth.

The moths lay eggs over the lawn area and seven to 10 days later the larvae hatch to construct their tunnels and begin feeding. The two to three generations per year will do the most damage during high summer when the grass is not actively growing and repairing the damage. In the South, a new generation is produced every five to six weeks.

Control Measures: A webworm infestation can be found and identified by using the soap solution trick on page 181. Alternately, a pyrethrin mix can be used by mixing 1 tablespoon of pyrethrin to a gallon of water and applying this to 1 square yard. The threshold for control is three to four webworms per square foot. Anything less and control is not indicated as necessary.

1. Cultural controls: Use plenty of water and appropriate fertilizer amounts. Healthy grass can often outgrow any damage. Stressed grasses are most often the ones to die.

SPOT CHECK

Some gardeners blame fertilizer burn or dog urine for lawn spots. The way to distinguish between grub or larvae damage and fertilizer or dog damage is to examine the edge of the dead patch. If the grass is growing the same on the edge as it is on the rest of the lawn, grubs are the problem. If the grass around the brown spot is growing luxuriantly and taller, greener, and more lush than the rest of the lawn—the dead spot is likely caused by fertilizer or dogs. With grub damage, you'll be able to pull the dead grass from the ground. With fertilizer or animal burn, the grass will still be attached to the roots and will not easily pull from the ground.

Close mowing is another way to stress the grass and encourage webworm damage.

2. Aim all control methods at the larvae, not at the flying moths.

3. There are several natural parasites (ground beetles and rove beetles), but if you've been spraying with pesticides you won't have these beetles in enough numbers to keep the webworms in check. *Bacillus thuringiensis* is effective on very young larvae, but by the time you'll likely notice a problem (populations seemingly explode in numbers) the larvae will be too old to be effectively controlled. Steinernema nematodes are the most effective. They can be purchased at good garden centers. This is true except in the South where the parasites do not survive well.

4. On home lawns, sod webworms are normally controlled by natural predators and are not usually a major problem.

5. Resistant turfgrass species exist. Look for cultivars of perennial ryegrass, tall fescues, and fine fescues that have "Endophyte Enhanced" labeled on their packages.

6. Contact and stomach poison chemicals are the last resort. Best control is achieved if the spraying is done in late afternoon. Late fall or early spring applications are often not effective because many larvae are deep in the soil.

Bluegrass Sod Webworm *(Parapediasia teterrella)*

This is a serious pest of bluegrass in the Midwest.

Identification: The head of the larva is darker than the green-gray body. These webworms are marked with a series of light brown spots around the body. Like all webworms, they live in silk-lined tunnels and cut off and drag grass leaves to their lairs to eat. Two generations a year mark this pest.

Control Measures: They are the same as for other webworms.

Tropical Sod Webworm *(Herpetogramma phaeopteralis)*

The larvae are yellow-green and 1 to 1½ inches in length. They have a pair of darker spots on each body segment and are fairly hairy. The head will be a slightly different color than the body. When disturbed, the larvae sometimes go into a C-shape. The adult moth is 1 to 1½ inches long with a wingspan of 1 to 2 inches. They have a prominent forward projection on their head so that when they are resting with their wings folded over them like a tent, the head projection is quite noticeable.

This particular pest is mostly a problem in Florida, where tropical sod webworms may produce a new generation every five to six weeks.

Control Measures: They are the same as for other webworms.

Cutworms

Black Cutworm *(Agrostis ipsilon)*

Generally speaking, cutworms are more of a problem on golf courses than they are on home lawns. This is because the regular aeration of golf course turf (making little tunnels) allows the cutworms to find and inhabit the vertical tunnels they use to survive. The cutworm crawls out at night to browse on the grass leaves and crowns around the rim of its tunnel. Usually, it affects only small areas of lawn unless there is a rather large population present for some reason.

This is also more of a problem the farther south you go. The cutworms themselves do not overwinter readily in freezing climates, but the adult moths overwinter in the South and are carried by the prevailing southeasterly spring winds north to greener pastures. The night-flying moths lay their eggs on the tips of grass blades and the young larvae hatch five to 10 days later. Hungry from birth, they eat all night and shelter during the day. In southern lawns, the larvae will pupate in the fall and hatch out the moths in time for the next spring's egg laying and flight north.

Identification: The adult moths are a dull gray or brown with a wingspan of 1 to 1½ inches. You won't see them during the day as they are night flyers. If you do see them resting, they hold their wings in the shape of a triangle. The larvae are dull gray with a row of black dots on their abdomens. When disturbed, they will curl up into a tight circle.

Control Measures: Contact or stomach poison

ENDOPHYTES

New concepts in insect control also use the symbiotic endophytic fungi (*Neotyphodium* sp.) that live and grow inside certain varieties of grass. The grass feeds the fungi and the fungi protects the grass from insect damage and does not harm the grass—a true symbiotic relationship. The fungi repel insects such as chinch bugs and webworms. The breeders are working to develop endophytic cultivars for all grass species. Check with your local garden center for availability.

KEEP OFF THE GRASS

IF IT AIN'T BROKE, DON'T FIX IT

Living in the North, I've never seen a cutworm infestation on my home lawn. I know there are a few of them out there because I turn them over in the vegetable and flower garden when I'm digging in the spring. This is one of those wonderful parts of gardening. I know the pest is likely in my lawn, but because it's not doing any serious damage—why worry about it? I watch the robins and other birds hunting and pecking in the spring and in the morning dew, so I know that they are being fed and I'm not worrying. Can life get any better than that? Relaxation is one of the best things that a garden encourages. Taking a type A personality to the garden really is counterproductive. That's the end of that sermon.

Threshold limits can be evaluated by using the soap solution technique (see page 181). Soap will force the cutworms to the surface for counting. The threshold for cutworms is five worms per square yard, anything above this number indicates control is necessary. You must apply the insecticide in the evening when the cutworms are active, not during the day when they are hiding and protected.

Bronze Cutworm *(Nepholodes minians)*

Identification: The bronze cutworm is a handsome fellow (as cutworms go) with dark brown to black on his upper side and slightly paler coloring on the lower. His upper surface has three narrow yellow stripes running the length of his back while a single broad white-yellow stripe runs down each side. There is a bronze sheen to the entire body (hence the name).

Bronze cutworms overwinter as eggs and hatch out in early spring. By April, the larvae are fully grown and they start pupating in mid-August. They hatch out shortly afterward to lay eggs and start the cycle again. Generally the bronze cutworm has only a single generation per year.

Control Measures: They are the same as for all cutworms.

Variegated Cutworm *(Peridroma saucia)*

Identification: The variegated cutworm is gray to brown with an orange stripe on its sides as well as a series of somewhat darker marks. A row of yellow (sometimes white) dots runs right down the middle of its back.

This cutworm overwinters as a partially grown larvae and starts feeding again as soon as the grass starts to green up in the spring. It pupates and in late spring the adults emerge to lay eggs and start the process again. A female can lay up to two thousand eggs in clusters of a hundred on grass sheaths. Two to four generations per year is the norm for the variegated cutworm.

Control Measures: They are the same as for all cutworms.

Armyworms

Common Armyworm *(Pseudaletia unipuncta)*

Armyworms are an interesting pest. They get their name from the habit of the larvae of traveling together in search of food. All grass plants are considered delicacies by these ravenous creatures. They skeletonize the surface of grass leaves by rasping all the tender parts but leaving the tougher veins. Older, hungrier armyworms may indeed eat the entire plant, leaving nothing but a bare circle in the lawn. Armyworms overwinter as partially mature larvae and then start feeding again in early spring as soon as food exists. The larvae pupate and the first generation of moths appears in May or early June. The females start laying eggs after about three days of sipping plant nectar and can lay up to two thousand eggs that hatch out in six to 10 days.

Identification: The young larvae are a pale green color, but as they mature they turn yellow to brown-green with stripes. They are 2½ to 4 inches long. These worms may curl into a C-shaped ball when you pick them up. The adult moth is pale brown to gray brown with a wingspan of 3 inches. The forward wing has a white spot near the wingtip (which is characteristic of armyworm moths)

Control Measures: As for all caterpillars, use contact or stomach poison.

Fall Armyworm *(Spodoptera frugiperda)*

The fall armyworm is a tropical pest whose moth adults hitch rides on winds to expand their summer eating range as far north as Michigan and Montana. The cold weather kills them off, and infestations are largely controlled in this manner for northern states. In the southern states, infestations may persist year round only in the warmest sections of the Gulf Coast. Like many armyworms, the fall armyworm will eat just about anything if it is hungry but its preferred food is grass plants, particularly Bermuda grass, fescues, ryegrass, bluegrass and Johnson grass.

The armyworms move about as an "army" of worms and when they hit a lawn, they consume all parts of the plant that are aboveground without discrimination. If it's green, they'll eat it. As you

CURES FOR CREEPY CRAWLERS

This isn't exactly about lawns, but I know that gardeners worry about caterpillars and other critters crawling up into trees. Although it's normally not an issue with lawn-specific pests, here's an easy way to lay your concerns to rest and protect your trees from being a lunch stop for caterpillars and other crawlies.

Wrap the trunk of the tree with a 2- to 3-inch band of masking tape. On heavily ridged bark, stuff cotton batting or some similar material under the tape to ensure that an insect can't get underneath the tape.

Spread horticultural glue onto the tape. Horticultural glue is made by several different companies (Tanglefoot is the best known), but the important characteristic is that this kind of glue does not dry out in a season. It stays sticky. With a sticky band around the tree trunk, insects will not cross the barrier. If they can't get up into the tree, they can't eat it. This works on trees of all ages and sizes.

might imagine, having the top of the plant eaten off will stunt the growth of most grass plants and kill the weaker plants.

The moths migrate north throughout the spring and summer. Each female moth lays about 1,000 eggs in clumps of 50 to 200. In two to 10 days, the larvae hatch and wander about looking for food. Unlike true armyworms that eat only at night, fall armyworms are not discriminating—they'll eat anytime they can find food, day or night. After feeding for two to three weeks, the larvae dig themselves into the ground and two weeks later emerge as moths to fly farther north. Several generations can occur at their midpoint of travels in North Carolina.

Identification: The larval stage or worm is 3 to 4 inches long and green, brown, or black with a dark head (the head is usually marked with a pale but distinct inverted Y-shape). The sides of the body have a long black stripe with four black dots on the top of each stomach section. The moth is brown with a wingspan of approximately 3 inches. The hindwings are white, while the front wings are a darker gray, mottled with lighter splotches. Each of the forewings has a white spot near the tip of the wing.

Control Measures: As for all caterpillars, use tomach or contact poison.

Mole Crickets
Mole Cricket *(Gryllotalpa hexadactyla)*

Being tropical pests from South America, mole crickets are southern pests and not northern. As a rule, they thrive in light, sandy soils and are particularly attracted to soils with high organic matter or where manure has been added. They are not particularly fussy about which plants they eat. Grass lawns are only one of many plants on their menu. Mole crickets burrow into the soil and come out at night to feed on the stems and roots of plants. The burrows also dry out the nearby soil so turfgrasses die because of localized drought around the rootzone and root damage. One mole cricket may cover several square yards in a night snacking on whatever strikes its fancy.

The mole cricket nymphs overwinter and become active in March, feeding in the soil until they mature in spring. In May or early June the new adults emerge to breed and lay eggs. They are attracted to light as they fly their mating flights. The females construct small "rooms" in the soil and lay approximately 35 to 50 eggs in each room. Depending on temperature, the eggs will hatch 10 to 40 days later. Nymphs develop through eight instars (stages) to become fully grown adults. They will overwinter either as final stage nymphs or as immature adults. Fortunately, there is only one generation each year.

Identification: Resembling grasshoppers, mole crickets are light brown and covered with fine hairs that makes them appear quite velvety. Their beady eyes and shovel-like front legs for digging are all contained on a 1 to 1½ inch long body. The nymphs resemble adults, except they are smaller and wingless. The physical differences between the different species are reserved for the connoisseurs. Most of us wouldn't recognize the minute differences between the wings if we could convince one of them to sit still long enough to use a measuring tape.

Control Measures: Population levels can be discovered by using the soap solution technique (see page 181). The threshold is approximately one per square foot. Fewer than that averaged out over the entire lawn does not indicate control is necessary. If there is an infestation in one area of the lawn and not in others, consider controlling the pest population where it exists rather than spraying the entire lawn (if there are no pests there to kill—why spray?).

A predator nematode (*Steinernema scapterisci*) kills different species at variable levels. Although control of tawny mole crickets is quite complete, the nematode only obtains 75 percent control on short winged mole crickets.

Luckily, a predator wasp (*Larra bicolor*) reverses this statistic. Introduced into Puerto Rico in the 1930s, it offers quite good control on the short-winged mole cricket.

Another predator, the red-eyed fly (*Ormia depleta*) is quite effective at attacking the tawny and southern mole crickets. But the short-winged mole cricket does not sing (remember crickets "sing" by rubbing their wings together) so the fly can't find it unless it's sitting right next to it.

Some chemical baits are available as stomach poisons.

Short-Winged Mole Cricket *(Scapteriscus abbreviatus)*

This cricket arrived in the United States about 1900 from South America, probably aboard some boats. Without wings for flying, it has not spread very far inland from the original points of entry. Currently it is found in Florida, Puerto Rico, and St. Croix in the Virgin Islands.

Its main claim to fame is that it is the dominant mole cricket where it exists in terms of damage, given that it is a great digger and burrower.

Control Measures: They are the same as for mole crickets.

Southern Mole Cricket *(Scapteriscus borellii)*

Southern mole crickets resemble other mole crickets except that they are largely carnivorous. Stomach analysis indicates they eat mostly insects such as ants rather than vegetation. The damage to turf comes from their tunneling activities rather than eating the roots.

This cricket is found as far north as North Carolina and throughout the South across Texas and Arizona into California. Cold weather is its limiting factor, it will not overwinter in deep freeze conditions.

If captured, this cricket will often play "dead." Then when freed from its constraints it will suddenly become "alive" again, exhibiting frenetic activity to escape.

Control Measures: They are the same as for other mole crickets. In addition, the tachnid fly (*Ormia depleta*), native to South America, is a major predator.

Tawny Mole Cricket *(Scapteriscus vicinus)*

The tawny mole cricket does not play dead when captured and has almost as wide a range as the southern mole cricket. Originally from South America and introduced into the United States about 1900, it now claims a range that goes as far north as North Carolina and all through the Southeast. Its spread will only be limited by freezing cold weather and perhaps dry climates. It doesn't like the dry soils, preferring irrigated soils and lawns to natural areas.

NORTHERN CRICKETS VS. SOUTHERN CRICKETS

As this is a southern pest, gardeners not living in the South should relax about crickets. The crickets we see in the North are not a problem for lawns or really for any garden plants. The only thing they do is keep us awake at night and bring good luck if they decide to live in our houses.

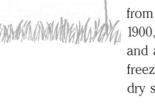

The tawny mole cricket is the biggest pest in the mole cricket family. It can be a major pest of vegetable seedlings, turfgrass, and pasture grasses because it feeds almost exclusively on plant material.

Control Measures: They are the same as for other mole crickets.

Aphids

Greenbug Aphid *(Schizaphis graminum)*

Greenbugs are found throughout North America but usually only need control in the Midwest, where they can also chew on small grains such as oats and barley. Greenbugs prefer Kentucky bluegrass over other species if given a choice. This aphid has a piercing mouth that injects toxins into the leaf and sucks out the juices. The toxins cause a yellowing around the feeding hole and severe infestations cause the grass blades to turn yellow or take on a yellow tone rather than a lush green. Damage is more severe early and late in the growing season because the greenbug prefers temperatures between 40° and 65°F. During the heat of the summer, feeding decreases significantly.

Identification: Approximately ⅛ inch long, they are usually light green. Under the lens, the tips of the legs and antennae will be black. They come winged and wingless and the young nymphs look like small adults and do not have wings.

Control Measures: Use contact insecticide or natural predators. Many predators such as the ladybird beetles (ladybugs) love aphids.

Chinch Bugs

Chinch Bug *(Blissus leucopterus leucopterus)*

The chinch bug uses its four-part beak to pierce and suck out the juices of the grass leaf. As you might expect, with severe damage the plant is not able to grow normally. Yellowing of the grass turf occurs with slight damage and death with heavy infestations. The damage normally occurs in irregularly shaped patches and normally is near the edges of the lawn in larger lawns, closest to where the insects overwinter and breed in protected areas.

This particular pest is found from the East Coast over into the western plains states, into Canada and as far south as Louisiana. It is the major pest in the Midwest and causes lesser amounts of

MOWING HEIGHTS FOR MOLE CRICKET CONTROL

You'll get better survival on your lawn with mole crickets if you do not mow below the following heights:

Centipede grass	1.5–2.0 inches
Bahia grass	3 inches
Common Bermuda grass	0.5–2.0 inches
Hybrid Bermuda grass	0.25–0.75 inches
St. Augustine grass	3 inches in sun, 4 inches in shade

damage in other areas. The chinch bug is more of a problem in years where the temperatures are hotter than normal and rainfall is lower than normal. Think hotter and drier, and you have a potential infestation of chinch bugs.

Chinch bugs overwinter as adults in protected areas next to building foundations and in long grasses. The adults emerge in the spring to lay their eggs behind the leaf sheath or in the soil at the base of a newly planted crop. These eggs hatch in a few days and the nymphs immediately begin feeding on any part of the plant they can reach. Two to three generations are possible each year.

Identification: The adult chinch bug is about a third of an inch long and black. The wings are variable in length, from as long as the body to only half the length. Each wing bears a very distinctive triangular black mark. The wingless nymph is smaller than the adult but similarly shaped. The head and body are brown, the eyes are dark red (use your lens), and the stomach area is pale yellow or light reddish.

Control Measures: Use the coffee can system (see page 181) to identify whether there is a chinch bug problem. The threshold is 20 pests per coffee can—any fewer and no spray is necessary. Nymphs are fairly easily killed with a contact spray. Adults tend to be a bit harder to kill.

Hairy Chinch Bug *(Blissus leucopterus hirtus)*

To begin with, this pest mostly enjoys home lawns rather than commercial sod farms. Don't ask why, we don't know. What we do know is that come August, there will be brown patches appearing on the lawn as a result of chinch bug feeding. A key fact in initial identification is that the brown patches are typically next to gardens or shrub borders or even under trees. Initial damage is rarely out in the middle of the lawn. After the initial brown patches, the pests can ruin an entire lawn if left unchecked.

Hairy chinch bugs overwinter as adults in protected areas under trees, in flower gardens or near the warm foundations of your home. The adults go dormant over the winter to recover and start feeding in the warm days of spring. Females lay the eggs by putting them inside the plant tissues of the grass stem. This activity

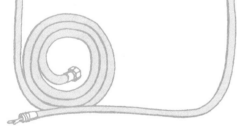

ORGANIC OPTIONS

When we suggest a contact spray for chinch bugs, there are a whole range of organic sprays that will do the job. From soaps and neem products to liquid rotenone sprays—almost any organic contact spray will do the job. Like their chemical brethren, it is important to read the label for registration and safety issues as well as application rates. Remember that just because a product is organic does not mean that it is harmless to humans, particularly pregnant women and children.

reaches a peak in early summer—mid-June in our zone 4 garden. The small nymphs hatch and start feeding by piercing the outer layer of the grass plant and sucking the juices out of the plant. The older the nymph, the more damage it creates. Naturally, if there is a good survival rate, damage can be extensive by the time August rolls around. The nymphs mature into adults and start searching for a place to overwinter.

Identification: Adult chinch bugs are fairly small, (¼ inch or less) and are black and white. When the wings are folded over the back, there appears to be a band or spot on the back of the bug. Nymph stages look similar to adults except that their white spot is less pronounced. Nymphs do not have wings. The legs on both adults and nymphs are reddish in color.

Control Measures: Use the coffee can system to identify whether there is a chinch bug problem. The threshold is 20 pests per coffee can—any fewer and no spray is necessary. Nymphs are fairly easily killed with a contact spray, although adults tend to be a bit harder to kill.

Southern Chinch Bug *(Blissus insularis)*

You'll find our friend the southern chinch bug almost anywhere you find St. Augustine grass. In fact, some research indicates that this is the worst pest of this grass, even worse than grubs or mites. Fortunately, it is not a pest of most other grasses. The southern chinch bug is much like its northern counterparts in that it sucks the juice and the life out of grass blades resulting in yellowing and browning of the leaf. Heavy infestations can weaken and kill the grass plant.

In the northern ranges of St. Augustine grass, eggs begin hatching about the middle of April. It is possible in these areas to produce three and sometimes four generations of southern chinch bugs in a single growing season. In warmer areas such as southern Florida, the eggs begin hatching in late February. There can be up to seven generations per year, which is why it is a serious pest the farther south you go.

Identification: The immature chinch bugs or nymphs are about the size of a pinhead when they hatch and are bright red with a

PESTS LEAD TO WEEDS

One of the problems associated with pest lawn damage is weakened grass plants. Weak plants are thin plants and don't make a tightly packed turf area. Thin turf areas allow weeds to get established. So, not only do the pests destroy the grass plants, but they make it easier for weeds to thrive and harder for you as a homeowner to repair the damage. (You have to kill the weeds before you can get a good lawn established, see Chapter 4 on renovation.)

KEEP OFF THE GRASS

white band across the back. Late-stage nymphs (they molt five times before reaching the adult stage) and adult chinch bugs are about a fifth of an inch in length and black; the adults have white wings.

Control Measures: Test for existence of the pest by using the coffee can technique. The threshold is 20 bugs per square foot.

Interestingly enough, there are quite a few good controls for this pest that do not entail using chemicals.

- Do not use water-soluble nitrogen fertilizers to feed your lawn. Studies have shown that lawns are more prone to attack when these products are used.
- Feed minimally. Do not create lush lawns, even with dry or granulated fertilizer products.
- Do not allow moisture levels to get too low. Moisture stress encourages the problem.
- Control thatch. Chinch bugs love thatch.
- Mow to 3 to 4 inches. This keeps the grass healthier than short mowing and healthy grass is less likely to be attacked or if attacked, less likely to be badly damaged
- Use resistant varieties of grass. Floratam and Floralawn are quite good in that the bugs do not like this grass and will not feed on it. Floratine is only resistant to bugs and not as good as the first two. New lawns should always use one of the first two varieties.
- Consider the use of beneficial predators. Big-eyed bugs love this pest and are sometimes confused with the chinch bug, so make sure you are not killing the predator. A predator earwig (*Labidura* family) really chomps down on chinch bugs, and research has shown that they'll eat up to fifty bugs every night.

Control with contact pesticides is possible if all else fails.

Mites
Bermuda Grass Mite *(Eriophyes cynodoniensis)*
As can be seen from the name, this pest is primarily a pest of Bermuda grass and is found only in the southern states along

a border between Florida and Arizona. The first symptom is usually first thing in the spring when the grass fails to spring into full green lush life. Some grass areas may be yellowish or brownish, not in patches like animal or grub damage, but in overall intensity. The grass may appear shorter—the internodes between the leaves are shorter than normal and this may cause the grass to grow in tufts. Individual plants may have brown, distorted stems that wither and fade. The lawn will be thin and weeds will colonize the open spaces.

Identification: Primarily active in late spring and summer, this small pest is approximately the size of the head of a pin, and it sucks the juices out of plant leaves. Adult mites hide under the leaf sheaths and are quite difficult to find and control. They lay very small eggs and the eggs hatch shortly after. The interesting thing is that the young nymphs are two-thirds the size of the adults and it only takes five to seven days for the mite to move from egg stage to fully grown adult and be quite capable of laying more eggs. If you can find some to put under your 20X lens, they will appear slightly cigar-shaped and creamy white with four legs.

Control Measures: Use contact insecticide or registered miticide.

Clover Mite *(Bryobia praetiosa)*

You'll be hard-pressed to tell the difference between this mite and the banks grass mite. The only difference is that this mite is a bit larger and its front legs are almost twice as long as its back legs. There is a world of difference in how they live. The clover mite spends the summer as a small reddish egg on the bark, stems, and twigs of other plants as well as in the cracks and crevices of buildings. When the temperatures cool after the heat of the summer, they hatch out and move to their feeding grounds to produce several generations of mites before winter sets in.

When colder temperatures arrive, the adult females move to more sheltered areas where they continue to lay eggs until really cold weather drives them into dormancy. The next spring, these adults and immature mites from newly hatched eggs start feeding and begin laying the next crop of eggs for fall hatching.

NO GUARANTEES

"Resistant" means that a pest will eat or colonize the grass, but it has to work at it. A "resistant" variety does not mean that a pest or problem will never bother the grass. Pests might prefer to eat other species or varieties of the grass, but if there's nothing else to eat, "resistance" is futile. Similarly, if a resistant variety of a grass is weakened by poor management, it will be attached by fungus or insect predators as well. "Resistant" varieties are great, but they are not foolproof.

Damage is the same for all mites. The rasping sucking of plant juices leaves brown patches on the grass blades and weakens the plants. With this mite, grass areas next to the overwintering sites are particularly hard hit.

Control Measures: Use contact spray or miticide beneficial predators.

Banks Grass Mite *(Oligonychus pratensis)*

The banks grass mite is a tiny mite (less than $1/32$ inch long) oval shaped, ranging in color from green through reddish brown to almost black. If you can distinguish such things, the males are slightly smaller than the females. I can never tell the difference. I suppose it's only important to the mites themselves.

As with all other mites, it is capable of producing seven to 10 generations in a single season and the high numbers simply suck the life out of grass blades. With this mite, you may see some very fine webbing on the underside of the grass blades.

The adult females and young nymphs overwinter on garden debris and protected spots near the lawn and then emerge early in the spring to begin feeding and breeding. As with all mites, the nymphs are smaller forms of the adults and can be controlled in similar ways. They reproduce very quickly under conditions of hot and dry and reach their highest population levels late in the summer.

Control Measures: Use contact sprays and miticides plus beneficial insects.

Winter Grain Mite *(Penthaleus major)*

This pest is widespread through most of North America and, given a choice, seems to prefer cool season grasses over warm. To feed, the mite rasps off the leaf surface of the grass blade and sucks the juices. This rasping creates a brown, almost-burned look on the grass blade. Some authorities refer to it as "brown stippling." I've never been able to figure out what that means. I just know that mite damage makes the grass look unhealthy. It has a brown tinge caused by losing the chlorophyll the mite has eaten. The exposed

parts left after feeding go brown, much like uneaten apples when exposed to air.

Identification: This is a very small insect and, under your lens, will be dark brown with a very distinct white dot on each side of the back. The body may be tinged green while the legs are usually reddish. The anus is surrounded by a reddish orange spot. This is its main distinguishing characteristic. Females lay their eggs singly and attach them to the base of a grass leaf or onto the thatch. The eggs hatch into a six-legged larva and shortly afterward, the larva pupates into an eight-legged nymph that matures into the adult form. If you're really interested, the nymphs have yellow-orange legs that mature to the red-orange as it becomes an adult.

In the South, the mite eats during the winter and goes dormant during the hot summer as an egg. Up to two generations can be produced in a year by this pest.

Control Measures: This is the food insect of choice for many beneficial predator insects. Spraying to control this pest will eliminate the beneficials as well as the mite. In the South, avoid any fall spraying because the beneficials will not be able to control the pest over the winter. Use contact sprays and miticides.

Scale

Bermuda Grass Scale *(Odonaspis ruthae)*

Female scale lay eggs under their own protective covering to protect their offspring. It is only when the eggs hatch into "crawlers" that they move into the wild world. The crawlers move to a new site on the grass blade and begin feeding by sucking the juices from grass blades. Once they've eaten enough, they lose their antennae and their legs, becoming quite immobile. At the same time as they are losing their legs, they secrete a waxy coating to protect themselves. They feed in this spot for several months and then begin the egg-laying process all over again.

This small (approximately $\frac{1}{64}$ inch across), circular white pest can be found in almost all Bermuda grass plots but is seldom a major pest worthy of control. The only time it becomes a problem is when the grass is already under stress from environmental condi-

CHEMICAL CONCERNS

The debate over chemical versus organic controls will continue to rage. What is clear in my mind is that while some chemicals are safer than others, there are few pesticides that are safe for pregnant women or small children. If you choose to use chemicals on your lawn:

- Keep all pesticides away from children. Remember, label warnings are based on adults. Children are affected by much smaller doses.
- Pregnant or nursing women should avoid contact with all lawn and garden chemicals at all costs. Many pesticides are fetotoxins (they poison the fetus at extremely small doses) or are fetal hormonal disrupters (disrupting the normal fetal development to increase the risk of birth defects or later-life learning defects).

tions or poor management. As you can imagine, the cure is to reduce the stress and the pest will once again slide into obscurity. Heavily thatched or shady areas are more prone to problems than are sunny lawn areas.

Turfgrass Scale *(Lecanopsis formicarum)*

This pest is quite a sight if the infestation is heavy. The damage will initially appear as thinly growing grass that never seems to get off to a good start in the spring growth period. Some of the grass plants might even be killed in early spring and you may think that winter damage has been responsible. If the infestation is quite heavy, it will appear as though the grass is rusty since the scale is a rusty red color and attaches itself to the grass plant to feed.

Mature nymphs overwinter in garden debris and grow up into adults in May and June. They immediately lay eggs. If you look quite closely, you'll see these silky masses containing the eggs. The eggs generally hatch during June and July, and the baby scales crawl to the tips of the grass blades for breakfast, lunch, and dinner. This crawler stage is when the grass tips will appear to be reddish if infestations are high. Crawlers are normally blown off the grass blades and carried by the wind to their new home.

Identification: The adults are oblong (approximately $1/32$ inch wide by $1/16$ inch long—pretty tiny but they make up for it in numbers) and have a yellowish tone. If you look through your lens, you'll see a broad brown stripe down each side of the adult scale. On the underside of the body is a rasping mouth that scrapes off the grass cuticle for feeding. Each female will produce approximately 400 eggs in a season.

Control Measures: As with Bermuda grass scale, control is not usually needed on healthy grass. Contact insecticides will kill the crawler stage, but the adults with their waxy coatings are more difficult to kill.

Other

Ground Pearls *(Margarodes meridionalis)*

This is a pest of southern lawn grasses; Bermuda, St. Augustine, zoysia, and centipede grass are the most commonly infested. The young nymphs suck the juices from the roots and underground parts of the plants. Damage will become apparent during the heat of the summer when the grass growth slows down. Irregular brown patches will appear. The damage will continue to grow in these areas and by fall, the turf will be dead.

The young nymphs overwinter as "pearls" rather than as adults and mature in the spring to emerge and begin feeding. They move about for a very short time and then dig themselves into the soil to cover themselves with a waxy coating and begin to lay eggs. The eggs hatch into this year's crop of slender nymphs. When they emerge, they penetrate the grass stems and begin feeding to do the damage described. Once the nymphs eat enough, they develop the globe-shaped appearance of the mature "pearl," ready to overwinter to start the process again. There is usually only one generation per year. However, if conditions are favorable, nymphs can remain underground in pearl form for up to two years.

Identification: The adult female is a pinkish scalelike insect, but unlike common garden scale she has well developed forelegs and claws for mobility. The male is a very small gnatlike insect (about $\frac{1}{32}$ inch long). Hatching from pinky white eggs lumped together in a white waxy sac, the young nymph is covered with a hard, globe-shaped yellow purple shell (approximately $\frac{1}{64}$ inch around). We're talking about a very small pest here, which makes it difficult to identify unless you have a magnifying lens.

Control Measures: Good cultural practices will help the grass recover from this problem. Check with your state's agricultural extension office to see whether your state has a product registered for control of this pest (some do, some don't).

The table on pages 220–223 lists the *most commonly available* pest controls at the time of printing. It does not list all the available pest controls (see the Resources section for finding the lesser-used products), particularly those that are only available to the commercial user. The availability of garden chemicals is in a constant state of flux. This table is meant to be a guideline, not a recommendation.

The name of the chemical is the active ingredient (the chemical that does the killing). The other names are simply marketing names used by different companies.

RESIDUAL EFFECTS

Systemic insect controls are chemicals that are absorbed into every cell of the plant. When a pest takes a bite, it gets a dose of poison and dies. Systemic controls are typically long-term controls; they have good residual ratings.

Contact sprays have to hit the pest (contact it) to kill it. Some contact sprays, such as insecticidal soap, only work when they are fresh and wet. They have no residual action. Other contact sprays have good residual effects. Even when dry if the pest eats or contacts them, the pest dies.

Residual effects vary from chemical to chemical. The label will tell you how long the product lasts.

For up-to-date product recommendations and usage guidelines, you can contact local suppliers or your local agricultural extension office, or read the labels of the products themselves. As the rates of application are also changing, we highly recommend you read and follow the directions on the product label rather than relying on memory or what you think is best. The label is the most important part of the information package—follow its directions.

Nuisance Pests: Chemical and Organic Problem Solving

"Nuisance" pests aren't harmful to your grass, but they are considered pests because some humans find them bothersome or annoying. Before you decide to blast away at them with sprays, figure out how much their presence upsets you, and treat accordingly.

Ants

Garden Ants

To begin with, ants do not directly cause any damage to the grass plants or lawn. They are scavengers, cleaning up the organic plant debris and garden garbage. In many cases, they even use fungus organisms as food sources. However, some lawnowners consider them unsightly and a problem.

It has always amazed me why anybody would want to eliminate an insect that is doing good things in the lawn, but I've often had requests for methods of eliminating ants. One time it was because the customer didn't "like the look of their anthills."

If you can see the anthills, either you have a huge new form of garden ant or you are cutting your lawn too short. Mow at the correct height for a home lawn and not a golf putting green, and you'll never see the anthills again.

Fire Ants

Having said all that about the good garden behavior of ants, I want to make it clear I was not talking about fire ants. Yes, they too are scavengers, but what a bite they pack. My wife and I vis-

PESTICIDE GUIDELINES

If you have to use pesticides of any kind (organic or chemical), keep the following guidelines in mind.

- *Use pesticide only when the pest is present in numbers that will actually cause turf damage.*
- *Apply sprays when the pest is most susceptible to it.* For example, don't spray to kill a ground-based larval form of a pest once the pest is hatched and flying around.
- *Use a properly calibrated sprayer to apply the correct amount of insecticide.* More is *not* better.
- *Keep in mind when the target insect population is feeding.* If the pest is nocturnal, avoid spraying at high noon because it will be hiding and resting for the day.
- *How you place the spray is important.* If you are trying to kill off a soil-borne pest, then remember to water the spray in after you apply it to force it down into the soil. There's little point to spraying the tops of the grass plants if your pest isn't there.
- *Do not spray when there is a wind.* The spray will move from your property to your neighbor's. This is a waste of spray material and a potential source of lawsuits.
- *Alternate your pest control products.* Any pest—from weeds to insects—will become acclimatized to almost any control method. Once a pest is not controlled by a product, it is useless to apply the product.

COMMONLY USED PEST CONTROL PRODUCTS

NAME	NAME SOLD UNDER	CONTROLS	CHARACTERISTICS	CONCERNS
Biologicals				
Predator Nematode *Steinernema riobravis, Steinernema carpocapsae*, and *Steinernema feltiae*. Different nematodes are sold in various regions, depending on availability and usefulness. Check with local suppliers.	Predator nematode Vector Devour Biosys	• Most pests whose larval stage is underground. All beetle larva (grubs), flea beetles, cutworms, crickets. • Over 200 lawn and garden pests are controlled. • Ants and fire ants.	• Small, living wormlike predator attacks and eats prey. Lays egg on grub host. Newly hatched predators feed on host. Extremely environmentally friendly; nematodes are naturally occurring.	• None. Quite environmentally friendly. • Soil has to be wet and directions for use have to be carefully followed for success. • Fire ant success depends on environmental variables.
Bacillus thurengiensis. Different species for different pests. Check with local sellers and extension agents.	BT Dipel Condor Biobit	• Caterpillars and webworms.	• Bacteria paralyzes the stomach and digestive system of pest. Pest stops eating immediately and dies of starvation after a few days.	• None with bacteria. • Naturally occurring.
Milky Spore—*Bacillus popillae*	Doom	• Grub of Japanese beetle.	• Bacteria infects the host grub, multiplies and kills the grub. Stays alive in soil to infect future generations of grubs.	• None. Naturally occurring. • For best results, apply when soil is warm.
Potassium salts of fatty acid (soaps)	M-Pede Insecticidal soap	• Most soft-bodied insects.	• Soap either kills by contact or is ingested as liquid and disrupts internal chemistry.	• None. • Some gardeners may have skin sensitivity to soap concentrate.
Cyfluthrin	Baythroid Baythroid H Attatox Contur Laser Responsar Solfac Tempo Tempo H	• Cutworms, ants, beetles, weevils, moths, armyworms. • Its primary use is for the control of chewing and sucking insects.	• A contact and stomach poison action.	• A synthetic pyrethroid insecticide moderately toxic to mammals. • LD50 = 869–1,271. • Although cyfluthrin is a skin and eye irritant in humans, pyrethroid poisonings are rare. • Highly toxic to aquatic life, bees, many beneficial insects. • Moderate toxicity to birds.
Methoxychlor	Marlate	• Weevils, leafhoppers, Japanese beetles, armyworms, scale (crawlers).	• Very persistent in the soil—up to 6 months. • Stomach and contact killer.	• One of a few organochlorine pesticides that have seen an increase in use since the 1972 ban on DDT. This is due to its relatively low toxicity. • LD50 = 5,000 to 6,000. • Few hazards to birds and fish. • Small effects on bees.

COMMONLY USED PEST CONTROL PRODUCTS *(continued)*

NAME	NAME SOLD UNDER	CONTROLS	CHARACTERISTICS	CONCERNS
Dichlorvos (DDVP)	Vaportape® II No-Pest® Strip Vapona®	• When used in traps, adult moths are killed. Control of armyworm, webworm.	• Dichlorvos has both contact and stomach action in insects, and it also is a fumigant. • It inhibits the enzyme cholinesterase and interferes with the function of the nervous system.	• Classified as a mutagen and a possible human carcinogen (Class C). Not classified as a teratogen. • Laboratory tests have shown that dichlorvos may affect the immune system. In 1995, EPA proposed to restrict the use of DDVP to licensed operators but not restrict the use of outdoor traps as the exposure to humans is neglible through these traps.
Bendiocarb	Turcam Dycarb Ficam Garvox Multamat Multimet Niomil Rotate Seedox Tattoo	• Variety of insects, especially those in the soil. • Caterpillars, armyworms, web-worms, scale, ants, chinch bugs, white grubs, including Japanese beetle and crickets.	• Cholinesterase inhibitor, it kills by disrupting the nervous system.	• Moderately toxic to birds. • Highly toxic to fish and worms. • A carbamate type with an LD50 between 34–156 in rat studies. • Toxic to humans with repeated exposure.
Carbaryl	Sevin	• Ants, armyworms, bluegrass billbugs, centipedes, chiggers, chinch bugs, cutworms, earwigs, European chafer, fall army-worms, fleas, grasshoppers, leafhoppers, Lucerne moths, May/June beetles, millipedes, sod webworms, sowbugs, ticks (including ticks that cause Lyme disease), white grubs.	• Moderate reversible cholinesterase inhibitor. • Works by disrupting the nervous system.	• One of the top five best-selling pesticides. • Quite controversial. • Moderately toxic and is labeled with a WARNING signal word. Adverse effects in humans by skin contact, inhalation, or ingestion. • LD50 is 250 to 850. • EPA says if used properly, there is no risk to humans. • Lethal to bees, fish, worms, and moderately toxic to birds.

COMMONLY USED PEST CONTROL PRODUCTS *(continued)*

NAME	NAME SOLD UNDER	CONTROLS	CHARACTERISTICS	CONCERNS
Imidacloprid	Merit Admire Condifor Gaucho Premier Premise Provado Marathon	• White grubs, billbugs, scale, and ground pearl	• Works by interfering with the transmission of stimuli in the insect nervous system. • Nerve blocking action similar to nicotine poisoning. • Systemic control with contact and stomach action.	• LD50 is 450, which makes it moderately toxic. • Weakly mutagenic and noncarcinogenic. • Toxic to game birds. • Moderately toxic to aquatic life and highly toxic to bees.
Acephate	Orthene Asataf Pillarthene Kitron Aimthane Ortran Ortho 12420 Ortril Chrevron RE 12420 Orthene 755	• Sawflies, chinch bugs, cutworms, armyworms, webworms, grasshoppers, ants, leafhoppers, crickets	• Organophosphate with residual systemic action of 10 to 14 days. • Stomach action • Organiphosphate chemicals act by interfering with an essential nervous system enzyme, cholinesterase.	• LD50 = 500–5,000. • Relatively nontoxic to birds and fish. • Lethal to bees. • No long-term health problems to humans, but acute short-term problems with exposure. • Do not expose pregnant women to this product.
Malathion	Malathion	• Aphids, mites, scale, and a large number of other sucking and chewing insects. Very wide spectrum of insects killed.	• Kills by contact or digestion. • Organophosphate.	• One of the most widely used pesticides, controversial. • Possible mutagenic and carcinogenic effects. • Moderately toxic to birds, highly toxic to aquatic life. • LD50 = 480–10,700. • Variability seems related to protein in diet—less protein, the more toxic the chemical.

COMMONLY USED PEST CONTROL PRODUCTS *(continued)*

Name	Name Sold Under	Controls	Characteristics	Concerns
Trichlorfon	Dylox Proxol Dipterex	• Crickets, fleas, cutworms, Japanese beetles, white grubs, sod webworms	• Works by contact and stomach action. • Organophosphate.	• Highly toxic by all routes of exposure (skin, breathing, ingestion). Note symptoms may be delayed 1 to 4 weeks after exposure. • LD50 = 150–649. • Pregnant women or nursing mothers should avoid exposure. • Highly toxic to birds and aquatic life. • Minimum to moderate danger to nontarget beneficial insects including bees.
Chlorpyrifos	Dursban Lorsban Pageant Pyrate	• Cutworms, rootworms, grubs, fire ants, and many others	• Broad spectrum use. • Contact with minor stomach action. You have to get it to the pest to kill it. • Organophosphate	• LD50 = 82–270 so this is a moderately toxic product. • Easily absorbed through the skin. • Moderately toxic to birds. • Highly toxic to aquatic life and bees.
Diazinon	Diazinon	• Very broad spectrum control. Ants, aphids, wasps, billbugs, chinch bugs, cutworms, army-worms, white grubs, Japanese beetle grubs, fire ants, leafhoppers	• Non-systemic organophosphate. • Kills by contact and small stomach action. Stays active in soil for up to 6 months under ideal conditions of cool and damp. Stays on plants from 2 to 14 days.	• LD50 = 66–635. • Toxic to most birds and aquatic life. • Caution in humans is because it is easily absorbed and is a cholinesterase inhibitor (nerve damage). • One of most commonly used pest controls.

ited some cousins in Louisiana and she was bitten by one of these pests. She described it as being hit by a red hot needle that would not go away. Quite the swelling and quite the bite mark. Quite the pest.

Fire ants are a particular problem and I have read of many solutions. Not one of them claims to be effective in all cases. Here are a few ideas:

- Some homeowners swear by pouring gallons of hot water over the new nests to drive the ants away.
- Some use potent chemical drenches in hopes of killing the queen. For the latest in chemicals, check with your local garden center. Old chemical solutions such as Diazinon are no longer effective against fire ants and are therefore a waste of money.
- Predator nematodes will eat the larvae and destroy the colony if you apply enough of them to get to the nest before the guard ants discover them and kill them off. It's a battle down there.
- Traps exist that use a sugary bait to entice the workers to enter. They are then fried by solar energy. The theory is that if you capture enough of the workers, the colony will wither and die. Don't bet the farm on this one, but it helps. These are available at garden centers, through mail-order catalogs, or on the Internet.
- Researchers are working on fungus strains and establishing natural predators to control the pest.
- Diatomaceous earth is registered for the control of ants. It's hard to kill an entire colony but every little bit helps. Diatomaceous earth is the fossilized remnants of microscopic marine organisms. Their shells are razor sharp if you are ant-sized, and when the ant grooms the product off, it gets cut up and desiccates. It feels like talcum powder to pets and humans.

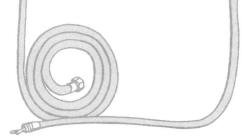

CHEMICAL HAZARDS

One problem that is starting to surface is the use of so-called inert products that are used in garden chemicals. If you look at the label of a garden product, it will have the amount of chemical and then a percentage of "inert" products. These products are sometimes more dangerous than the chemical they are working with. At the time of this writing, the EPA does not require them to be labeled as part of the warning. This is one more reason to consider the use of organic products.

Earwigs

Earwigs are another pest that prefer to eat decaying organic matter. They are a cosmetic problem around gardens where they take the odd chunk out of flowers, but they are not a lawn pest of any consequence.

Fleas

Fleas are not a problem for the lawn, although the lawn is a breeding ground. Beneficial nematodes can eliminate flea problems.

Wasps

Wasps sometimes nest in lawns and can be a real nuisance. I well remember the time I was tilling with my garden tractor and hit a wasp nest. Talk about your basic fast moving object! With a horde of them buzzing around me like crazy, I abandoned ship, left the tractor right where it was, and surrendered the field to the wasps. A few hours later, I was able to go back and retrieve the tractor—the wasps had moved on.

If you discover a ground-based wasp nest, there are two interesting methods of eliminating the problem. The first is to obtain one of the old-fashioned looking glass bell-cloches (available through mail-order catalogs) and put it over the hole. For the non-gardener, a bell-cloche is a glass bell that comes in various sizes ranging from only a few inches tall to 18 inches or slightly larger. The taller ones are best for wasp traps. The wasps don't realize there's something blocking their way and they don't dig a new exit. They just wither away.

The second method is to purchase a trap that is specific to ground wasps (again available through catalogue or Web retailers) and place it next to the wasp hole. Baited, the trap attracts wasps that can get in but can't figure out how to get out. You wind up with a trap full of dead and dying wasps and none left in the nest.

Or, you can discover the nest as I did and pay the price.

PESTICIDES TOXIC TO BEES

Do not apply these pesticides to flowering crops or weeds when bees are present.

Trade Name	Active Chemical Name
Ambush	Permethrin
Basudin	Diazinon
Cygon	Dimethoate
Guthion	Azinphosmethyl
Imidan	Phosmet
Lannate	Methomyl
Lorsban	Chlorpyrifos
Malathion	Malathion
Ripcord	Cypermethrin
Sniper	Aziinphos-methyl
Sevin	Carbaryl

Rodent Pests

Moles and Voles

Moles and voles love lawns—it's a ready-made source of dinner for these rodents. Moles are those lovable little fellows that creep around under the grass in search of grubs and earthworms. You know—Mr. Mole with the funny nose and terrible driving habits. Unfortunately, they leave little tunnels and entrance holes that resemble miniature volcanoes. Moles are meat eaters and do not bother the grass other then incidentally in their search for dinner. You can eliminate mole problems either by eliminating the grub problem on your lawn that they are searching for, or by using a product like Mole-med.

Mole-med is simply old-fashioned castor oil that is diluted and sprayed onto the lawn area. As far back as the late 1800s, garden writers were suggesting their readers should insert castor beans into the tunnels and spray castor oil over the garden to deter moles. These liquid products don't kill the mole, apparently the mole doesn't like the smell and moves on. (There is still debate over whether the castor bean is eaten or just avoided).

Voles, on the other hand, resemble short-tailed field mice, and they do love to eat grass roots. They are a bit harder to eliminate because the castor oil doesn't affect them. You might try a sonic torpedo. This is a tubular battery-operated apparatus that sets up a vibration when inserted into the ground that voles don't like. Other sonic devices are also advertised as effective against these creatures. Plug them in and the voles and mice will leave when the appropriate frequency is created. Check with your local pest management company.

Cats work really well. More than one cat owner has regaled me with tales of how much dear old tabby just loves to bring home "presents" to his owners.

I've heard mixed reports of the guillotine traps that are inserted into the tunnels. Some gardeners swear by them and some simply swear at them. I think this tool is one you have to try for yourself. I don't. Just for the record, I'm told that some of the traps with stronger springs actually do decapitate the rodents, while others merely break their necks. Dead is dead, however. And no, unless you go digging around in your lawn, you will not find the bodies.

DON'T TRAP AND MOVE

Often in garden writing, you'll see the recommendation to trap an animal and move it away from the garden. You might just as well trap it and shoot it.

Once you take an animal away from its territory and shelter you are simply exposing it to predators and the animal owners of the food territory you move it into. With no shelter and serious harassment from the territory owner, the moved animal cannot feed properly and is likely to be taken by a predator. So, instead of a clean quick death, you condemn the moved animal to a slow death by hunger, exposure, and predation.

Moving an animal away from your garden doesn't lessen the problem for you, either. With animals that have territories, another will simply move in and make your garden its territory as soon as the trapped animal is removed and nobody is defending that turf.

It is far better to come to some accommodation with the animal population or create conditions that naturally deter them from using your property as a restaurant.

Some gardeners carefully slice open the vole tunnel and insert a waterproof poison block for mice and rats. This works reasonably well—the poison is below ground where pets and children can't get to it, and it will last until the pest eats it. You'll get voles this way because they do eat the grain-based poison blocks. But remember that moles are carnivorous, so it probably won't attract them.

Mothballs do not work (the voles simply don't get moths) and chewing gum also doesn't work (except that the voles get cavities from all that sugar).

Large Animal Pests

Skunks and Raccoons

Sometimes when you go out on a clear summer's morning, your lawn will look like a miniature rototiller has gone over it. The sod will be turned back and chunks of grass will be lying about getting ready to die in the heat of the day.

This is the result of skunks, and sometimes raccoons. They have been going through your lawn looking for white grubs—and finding some. They seem to know where the grubs are and dig them up for supper.

There's good news in all this. First, you didn't know they were there last night because the dog still smells like a dog this morning. Second, you have a lot fewer grubs this morning than you did last night. But, you must admit, the grass looks a little the worse for wear. These nocturnal pests regularly visit our backyard. It's an improved farm pasture, really, where the dogs like to play. The skunks get the grubs and sometimes—they get the dogs. (I recommend a product called "Scent-off." Tomato juice doesn't work on Old English sheepdogs.)

A tight fence (it has to be a very tight fence because a skunk can get through spaces of only a few inches) will keep a skunk off your lawn, but the easiest thing to do is treat for lawn grubs. Once you eliminate the grubs, the skunks will stop making your home a lunch stop.

MOLE OR VOLE?

If you have trouble remembering which is which:

M = meat eater and these are Moles.

V = vegetation eater and these are Voles.

KEEP OFF THE GRASS

Armadillos

Although sort of a cute little animal (as opposed to skunks anyway), the nine-banded armadillo is a pest of lawns and gardens throughout the Southwest and Southeast. They burrow (sometimes as far down as 25 feet) into the soil around trees and their strong front claws are formidable digging tools. Besides fruit, armadillos simply have a craving for grubs, crickets, and earthworms. They use their efficient front feet to do some pretty impressive earth moving in their search for dinner.

Like a lot of nocturnal hunters, this pest is a creature of habit. Once it figures out that there is a food source in your lawn and garden, it will come back regularly to sample the menu. Like larger predators, armadillos establish a "run," a track they travel at regular intervals in search of the perfect night's food. If you are that source, you can expect to see armadillos almost every evening. The first one is cute, the second one is less so, and by the time you realize you're supporting the entire state's population of armadillos on your lawn (or at least the lawn looks like it), the fun has gone out of this curious little critter.

There are several keys here. The first is lawn grubs. If you don't have them, armadillos can't eat them. If they can't find and eat grubs, they won't visit your lawn. Just as with the more northerly skunk, control of lawn grubs is a first line of defense.

You may find that the armadillo is munching on other garden flowers and plants as well. In this case, use a squirrel or deer deterrent spray—one of the noxious tasting products—to convince this pest to eat elsewhere. The trick with these sprays is to use them regularly and often. Follow the label directions religiously. Like squirrels, if the pest thinks there's food there because he tasted something good once, he'll be back time and time again because he remembers the good taste. If you convince him on his first visit that everything tastes terrible, he won't put you on his "run."

There are a variety of noxious-tasting sprays on the market. Check with your local garden center. Some of these products have been pelletized so they can be used in the areas where creatures are digging.

CHAPTER EIGHT

Specialty
Lawn Areas

Golf Greens

The first thing that you have to understand about having your own golf green in the backyard is that it is a wonderful fantasy—and an incredible amount of work. The reality, unfortunately, is that this is the kind of project that many start and few finish. Of those who finish, only a few find they have the time, energy, and money to maintain the green in a usable form. You see, golf greens are probably the most highly managed bit of ground in use today. And if any single part of that management plan is missing or delayed, the green becomes unusable.

Having gotten that little bit of bad news out of the way . . .

Soil

If you decide that you really have to have your own grass golf green (and there are quite a few of you who do), then the first thing to understand is that the soil is the most critical component of the entire system. Water infiltration rates have to be high enough to handle almost any rainfall. The soil has to have adequate nutrient-holding capacity yet resist compaction, and it must be well aerated. All of these characteristics have to remain constant for a long period of time or you'll be rebuilding it constantly and expensively.

Golf course grass greens use sand as a base to build and sculpt the green. They also use a blend of sand to ensure the drainage is as good as the USGA table indicates it should be. Golf course construction pros mix and test the sand to ensure it meets the drainage specifications as well as the aeration specs. Then they test the soils for silt and clay content to make sure they are within bounds before adding them to the mix. Next, they add organic matter to ensure the soil will hold nutrients. Finally, the entire green is underlaid with drainage tiles to move water away from the green and sloped properly (at least a 1-degree slope) to keep the water moving and not flood out the bent grass.

USGA GUIDELINES

The U.S. Golf Association (USGA) has determined that these are the physical properties of the soils needed for good green construction.

Characteristic	Measurement
Bulk density	1.20–1.60 g/cm³
Porosity	40–55%
Total noncapillary porosity	15% or more
Water retention	12–25%, by weight
Infiltration rate	2–10 inches/hour
Silt content	5% or less
Clay content	3% or less

USGA Specifications for Physical Measurements of Greens Mixtures (USGA 1973).

FOR THE DIEHARD GOLFER

If you are truly a committed golfer, let me suggest you investigate the new forms of artificial turf that are available for practice golf greens. These nylon coverings look like and act like grass. They have hundreds of individual grass blades, and the balls roll exactly as they do on real turf with a roll factor of seven (same as for a real green). The turf "speed" can be adjusted by adding or subtracting sand (just as in the real world). So you can have variable practice conditions depending on your own needs. Want a fast green? Add a bit of sand. If you want slow greens today, sweep it off.

The size of the green and the surroundings (do you want sand traps or pond areas to surround your fantasy) dictate the final price. On average, figure between $20 to $30 a square foot. Twenty dollars for the bare-bones construction and $30 for sand traps, and so on. Get out the measuring tape!

Oh yeah, for the record—this cost is not that much different than for a real golf green (a PGA-size green can cost upward of $90,000 to construct), and you don't have to buy a special mower or do any work.

As the company says that installs these systems, "You can putt or you can cut."

On the home scale, the very first thing you should do is *ignore the entire USGA table and all thought of creating a sand-bedded green.* The only way you're going to succeed with a sand-based green is if you love growing grass more than you like golfing and if you are prepared to have the local grass company come and spray the darn thing every week for the multitude of diseases this kind of a lawn is prone to getting. These standards are set to handle the kinds of traffic the green gets from club play. Your small green won't get anywhere near this traffic, so you can make it a bit easier on yourself.

Bring in good topsoil—it should be on the sandy side—and create your green. If the soil is not sandy, then add sand to the soil to make a very sandy soil mix (70 percent soil and 30 percent sand). The green should be raised above the surrounding soil to increase the drainage. Don't just start mowing the grass short in one area, you'll likely kill it, and that won't help your golf game at all. Once you've created the shape of the green you want, at the height and roll you think appropriate, then the next step is to add organic matter. Get out the compost and add several pounds per square foot of green. Work it in with a tiller. Level and rake the green so all water will flow away from the green. You won't get this right the first time and after a serious rain, you'll see puddles forming on your green. Fill in these low spots with more sand-soil mix.

Grass

You usually get one of two choices for the grass on your green. Bent grass is the number one choice. If you live in the South, you can use Bermuda grass instead. You'll be disappointed if you try to use another species of grass. For example, if you try to use Kentucky bluegrass as your putting green, you'll kill it by cutting it short enough to putt on. Bent grass is really the choice here because it can tolerate this short mowing.

Greens should be in the full sun. Shade is not an option for the home putting green. There are enough problems to solve in establishing a home green without having to deal with shade.

Irrigation is almost a necessity, unless you like to stand for hours with a hose. Overhead sprinklers should be set on timers to deliver

MOW LIKE A PRO

Oh yeah—did anybody tell you that you can't mow a golf green with a regular lawn mower? A mower for the green will cost between $1,000 (used) and $5,000 (new). These are specialized mowers that can cut the bent grass at the correct height for golf.

KEEP OFF THE GRASS

water first thing in the morning when dew is on the ground. Try not to water if there is no dew; this will cut down on fungal problems by keeping the grass as dry as possible. When Mother Nature wets it with dew, then you can further wet it with your watering.

The problem with growing bent grass intensively is that it is prone to all manner of fungal and insect infestations. It will require cutting several times a week and a regular schedule of feeding and spraying. The big problem here is that the window of opportunity to maintain and solve problems is quite small. For example, if you miss mowing by a day or two, when you do cut, you'll take off too much leaf surface (remember no more than 30 percent at a time) to get the green back into playing condition. This stresses the grass and the next thing you know you have a fungal infestation. Unless you spray as soon as the fungus gets established (not when it has grown halfway across the green), you'll lose the stressed grass and large dead spots will trumpet your failure.

If this sounds pessimistic—well, it is. The construction of a golf green is fairly easy on a home scale. It's the maintenance that will kill you (and your green). If you like the challenge of growing grass—then this is your project. If you like golfing, then either go nylon or go to the course.

Play Areas

Kids are hard on grass. There are no two ways about it—the pitter patter of tiny feet can really ruin a grass plant's day. Grass is a resilient plant, but children and their playing are tougher than even this toughest of plants.

There are several tricks to keeping grass growing in areas where children play.

- Mow tall. The kids may not like it (they'll lose small toys in the grass), but if you mow the grass at least a half inch to a full inch taller than is normally recommended for your variety, the grass will be healthier and resist the stress better.

FURTHER THOUGHTS ON GOLF GREEN CONSTRUCTION

- Small home greens are fine because the short approach shot is from a chip shot off the green.
- Purchase a cup changer. Design your green so it has different approaches and several pin positions. Otherwise you'll get bored quickly.
- Slopes of between 5 percent and 2 percent will ensure good drainage yet still allow the ball to stop rolling after the putt. A steeper slope (especially just after mowing the grass quite short) will cause the ball to keep rolling. You can construct a steeper slope between golf greens or on the edge of the green. This slope can be 20 percent or more.
- The green will look better from the house if it is sloped from the back to the front (between 2 and 4 percent slope) as well as sloping in other directions for drainage purposes. Consider sloping part of the green to allow a run-up shot directly from the backyard approach.
- You can increase the enjoyment of the green by creating ridges, sand bunkers, and ponds around the green.

LAWN TRAFFIC TROUBLES

I often get questions about dogs playing in the backyard along with the kids. The question usually is, "I have these two dogs in a small backyard and they've killed all the grass with their running. How do I grow grass now because the dogs are all muddy when they come into the house?"

The short answer is that you don't. No matter what you do—if the traffic over the grass is too heavy, there is no other plant that will take the abuse better than grass. If grass won't grow there because of the traffic—you can either reduce the traffic or install a hard landscaping solution such as paving stones or outdoor carpet.

Sorry.

- If you have a chance to modify the soil, make sure it is not a heavy clay soil but rather a good sandy loam. The better the soil, the better the grass.
- Water thoroughly several times a week. Never let the grass go to the wilt stage or the blades will be broken off by passing feet.
- Pick varieties that handle stress better than others. Perennial ryegrass should always be chosen over Kentucky bluegrass for heavy traffic or play areas. See Chapter 1 for grass varieties.
- Use my spring repair system *every* year (see Doug's recipe on page 105) whether you think your grass needs it or not. Double up on the amount of compost you apply—the grass will need all the help it can get.
- Relax. The kids will be grown up pretty soon and then you can have a good lawn. In the meantime, enjoy the kids rather than the lawn.

Shade Lawns

Shade and lawn grass mix very much like oil and water. If you work at mixing the oil and water, they'll go together for a short time, but as soon as you stop, the blend comes apart. Similarly, if you work at growing grass in the shade all summer, you can accomplish a great deal. As soon as you stop, however, the shade will begin to weaken the grass and pretty soon your lawn is an advertisement for a "how not-to-do it" campaign.

The gnashing of gardener's teeth is not a pretty sound, but that's what I regularly hear when homeowners ask me about growing grass under the shade of evergreen or big deciduous trees. I have to explain that grass prefers full sunlight to grow well. Even the shade *tolerant* species prefer full sunlight. When the light goes down to 600 foot-candles under a tree, the grass is not going to grow. Evergreens create particularly dense shade conditions and grass simply will not grow under them.

Turf also needs good water availability to grow well. Tree roots, particularly from evergreens and big maples, suck up all available water with their extensive root systems. Remember that a big tree uses between 200 and 300 gallons of water every day, and they are much more efficient at scavenging for it than grass is.

Turf likes to be fed at the proper levels. Although tree needs aren't high, if the food is not available, the turf will be weaker. You see, tree roots get the food as well as the water.

So, how do you grow grass in shade? If you have enough sun to support life, here are some steps you can take that will help the grass look like a lawn and not like a war zone.

- *Use a proper grass species.* Some will tolerate shade more than others. Don't even bother trying to grow a full sun-lover species in the shade, it will only kill the grass and frustrate you. Within the shade-tolerant species, check with your garden center for new varieties of these grasses that have proved their ability to grow in the shade better than older varieties.
- *Use Doug's recipe* (page 105) every *spring*. Increase the grass seed from 2 pounds per 1,000 square feet to 3 pounds. You need to thicken up the turf and the only way to make the area look green is to increase the plant density.
- *Organic matter is very important as well.* Both the grass and the trees thrive on it. Add 50 percent extra compost over the recipe.
- *Water deeply at least once (preferably twice) a week.* If you don't water, you don't have grass. It's really that simple. To keep the grass you've planted alive, it must have water. In shady areas, the tree is getting the lion's share of the water. I can't emphasize this point enough. Other than the lack of sunlight, the lack of water is the number-one cause of death or lack of growth of grass in shady areas.
- *Mow taller than normal.* Add an extra inch to the grass height under trees. The grass needs every bit of leaf area it can get to capture sunlight. If you cut the shaded grass at the same height as the sun-site grass, the shaded plants will not have enough leaf area left to capture the low sunlight levels. Not enough sunlight equals weak grass. Yes, that means you'll have to adjust your mower before you take it under the tree to mow, and yes, that is a pain in the anatomy. You do, how-

SHADE TOLERANT HATES SHADE LEAST

Shade tolerant does not mean the grass likes the shade or even grows really well in the shade. It means exactly what it says—tolerant. A shade tolerant variety is simply the grass that hates shade the least.

KEEP OFF THE GRASS

ever, have a choice—mow tall or have poor grass. I suggest you leave your shade mowing to the end of the first mowing session and then adjust the mower once to do all the shade areas. Next time you mow, start with the shady areas and adjust the mower to do the sunnier areas. This way, you only adjust your mower once each mowing session.

- Only water when there is dew on the ground. Fungus and bacteria love dark, damp conditions. So, when Mother Nature puts water on the ground, take advantage of it to apply extra water to keep the grass happy. When Mother Nature leaves the grass dry, you should consider doing the same.

Finally, there are some shady conditions where grass simply will not grow. If you've tried the techniques I've suggested and your grass still looks weak and thin, read Chapter 9 for some alternatives to grass.

Pathways

Grass grown on pathways needs special care if the garden is to be heavily visited. Grow the pathway taller than you would a lawn (at least 1 inch taller), so the grass has a chance to store the energy needed to combat the foot traffic. Do not overfeed the pathway grass; this will create a lush turf, easily damaged by foot traffic. Pathways also require regular core aeration because the traffic will compact the soil.

The soil for a heavily traveled grass pathway should be more like a golf putting green than a lawn. Amend the soil with extra sand to combat compaction.

Use a perennial ryegrass in the North or Bermuda grass in the South; you need a grass species that will handle the foot traffic better than others.

Mechanically edge the edges of the path with a material appropriate to the garden. White plastic fencing looks slightly tacky if the garden is a mixed perennial border in the grand cottage garden style. The best edging for informal gardens is one that is invisible.

If you don't use a mechanical edging, you will need to become familiar with the lawn edging tool. This halfmoon–shaped cutting device is the tool of choice, and a well sharpened edger in the hands of an experienced gardener can make short (and really neat) work of a pathway border. A sharp edger does not have to be used like a shovel but can be used more like a knife, slicing through the roots trying to invade the garden soils.

Seats

The uses of grass are only limited by your imagination. One of the favorite garden seats in 1800s England was a bench with grass for a seat. The top of the bench had raised edges (some were hollow right to the ground) to hold the soil and the turf was grown in that space, much like a big, square flower pot. The turf was hand-clipped to keep it short. Gentlemen and ladies could have the pleasure of sitting on the grass without having to bend over.

Containers

Although ornamental grasses are often grown in large containers, there is no reason lawn grasses cannot be grown in similar ways. A pot of grass grown on a sunny windowsill and put into the bird's cage or left for "kitty" to chew on will liven up most household menageries.

Use a regular potting soil and sprinkle grass seed on top of the soil. Cover it lightly with an eighth inch of soil. Keep damp and warm, and within a few days, you'll have a small pot for the cat or bird to enjoy.

Tennis Courts

If you've always wanted to get to center court, but your backhand is holding you back—here's your answer. Make your own court. Follow these simple rules and you too can star on grass:

- Orient the court north and south so the setting sun does not shine into the face of one of the players.

- Make the grade quite low. Between 1:100 to 1:150 is ideal. This will move the water away from the court (you can't play with standing water on the court), yet still be level enough for fast tennis.
- You'll need a minimum of 144 by 56 feet for a single court. This will give you space for the court and the necessary backcourt area to enable you to play the ball on those wicked serves your partner has been working on.
- Remember, the grass mix has to recover from wear quickly. Perennial ryegrass and chewings fescue mixes are the best for this kind of recovery. A planting ratio of 50:50 will work quite nicely. Bermuda grass would be the best choice for a southern grass choice.

There is no particular soil recommended for a home grass court other than avoiding very sandy soils. They do not perform well under the rapid starting and stopping of a tennis game. They also tend to "scuff" and create divots more than clay soils would.

Keep the grass to ½ to ¾ inch in height. This will entail a serious regimen of disease and insect control because the turf will not appreciate being kept this short. During dry spells, you'll have to water at least twice a week to keep the turf growing. Aerating is a variable. The more you play on the court, the more often you'll have to aerate the soil. Three times a season is the maximum expected and never aerate during a dry spell but rather when the grass is actively growing.

Mow with a sharp reel-type mower for best ball action and plant health.

Good luck with that backhand.

Croquet Lawns

You *can* play croquet on any lawn but to have a really good playing experience a certain standard should be met. I mean, how can you expect your friends—suitably clothed in their summer whites—to play on anything less than perfection?

"It simply wouldn't do," as a grand old friend used to say.

To begin with, you need at least 105 feet by 84 feet to have a regulation-size croquet lawn. I know, I know—you've never played on one that big in your life, but that's the rule, folks. It must be flat; you obviously don't want the struck balls rolling downhill. The grass must be mown to ¼ to ½ inch in height (about the same as the average golf green). After all, there are standards.

Grow the grass exactly like a tennis court for best results.

Mazes and Labyrinths

The difference between a maze and a labyrinth is really quite easy to understand. You can get lost in a maze, but there is only one way into and out of a labyrinth so you can't get lost. A maze is for your amusement, while a labyrinth has a long history of meditative use.

We regularly cut a labyrinth in our back garden during the summer months. It makes a wonderful walking meditation area and is easy to accomplish. The first step is to allow the entire lawn to grow an inch longer than normal. Then readjust the mower setting so the mower deck is at its normal setting. Mow the pattern at this regular setting. You'll be creating a pattern in the grass that will allow you to see and follow the pathway without any problem at all.

On my lawn, I have a regular riding mower that I use for the bulk of my cutting and a much smaller (and narrower) electric mower that I use to cut the pathways. Once the pathways are cut, I just mow over the top of them with the riding mower to keep the path separations cut to the proper height. I mow the pathways after the regular lawn mowing just to keep them distinct.

With mazes, the sky is the limit. You start in exactly the same way, by letting the grass grow an extra inch or two taller. Then you use a narrow mower to cut the pathways you have already designed on paper. Trust me on this one. You want to design first on paper; behind a mower is not a good place to be making these decisions.

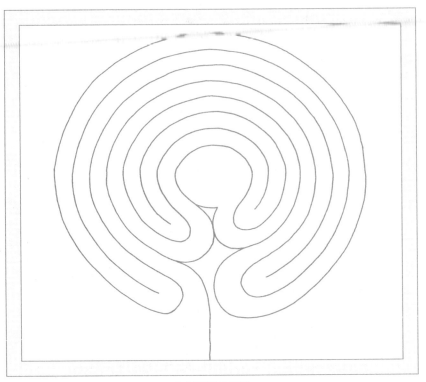

LABYRINTH

This is an excellent birthday party activity. Design and cut a maze and let the kids go figure it out. That should keep them out of your hair for—oh—two or three seconds. Speaking from the personal experience of four children and numerous parties, no other activity lasts that long during birthday parties. Consider it a challenge.

Once you are tired of having a labyrinth or maze, simple set the mower deck to the height of the pathways and mow. The pattern will disappear shortly because the grass heights are now consistent across the lawn. The wear traffic pattern may take a few weeks to regrow (depending on how often you used it), but within a month, the pattern will have disappeared.

CHAPTER NINE

Alternatives to Lawns

This is a book about lawns, but in many lawn areas there is always a place where the grass won't quite grow well or where it's too hard to mow or . . . I'm sure you get the idea. Quite likely, you've even got the spot. So, here's a quick primer on alternatives to grass.

Ground Covers

Ground covers have a tremendous appeal to gardeners. Just think, here's a plant that grows almost anywhere, spreads around, produces flowers, and will grow in your garden. Not only that, gardening folklore says that once a ground cover is established, it will prevent weeds from germinating and growing. Gardeners who don't know any better also say that ground covers will compete with grass and crowd it out.

Myths

The reality is that there are some good features of ground covers, but there are also some myths running around the gardening world as well. Here are a few myths I've heard.

- *Ground covers will eliminate grass from your garden.* I wish I had a nickel for every gardener who told me that because they had heard it somewhere. Grass is a strong grower and one of the most competitive plants in the garden. There is no ground cover that you can grow that will smother grass. In fact, the opposite is true; you'll have to kill off the grass to establish the ground cover, and then you'll have to weed out any invading grass on a regular basis. This is particularly true for sunnier areas. Shadier gardens have less trouble with grass-invading ground covers. After all, grass doesn't grow well in the shade; that's why we are using a ground cover in the first place. Having said all that, a well established ground cover will reduce weed-seed germination because it shades the soil, reducing the sunlight needed by many seeds to induce germination.

- *Ground covers are no work.* The reality is that a good ground cover is work. It is, however, a different kind of work. There is no weekly mowing, but you do have to weed and prune off dead chunks and replace winter damage and perform other chores associated with growing plants. You can grow one single plant or you can grow a bunch of them together and call them ground covers. The reality is that it is still gardening and will require some labor.

- *Ground covers are fast to establish themselves.* Well, maybe. Some such as English ivy are pretty fast, establishing a good mat in a year or two. Others such as Vinca major (periwinkle) will take a few years to establish themselves. In the meantime, you'll have an ugly bare spot to contend with. Using an evergreen shrub as a ground cover means a multiyear investment in patience. That's the reality of establishing plants. They work on their own timetables and none are as quick to establish as turfgrasses.

- *You don't have to water or feed ground covers.* Why not? They're in the garden and, if they're under the shade of a tree, they are competing with the tree for available water and nutrients. I guess you don't have to water and feed ground covers, and in return, they don't have to grow very well either.

- *Some ground covers will bloom all summer.* I know of only one ground cover that blooms for an extended period during the summer and it is a weedy plant not suited for a decent garden because of its rapacious nature. Crownvetch has a muddy pinkish flower that blooms for a long time in the summer and is suited only for wilder areas or holding down the soil on steep slopes. It self-sows so prolifically that, if allowed into a good garden area, it will quickly take over. It is quite difficult to eradicate once established. Ground covers are normally grown for their foliage and ability to . . . well, cover the ground.

So, is there a plant that will grow in the sunlight provided by the average closet, and flower all summer with absolutely no care? Sorry, only in our dreams. To make things easier though, here are a few things to think about before you plant your ground covers and then I'll give you a listing of some of the more popular plants.

Selecting a Good Ground Cover

Remember, this is a book about growing lawns so the only reason we're choosing a ground cover is that the grass won't grow in that spot. As the author, I can only say that if grass will grow and you don't want to grow it, then you bought the wrong book.

If drainage is poor and the area is wet, you have the option of either draining the ground or installing a bog garden. Similarly, if pH (acidity) is a problem, then you can modify the soil with either lime (to make it less acidic) or sulfur (to make it more acidic). If grass won't grow because of soil fertility problems, get out the compost and fertilizer and correct the problem.

This leaves shade as the final reason the grass won't grow. So, you can either cut down the trees creating the shade (a poor idea in my opinion) or grow an alternative ground cover in this area. I've listed some of the more common ground covers on the next few pages along with some comments about how to grow them.

Preparing the Bed

This is the easy part to write about; the instructions are quite simple. Prepare the ground cover bed in exactly the same way as you would any other lawn area. Remember these rules:

- Make sure the ground is level and free of all stones, weeds, and debris.
- Till organic matter such as compost into the soil if possible. Otherwise, if there are too many tree roots, spread it over the ground where you can incorporate it as you plant.
- Use a starter fertilizer, something with a high phosphorus (second number) and low nitrogen (first number) ratio to boost root growth.
- Rake the area to prepare for planting and then install the plants.

The only difficulty you may have is tree roots in the planting area and you don't want to chop them up to cultivate the soil. Neither do you want to bring in soil to raise the soil line above the roots (this cuts off oxygen from the tree roots and damages the tree). The only option here is to work manually around the major roots, hand-digging the spaces between the roots and adding compost to these areas. You will wind up chopping up many of the tree's smaller feeder roots but, although this isn't ideal, the tree will survive.

Install the ground cover plants in the worked areas. If you adequately water and feed them, they will colonize over the top of the roots.

The only caution is that if you are planting ground cover plants this far under a large tree, make sure the ground cover plant is one that will tolerate such deep shade conditions. Remember that grass won't grow under there; you have to plan for a deep shade-loving perennial. We had the perennial plant Hosta growing under a very large wild apple tree, and the difference between the plants on the outer edges of the tree's shade and those right up against the trunk was quite pronounced. Those on the edges were bigger and healthier than their more deeply shaded neighbors. Given that watering and feeding was the same for the entire bed, the only difference was in the amount of sunlight the plants received. Even shade-tolerating plants will not grow as quickly or bloom as heavily in the deep shade close to tree trunks. This problem is worse under evergreen trees than under their deciduous cousins.

Planting

The closer you plant your ground cover, the faster they will fill in. That seems pretty obvious. The problem is that the closer you plant your ground cover, the more plants you require, and the more expensive it becomes to create that perfect garden carpet. Hey, nobody said gardening was cheap. If you need a large number of plants, you can usually make a deal with your local garden center (particularly if you order them several months ahead of time) to obtain landscaper plants at almost-landscaper pricing.

SLOPED GROUND

One other reason why you might want to consider a form of ground cover is the slope of the ground. If it is too sloped to easily mow, ground cover can be a good alternative.

Landscaper plants differ from retail plants in that the retail plants are almost always sold in small pots with a tag or in four- or six-packs with a tag. These are more expensive. Landscaper plants come in a large flat with no pots, no tags, and minimum amounts of soil on the roots. They are much cheaper, but they take a bit more care to plant (due to the lack of soil on the roots) and more care (more watering) after planting to compensate for the reduced root surface. So, if you have a lot of plants to install—at least several hundred (each landscaper flat will have 50 to 100 plants, depending on the variety)—then you might try seeing if your local garden center can help you out. Plan ahead. Do not go in on the day you want to plant and ask for landscaper pricing—it isn't going to happen.

The actual installation of each plant is as simple as digging a hole and burying the roots. The key is to make sure that the soil is damp

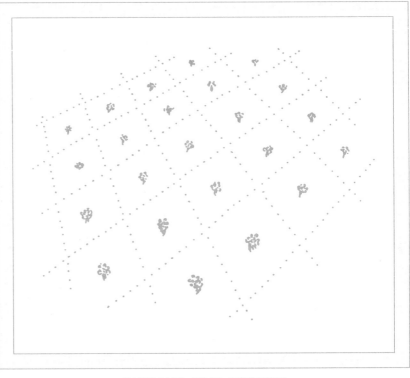

DIAMOND GRID PATTERN

when the plants are installed and to water the area well immediately after planting. When I say well watered, I mean turn the area into a mud pie. The plants will look horrid—half-wilted, mud-spattered, with leaves half covered in mud—but they will quickly recover and start growing. Without the mud bath, the plants will struggle. Water daily for the first two weeks and then slowly cut back. Make sure the ground stays moist for at least the first two months if you want to get those ground cover plants to grow and compete with the trees.

When the pros install ground covers, they plant them in a diamond grid pattern. Each plant goes in the middle of the diamond so if you look at the planting from a distance, each plant lines up in several different directions with other plants. This ensures a quick fill-in time with a consistent root area given to each plant.

Hardiness and Winter Protection

For the most part, ground covers should not require winter protection. If you have to work to protect your ground cover with mulches or covering insulation, get a new ground cover. Ground covers are about reducing work. They are not a garden feature that should demand extra work.

Do not feed ground cover in the fall. Feeding only stimulates tender growth and this tender growth is more easily winterkilled.

A local garden center will be able to give you hardiness ratings for most of the ground covers in your gardening zone.

Watering

Ground covers require water, particularly if they are in the shade and rootzone of large trees. You can plan on applying at least 1 to 1½ inches of water a week to the ground cover to keep it growing. Slightly heavier watering, at 2 inches a week, will be necessary during the heat of the summer when the trees are at their greediest, sucking up all available moisture.

As with lawns, the best thing to do is establish a sprinkler system or in this case a drip irrigation system to automatically do the watering for you. Not only does the sprinkler ensure you have equal water applied to all plants, it also cleans the plant leaves since it doesn't create the same water flow as a hose.

HOW MANY PLANTS TO FILL YOUR BED?

Use this table to find the number of plants you require to fill your bed. The left-hand column is the spacing you've chosen. Divide the square footage of your bed by the number in the right-hand column. The resulting number is the number of plants you need to fill your bed at your chosen spacing.

SPACING IN INCHES	DIVIDE YOUR BED FOOTAGE BY:
4	0.11
6	0.25
8	0.44
10	0.7
12	1.0
15	1.56
18	2.25
24	4.0
30	6.25
36	9.0
48	16.0
60	25.0

As with all garden plants, do not water after August to allow the plant to begin to harden off. This bit of water stress at this time (remember that the fall rains will be ample to sustain life) will help the plant get a bit tougher in preparation for winter.

Controlling Weeds

Controlling weeds in ground covers is mostly done using the Armstrong method. (Arm strong—strong arm—get it?) Yes, that's right—by pulling the weeds out by hand.

Hand weeding is a time-honored tradition in ground cover patches. Give it a thorough going-over first thing in the spring as soon as the weeds start to germinate.

Corn gluten will stop weed seeds from germinating in any ground cover plant and does not harm established plants. Unfortunately, the same cannot be said about other pre-emergent herbicides used on ornamental crops. Read the label before you use any chemical as a pre-emergent weed control in ground covers.

Mulches work well for many ground covers. Lay down the mulch in the fall and the perennial ground cover will grow up through the mulch while the annual germinating seeds either will be prevented from germinating or can easily be weeded as they try to establish themselves. This, of course, implies that you have removed all perennial weeds (or stopped them from establishing themselves), because they will grow through a mulch as well. It is difficult to mulch evergreen ground covers or ground-hugging plants such as Ajuga; the mulch is difficult to apply in the first case, and smothers out the plant in the second.

Do not use lawn herbicides on ground covers. These will, for the most part, treat the ground covers as weeds and either kill them or stunt their growth. Also, when applying chemicals to the lawn, take care that they do not drift over onto the ground cover area.

Feeding

A ground cover is much like any other garden plant, it will only thrive if it is fed properly. The easiest way is to spread compost over the plants in the very early spring before they start to grow. The compost will settle down to the soil and the new growth will come up through it. With evergreen ground covers, still apply compost first thing in the spring, but then water the area heavily to wash the compost off the leaves down to the ground.

Do not apply lawn fertilizer to ground covers. Lawn formulations are too high in nitrogen and will burn the ground cover. Take care to avoid sprinkling lawn fertilizer onto ground covers that are on the edges of lawn areas. This is particularly true of weed-and-feed formulas, not only will the fertilizer burn the ground cover but the herbicide will damage it as well—a double dose of problems.

General plant food with a balanced formula, (e.g., 10-10-10) can be substituted for compost when applied at the correct amount (see the label for directions). However, compost is still the undisputed champion at feeding ground covers.

Pruning

Generally, if you want a ground cover for low maintenance, you just don't prune it. However, depending on the plant, you may find that some pruning is a good idea at certain times of the year. For example, some gardeners like to cut the dead flower stalks off spring-flowering plants with a string trimmer to neaten up the look of the ground cover. With plants that get too tall and leggy such as Aegopodium, a string trimmer or lawn mower set to 4 to 6 inches does a good job of bringing the plant back to size and thickens up the stand. Instead of a leggy mess, you'll have an attractive planting after the week or two it takes the plant to regrow. With either of these situations, do not scalp the plant too close to the ground or you'll weaken it. With some flowering plants such as geraniums, a heavy pruning after the first bloom flush will bring on a second bloom later in the season.

Never prune a plant in the late summer or early fall before it has been knocked back by a hard frost. Pruning in late summer will cause the plant to throw new shoots and these may not harden off enough by winter to survive. The mess of the dead foliage the following spring and the weakened plant (it spent all its energy producing a shoot that didn't survive to replenish the root) are not the kinds of situations you want in your garden.

GROUND COVERS: SNEAKY AND AGGRESSIVE

The reality of ground covers is that, by and large, they are aggressive spreading plants. They will not be content to stay where you plant them. For example, a common name for Ajuga is bugleweed. Once this plant escapes from the ground cover area into the lawn, we now call it buglelawn. The Ajuga is too low to be hurt by the lawnmower and it will take herbicide or determined hand-weeding to eliminate it.

We made the mistake of allowing a *Lamiastrum* cultivar out into the garden, because I thought I wanted its silvery foliage to mix with the plants that were already there. It took three years of steady digging to remove it from the bed after I decided it was no longer welcome. Most ground covers have a place in the plan of the garden, but that place is usually not in a flower bed.

A sharp shovel is necessary to limit the expansion of most ground covers once they are happily established where you want them. Use this shovel every spring and *immediately* on seeing an escapee.

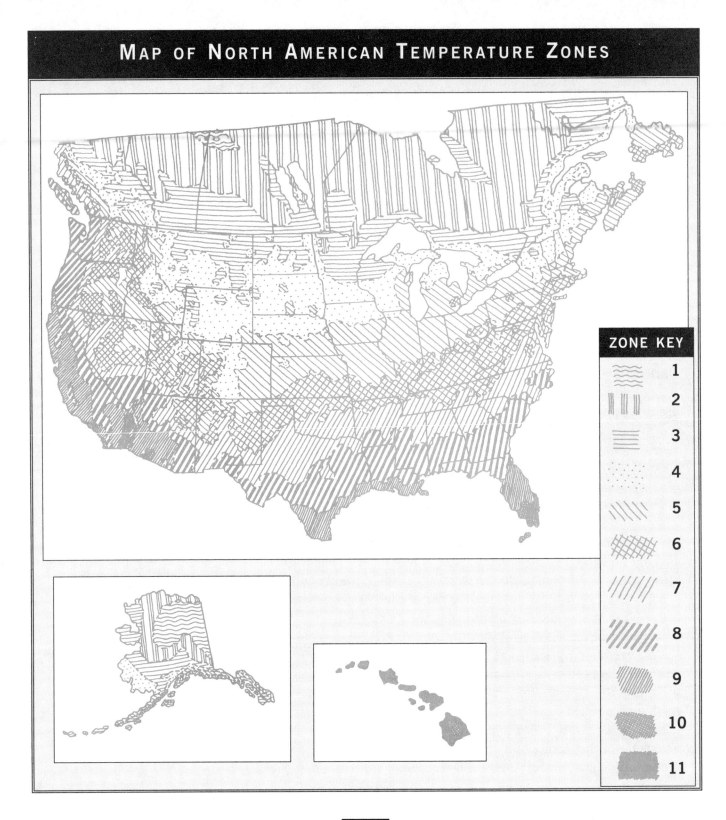

MAP OF NORTH AMERICAN TEMPERATURE ZONES

ZONE KEY

1
2
3
4
5
6
7
8
9
10
11

GROUND COVER PLANTING CHART

NAME	APPROX. ZONE HARDINESS	SPACING (INCHES)	COMMENTS
Aegopodium podagraria (Goutweed)	3	12	Vigorous grower, will smother less aggressive plants. Hardy and aggressive, 18 inches tall. Mow when it gets straggly. Easy to grow, hard to eliminate.
Ajuga species and cultivars (Bugleweed)	4	12–18	Vigorous, semi-evergreen. Dense mats, 4 to 6 inches tall. Full sun to heavy shade. Prefers moist but well drained soils. Shallow rooted, so dry soils are a problem. Protect from winter winds.
Asarum canadense (Wild ginger)	3	12–18	Deciduous, fast growing, 6 inches tall, hardier than the European form. Wonderful for shade to dense shade. Fast establishing.
Asarum europaeum (Wild ginger)	4	12–18	Evergreen, 5 to 6 inches tall, slightly more tender than native form. Likes organic soils in shade, slow to establish. Without snow cover, protect from harsh winter winds.
Brunnera macrophylla (Hardy forget-me-not)		18–24	Deciduous, forget-me-not type blue flowers in spring, rough foliage, 18 to 24 inches tall. Grows almost anywhere but does best in part shade with good organic soils. Plants grown in full sunlight will show **scorched** leaves in midsummer.
Campanula poscharskyana (Bluebells)	3	18	Self sows with abandon, and will pop up almost everywhere it can find a protected spot to germinate. Grows 12 to 18 inches tall. Long bloom time, excellent blue flowers. Grows in sun to part shade in almost any soil except heavy clay and hot and dry conditions.
Cerastium tomentosum (Snow on the mountain, Snow-in-summer)	3	24	Vigorous grower with silvery foliage, 18 to 24 inches tall. Inconsequential white flowers produced on this rampant grower in midsummer. Wants full sun. Well drained, poor soil is best. Feed it and it grows open, floppy, ugly stems.
Convallaria majalis (Lily of the valley)	2	12–18	Deciduous, shade lover that grows 8 inches tall. Very fragrant spring flowers. Will slowly expand to cover a wide area. Will grow in almost any soil. Too much sun burns the leaves. If grown under trees, feed every spring to help it compete.
Coronilla varia (Crownvetch)	3	18	Deciduous, sprawling, invasive grower, 18 to 24 inches tall. Good for banks in rough places, (e.g. steep banks beside highways). Slow to establish, hard to eradicate. Muddy pink flowers in June to July. Does best in full sun, tolerates shade. Mow to keep compact.
Epimedium species (Barrenwort)	3–4	12	Deciduous in North, semi-evergreen in warmer areas, 8 to 12 inches tall. Flowers in May, colors depend on species. Slow growing but nice plant for a garden setting. Best in part to full shade in rich soils. No dry soils. Does well under trees if kept damp. Excellent plant.
Galium odorata (Sweet woodruff)	4	12–18	Deciduous, (evergreen in warmer climates) delicate looking, does best in medium to deep shade in moist soil with adequate organic matter. Combine with English ivy.

GROUND COVER PLANTING CHART (continued)

NAME	APPROX. ZONE HARDINESS	SPACING (INCHES)	COMMENTS
Geranium species (Cranesbill)	3	18–24	Easy to grow, thrives in organic soils in sun to part shade, 6 to 18 inches tall. Do not fertilize or will grow sparsely. Prune heavily after blooming to rebloom. May need thinning or rejuvenation every 4 to 5 years.
Hemerocallis (Daylily)	2–3	18–24	Most are deciduous, some southern varieties are evergreen, 12 to 36 inches tall. Flowers heavily in July (although newer forms have longer bloom times). Grows best in sun to light shade, easy to grow. Fills in quickly but not an aggressive spreader. Not bothered by pests or disease.
Hosta species (Funkia, plantain lily)	2–3	18–24	Deciduous, part shade to shade lovers, 6 to 35 inches tall. Blooms in July with lilylike stems. Will grow in sun if kept moist, but otherwise does poorly in sun. Many different cultivars to mix and match for a wonderful garden design.
Lamiastrum galeobdolon "variegata" (Yellow archangel)	4	24–30	Deciduous, trailing, vinelike, aggressive spreader, mounding 18 to 24 inches tall. Yellow flowers in May to June. Grows almost anywhere except deep shade and dry soils. Give it water and it will grow anywhere! Easy to grow, hard to kill.
Lathyrus latifolius (Perennial sweet pea)	3	24–30	Wandering vine that mounds or scrambles up over banks. Self-sows but is not dense, plants can grow up through it. Flowers in midsummer. Grows best in full sun but will tolerate part shade. Once established, it survives neglect easily in rough places.
Lysimachia nummularia (Moneywort)	3	18	All of the Lysimachia family are rampant spreaders, from the shortest like L. nummularia (2 inches) to the taller like L. clethroides (3 feet). Grows in sun or shade and has bright yellow flowers in midsummer. Prefers damp soils. Will invade the lawn and is difficult to eradicate because of its low-growing nature.
Pachysandra terminalis (Japanese spurge)	4	12	Evergreen plant, slow to establish. Pest free, 12 inches tall. Grows best in damp shade with rich soil but will tolerate dry part shade once established. Will burn in the harsh sunlight.
Phlox subulata	3	18	Evergreen to semi-evergreen depending on cultivar, but may burn a bit over the winter, 4 to 6 inches tall. Sun to light shade. Blooms in a variety of colors in early spring. Grows best in well-drained soils; clay soils will kill it. Does not require heavy feeding.
Polygonum cuspidatum var. compactum (Fleeceflower)			Decidous, vigorous grower, 12 to 24 inches tall. Spreads by underground rhizomes—fast! Quite attractive foliage—reddish shades depending on season. Grows best in full sun, in almost any soil except heavy clay. Shear first thing in spring before new growth starts for best performance. Do not let loose in good garden.

GROUND COVER PLANTING CHART *(continued)*

NAME	APPROX. ZONE HARDINESS	SPACING (INCHES)	COMMENTS
Potentilla tabernaemontani	4	18–24	Deciduous (may be evergreen in warm climates), 3 to 6 inches tall. Spreads by aboveground rooting stems and is fast/invasive. Bright yellow flowers. Grows in well drained but not fertile soils. Best in full sun but tolerates some shade (flowers reduced in shade). Easy to grow, hard to contain.
Sedum	3	12–18	Large family of sun-loving, spreading plants. Normally 2 to 6 inches tall. Grows best in sunshine and well drained soils but will tolerate some shade. In shade, becomes thin and sparse. Damp soils and heavy clay will usually stunt them. Some species, (e.g. *S. acre*) classed as weeds in some jurisdictions. Easy to grow, long-lived. Most often used in rocky areas such as rock gardens.
Teucrium chamaedrys (Germander)	4	18	Deciduous in cold climates and evergreen in warm, 8 to 18 inches tall. Spreads 12 to 18 inches wide with wonderful purple-rose flowers in June to July, sporadically afterward. Mulch the first season or two until well established. Prune in early spring to remove winterkilled branches. Excellent, noninvasive plant for sun or very light shade.
Veronica species (Creeping speedwell)	4–5	12–18	Deciduous plant, 8 to 18 inches tall. Some species are classed as lawn weeds in some jurisdictions. Mostly spreads by seed or aboveground rooting stems. Bluish flowers in May and June. Easy to grow, hard to eradicate from lawn if it colonizes.
Vinca minor (Periwinkle)	4	12–18	Deciduous to evergreen depending on climate, 8 to 18 inches tall. Starts slowly but once established grows quickly. Forms a mat of stems and leaves with bluish flowers. Does well in most soils except heavy clay or waterlogged. Prefers shade and part shade garden areas. Shear in spring for thicker growth.
Waldsteinia ternata (Wild strawberry)	4	18–24	Evergreen to semi-evergreen, 4 to 6 inches tall. Does best in full sun but will tolerate shade. In shade, sparser growing. Grows well in almost any soil except heavy clay. Loves organic matter in the soil.

We've discussed the most commonly used perennial ground covers, but you should also understand that any plant—if installed closely enough together—can act as a ground cover. A perfect example of this is Nepeta or catmint. If planted 18 inches apart, Nepeta will grow together to form a wonderful mass of violet blooms and fragrant foliage. There are several ornamental forms that are a delight in the perennial garden and would be even more delightful planted in a mass of ground cover.

If you have a favorite plant and it grows well enough in the area you want to cover (instead of grass), then experiment with it as a ground cover by planting it close enough to its neighbor. Don't be side-tracked by a list of common plants if you have, or desire, an uncommonly delightful garden.

Ornamental Grass

In short, ornamental grasses require everything that your lawn grass varieties need. They do not differ in sunlight or watering needs, although they can and do respond well to much less fertilizer than turfgrasses. You only mow them once in the very early spring before they start growing to cut down last year's tall foliage. There is no summer mowing. In masses, they will be prone to many of the same insects or diseases that plague normal turfgrass lawns. However, they are so vigorous and tall that you'll never see most insects or disease conditions.

Ornamental grasses are primarily for ornamental purposes and not to replace a lawn, unless you like the look of masses of tallish grass that resembles a hay field more than a lawn. There is no doubt though that massed ornamental grasses can be very attractive. For example, some of the shorter species (such as *Festuca glauca*) growing between 8 and 18 inches, make a delightful show when planted closely together. The different colors and textures of these grasses give the area more of a garden look than that of a lawn.

Try them on a small scale on the edge of your lawn before you commit yourself to using them on a larger ground cover scale. Also, many of these grasses grow so quickly that you can divide and propagate much of your own needs from a few mother plants. If you plant a grass such as ribbon-grass (*Phalaris* species) next to a neighbor's yard, you'll quickly become unpopular as it spreads.

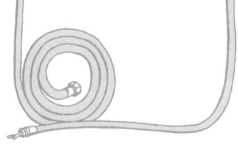

MORE IS BETTER

A general rule of thumb when planting perennials for wild-flower establishment is to use one plant per square foot in your design. This will fill in the garden area fairly quickly at a reasonable price. If you plant fewer than this, say one plant per 2 square feet, you'll have open spaces for weeds to colonize. If you plant more than this density, it will fill in more quickly.

As with much of gardening with plants—more *is* better.

Wildflower Lawn

A wildflower lawn swaying in the breeze is a visual delight and a dream shared by many gardeners. Unfortunately, the reality is not quite so easy as the dream would suggest. If you simply toss some seeds from a can around your garden and hope for the best, you'll be disappointed. If, however, you follow a well-defined plan, you can create a wonderful wildflower garden that will be the envy of your neighborhood.

The first thing you have to understand is that lawngrass and wildflowers do not mix in the same area. You'll have to eliminate the grass before you can plant your flowers. This is the mistake that many gardeners make when trying this lawn alternative because instructions are not all that clear on this point. Grass will invade this bed and it will smother out the flowers if you let it. In addition, your major difficulty in both establishing the bed and maintaining it will be the annual and perennial broadleaf weeds that want to colonize this area. Make no mistake about it, you'll have to become very familiar with your hand-weeding spud in the first few years of your wildflower lawn.

Step 1, therefore, is to kill all the grass in the area you want to use as a wildflower lawn. You can do this with a herbicide or you can smother it with black plastic (2 to 3 months) or solarize it with clear plastic (2 to 3 months but no weed seeds are left either). Or you could constantly till up the area to kill the grass plants and emerging weeds. Constant tilling will kill the grass over the course of a summer. This is probably one of the most important steps in the whole process and your success or failure at this step will determine the beauty of your wildflower patch.

Step 2 is to decide on the species of flowers you want by reading books or catalogs on native wildflowers (you do want to use natives, don't you?). You'll find resources for seed and plants in these books and catalogs.

Step 3 is to decide whether you want to use seeds or plants. Seed is cheaper by far, but it will take longer to establish the wild-flower lawn than if year-old plants are purchased. Wildflower mixes sold in seed racks contain a high proportion of annual plant seeds. This ensures you obtain some color the first year, but after that, the lower proportion of perennial seed is not going to fill in the garden area very quickly. Seed has the advantage of being whimsical in its layout; with plants you can design the color scheme and planting mix. Purchasing plants is also a faster route to success because the nursery has already germinated the seed and grown the plant for at least a year.

Small areas can easily be hand-sown. A small seed spreader (you can rent them) will do the job more evenly.

After sowing, roll the area with a quarter-filled roller to ensure the seed is in contact with the soil. You can cover with a thin layer of compost and water the garden area thoroughly to aid in germination.

Water the lawn area regularly every few days to keep the soil damp. This will aid seed germination. Many of the perennial seeds will not germinate the first year but will wait until the second (or sometimes third) year before germinating. Your job is to create as good a seedbed as you can to encourage the seed to start. After two months of keeping the soil damp, stop watering. New plants will have a good root system by then and should be encouraged to develop deep roots. Forcing the roots to grow deeper in search of water will create a very healthy plant.

Many native plants do not look like much for the first year or two. They are developing root systems rather than fancy top growth. As long as you are growing the plants you want and not weeds, you'll have to grow some patience as well. Once the natives develop good root systems, they will put on their flowering show. It is quite common for beginning gardeners to be extremely disap-pointed in native plants for the first two to three years. Year 2 will see plants such as the biennial black-eyed Susans start to bloom but expect most of the blooms in year 3.

It is extremely important to keep the common lawn weeds out of the wildflower lawn for the germination and developmental phases. You will have to remove them or they will grow much faster than the wildflowers will.

Moss

Moss gardening—led by example in Japan—is becoming fashionable again. Although some lawnowners fight the invasion of moss, others encourage it. In shady areas where grass will not grow, moss can be particularly attractive. To encourage moss, these conditions are useful:

- *Shade.* Moss does not grow well in most of North America when exposed to sunlight. The high heat of the average summer will desiccate the moss, killing it outright. It wants protection from direct sunlight.
- *Acidic soils.* The addition of sulfur to soil will greatly assist the moss in establishing and maintaining itself. Do not use an acidification fertilizer as you would for rhododendrons, because you do not want to raise the fertility of the soil. You only want to increase the acidity.
- *High humidity and standing water.* If moss cannot tolerate direct sunlight, it also cannot tolerate drying out. However you arrange to provide moisture—from natural sources because you live in the Northwest or from misting systems on time clocks—moss demands high moisture and humidity to thrive.
- *Low fertility in the soil.* With high fertility levels, other plants will be prone to invading the moss area. Without fertility, moss will gather what it needs and create thick mats that eventually become self-supporting colonies.

I have established moss on some parts of my gardens by following these rules. To get the initial colony going, I followed an old recipe that seems to work. I took my nursery blender (the kitchen

EVERGREEN WARNING SIGNS

If you try to grow an evergreen in the shade, the first sign that it is not happy will be stretching of the branches. The second sign will be an excessive dying back of the center of the plant.

KEEP OFF THE GRASS

one is likely not a good idea) and whizzed up some chunks of moss in a bit of milk. I used a paintbrush to paint the mix onto the surfaces where I wanted to establish moss. Several times a day after the painting, I sprayed a weak solution of compost tea over the area as well. This had the effect of increasing the humidity for the moss as well as providing low-level nutrients to the rock surface for the baby moss plants to use.

On another project, I simply transplanted some moss from the bush on the edge of my property to a rock I wanted to "mossify." This rock was then kept quite damp and well shaded for several weeks until the moss started to grow on its own. I did spray it with a weak compost tea at least once a day.

The key to survival or propagation of moss is constant humidity and moisture. Provide that and you can grow moss darn near anywhere with any recipe. Once you dry out the starter moss, you risk losing it no matter what recipe you use.

Once moss is well established, it is a tough plant. You can walk on it as a pathway and even dry it out and it will recover quite nicely once it is provided with water. It can be difficult to establish moss on a slope unless the watering is quite mistlike. Any heavy watering will dislodge the moss spores and carry them to the bottom of the slope. Establishing moss on slopes is best done by transplanting rather than trying to establish the spores.

Shrubs

Whether evergreen or deciduous, shrubs are wonderful ground cover. The evergreens are particularly well suited for landscape use because they retain their greenery all year-round to give a sense of permanence and continuity in the garden design. Note that the vast majority of evergreens demand full or at the very least six hours of sunlight a day to survive. Evergreens therefore are competitors to the grass lawn, requiring at least the same amount of sunshine. This means that evergreens are best suited for areas where it is difficult to grow or maintain a lawn. Steep slopes are an excellent place for shrubs because of the difficulty of mowing the lawn in such areas.

STEEP SLOPES

I am constantly asked about plants for very steep slopes where a lawn mower cannot operate. Although perennial ground covers are an option, one of the nicest choices for a steep slope that is part of a visible landscape is to use shrubs. Lay a landscape fabric under the shrubs to control weeds and mulch with an attractive bark chip. A few minutes of weeding once or twice a summer to remove weeds that try to grow in the mulch is the only work that needs to be done on such a bed. Once the shrubs grow up, it will be an attractive, low-labor garden area.

EVERGREEN PLANTING CHART

Name	Hardiness Zone	Spacing (inches)	Comments
Arctostaphylos uva-ursi (Bearberry)	2	24–36	Very hardy evergreen with attractive red berries. Growth is slow but consistent. Grows best in poor but well-drained soils. Damp or clay soils will kill this plant. Sun to light shade is preferred. Generally pest and trouble free.
Cornus canadensis (Bunchberry)	2	12–18	Deciduous ground cover to 12 inches tall. Red fruits cover this plant from August onward. Requires shade in cool, moist, acidic soils with adequate organic matter. Transplant carefully. Not aggressively invasive.
Cotoneaster adpressus plus others (Creeping Cotoneaster)	4	24–36	Deciduous ground cover, spreading branches root where they touch, 12 to 24 inches tall. Prefers full sun for best fruit production but will tolerate some shade. Prefers well drained, slightly acidic soil. Does not grow well on clay or wet soils.
Euonymus fortunei (Wintercreepers)	4	24–30	Semi-evergreen to evergreen depending on warmth of winter. Grows 12 to 36 inches tall depending on cultivar. Prefers fertile soils in full sun to part shade but not wet soils or clay. Will winter burn in harsh winters or if unprotected in winter winds.
Hedera helix (English ivy)	5	18–24	Low-growing evergreen vine, 8 to 12 inches tall. Roots at leaf nodes as it spreads. (Can also climb if given a chance.) Grows best in rich, well drained soils but tolerates a wide range of soils. Tolerates dryness once established. Grows best in shade but will tolerate sun with adequate water. Trim to keep in bounds.
Juniper species	4	24–36	Grows in full sun, heights range from 6 to 36 inches, depending on cultivar. Spreading junipers make good dense ground covers in almost any soil, except clay and damp conditions. Survive dry soils once established. Does not tolerate shade.
Mahonia repens (Creeping Mahonia)	5	18–24	Prefers a moist, well drained, slightly acidic soil. Grows 12 to 18 inches tall. Prefers slight shade but will tolerate sun in all but the hottest and driest of soils. No clay or damp soils. Protect from winter winds that burn foliage. Be careful when transplanting.
Stephanandra incisa "Crispa"	5	24–30	Grows best in an organic soil that is slightly acidic. Likes a damp soil. About 2 to 3 feet tall. Prefers full sun but will tolerate light shade. Protect from winter winds.

Herbs

Isn't it romantic to think of a scented lawn? To smell the fragrance wafting up as you walk over the herb plants is a gardener's delight. The two herbs often recommended for this purpose are chamomile and thyme. Both give a delightful fragrance when crushed and both have been used as part of walkways for centuries. Neither make a particularly hardy covering in areas where there is a great deal of foot traffic. In other words, you can walk on them once or twice, but if they are on your main traffic pattern into your house, they won't last long.

Plant them in the spaces between patio or paving stones. They'll grow quite nicely there and if the bulk of the foot traffic is on the paving stones, the plants will survive and slowly expand to fill the cracks.

The major problem is drainage. Because water will not seep into the paving stones themselves, it runs into the cracks between stones. If the soil is clay underneath these stones, too much water can accumulate and drown the roots. All patio stones and walkways should sit on a good layer of sand, which will provide drainage and enable the herb to thrive in the small space.

Vines

Some gardeners find that vines make excellent ground cover. Clematis, honeysuckle, and roses, for example, are well suited to make an excellent flowering show. The difficulty with using vines is that they do not completely cover the ground. They have a very open growing habit. Normal ground cover will prevent some weed-seed germination by shading the soil, but vines will not prevent the weeds from invading at even the slightest level. This means that you will have to weed the ground cover vines. Most of the flowering vines require enough sunlight to flower that turf can be easily grown in these areas. Save the vining ground covers for the flower garden.

Hardscape

When all else fails—pave it. Just kidding, sort of.

Many folks find that using what landscapers call "hardscape" in areas where grass is difficult to grow is an excellent choice for low maintenance and appearance. Let's face it—what will look better, scraggly grass or a well designed constructed deck or deck and water feature combination? How about a shady, vine-covered gazebo with areas to sit and watch the birds play in the naturalized berry shrubs?

Indeed some form of hardscape will permanently and attractively solve the problem of what to grow and how to grow it in that particularly tough area. Think about it.

One common solution for the area against the trunk of a large tree is to use what is called a "paver" in the trade or a paving stone or cobblestone by consumers. A very attractive pattern can be constructed and set relatively easily under the tree to form a permanent mulch around the trunk. You won't have to mow or cultivate this area (other than to keep the inevitable weed from becoming established), and it will continue to lend a sense of design to the garden. Your local garden center will have pamphlets that show you this kind of installation and give tips on doing it yourself.

Having said all that, of course grass is simply the best ground cover there is.

Glossary

Abiotic plant disease: Disease caused by unfavorable growing conditions.

Alternative turf area: An area in which it is difficult to grow grass.

Annual weeds: Weeds that grow and set seed in a single growing season.

Antenna: A sensory organ on each side of an insect's head.

Bacteria: Very small unicellular organisms that lack chlorophyll and are the chief causal agents of decay and fermentation.

Bactericides: Pesticides used to kill bacteria.

Bacteriostats: Pesticides used to stop bacterial growth and reproduction.

Beneficials: Or beneficial predators. Insects that are harmless to grass plants.

Biological control: The use of natural organisms to control pathogenic organisms.

Biotic plant disease: Disease caused by plant pathogens.

Blight: A disease characterized by a rapid dying of living tissue.

Blotch: A disease characterized by large irregular spots or blotches.

Burr: A type of grass seed, like the burrs that stick onto clothing.

Canker: A dying, often sunken, lesion on grass tissue—stems or leaves.

Chlorotic: Yellowing of the normally green plant tissue caused by a lack of chlorophyll.

Contact spray: A spray that has to hit the pest to kill it.

Cultivar: A form of the plant that is different from the species in some way as a result of horticultural breeding or hybridization: a *culti*vated *vari*ety.

Cuticle: The thin outer cell layer of a plant, responsible for keeping bacteria and other pathogens out of the plant.

Damping off: Seedlings die at the soil line.

Diamond grid pattern: For planting ground cover, all lines are equidistant and plants are installed in the center of each diamond shape.

Dieback: The progressive dying back—from the tips of the new shoots back to the leaves and roots.

Disease cycle: The entire chain of events in disease development.

Dormant: A reduced physiological state.

Drench spray: A spray that is applied to soak into or drench the soil underneath the plant.

Endophyte: Any organism living within another organism.

Evapotranspiration: The amount of water lost by the soil and the plant combined.

Foliar spray: A spray that is applied to the leaves or foliage of a plant.

Frass: Solid larval insect excrement.

Fungi: A large group of organisms that do not have chlorophyll, such as molds, mildews, mushrooms, rusts, and smuts.

Fungicide: A substance that is toxic to fungi.

Gall: A swelling on a plant produced as a result of infection.

Herbicides: Pesticides used to kill weed pests.

Hypha: A fungal strand—a single branch of a mycelium.

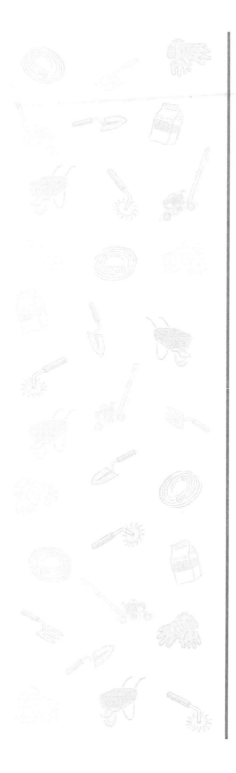

Insecticides: Pesticides used to kill insects.

Instar: The stage between insect moltings.

Larvae: Young insects that have hatched and are an immature form of the adult—a caterpillar, maggot, or grub depending on the kind of insect.

Lesion: A localized area of discolored, diseased tissue.

Metamorphosis: A series of changes that an insect goes through between the egg and the adult stage.

Mildew: A fungal disease of plants in which the mycelium is often seen as whitish threads on the surface of the plant.

Molt: To shed an outer skin.

Mycelium: The mass of filamentous strands that make up the body of a fungus.

Necrotic: Dead or diseased.

Nematodes: Microscopic wormlike animals that parasitize animals or plants.

Nurse grass: A fast growing, short lived grass species that is planted with a slow growing, long lived species to prevent water erosion and soil compaction. By the time the nurse grass dies out, the long-term grass is established in the good soil environment.

Oomycete: A class of fungi that that produce water molds.

Parasite: Any living thing that lives on or at the expense of another living organism

Pathogen: A disease-causing organism.

Perennial Weeds: Weeds that live for two or more years and do not need to reseed themselves every year.

Pest: An organism that creates a problem for a lawn by interfering with its normal growth (e.g., weeds, insects, nematodes, bacteria, fungi, and viruses).

Pesticides: All chemical sprays.

Pheromone: A substance secreted by an animal that influences the behavior of other animals.

Phytotoxic: Toxic to plants.

Protectant: Any substance that protects an organism against infection.

Pupa: The resting or inactive stage of an insect's development.

Resistance: The ability of an organism to overcome the effects of a pathogen or other damaging factor.

Ringspot: A circular area of chlorosis with a green center.

Rust: A disease characterized by rust-red spores.

Scorch: A burning of leaf margins as a result of infection, pesticide injury, or unfavorable conditions.

Seed blend: Contains two (or more) cultivars of the same species.

Seedhead: The flower part of the grass that has gone to seed.

Seed mixture: Contains at least two (or more) species of grass.

Shade tolerant: A variety of grass that hates shade the least; it does not mean that the grass likes the shade or even will grow well in it.

Sign: the visible expression of a pathogen (e.g., visible mycelium masses).

Species: A form of the plant that has come from nature.

Spore: A reproductive unit of a fungi.

Striate: Marked with thin, parallel lines.

Symptom: A visible expression of a disease on a grass plant (e.g., yellowing of the plant).

Systemic: Something that spreads internally through the plant's body.

Thatch: A dense layer of living and dead organic matter that accumulates between the soil surface and the green matter.

Threshold: Term used in the turf industry to determine whether pests are causing a problem.

Topdressing: To put new seed, special feed, sand, or compost on top of the existing lawn without killing off the old grass.

Vector: An organism that transports a pest problem.

Virus: Microscopic disease-causing agents capable of multiplying only in living cells. They cause a variety of turf problems.

Wilt: Loss of rigidity resulting in a drooping or plant leaves. Normally caused by a lack of water.

Resources

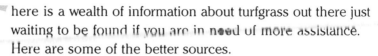

There is a wealth of information about turfgrass out there just waiting to be found if you are in need of more assistance. Here are some of the better sources.

General Internet Search Engines. I use *www.google.com* quite a bit when I start searching the Net. It has seldom failed me.

General Internet Sites

If you have questions, visit my site at *www.simplegiftsfarm.com* to read other lawn articles or to ask me a question. I'll try to help.

If you have a question about a specific lawn chemical for insects, weeds, or diseases, the absolute best resource is Extonet at Cornell University: *http://pmep.cce.cornell.edu/profiles/index.html*.

If you need general information about insect pests, try visiting the University of North Carolina: *www.ces.ncsu.edu/TurfFiles/pubs/insects/mip-doc.html*.

If you need general biocontrol information, try *www.biconet.com*. This is a commercial site that wants to sell you stuff, but it has a lot of information about lawn pest control using natural systems.

Do you need to know about southern lawn grass? Try this University of Florida site—it's one of the best: *www.floridaturf.com/index.html*.

If you need more southern lawn information plus just about anything else in the southern garden—try Texas A&M's *http://aggie-horticulture.tamu.edu/tamuhort.html*. You'll love the breadth of information found here.

Another excellent site for more northerly gardeners is the University of Guelph's Turfgrass Institute. The main page is *www.uoguelph.ca/GTI*, and there are many other links and articles to be found on this site.

One of the largest sites on northern turfgrass is found at Michigan State University: *www.lib.msu.edu/tgif/*.

I know that many of you southerners are concerned about fire ants in your lawn. Here's the update Net page from the United States Department of Agriculture: *www.ars.usda.gov/is/AR/archive/sep99/ant0999.htm*. I've found this area changes quickly. Use a search engine to find up-to-date reports on fire ants.

"Pesticides and Children" is an article on the Physicians for Social Responsibility Web site describing the report of the National Academy of Sciences on children and pesticides: *www.psr.org/pestkids.htm.*

"Golf Courses and the Environment" is an excellent summary of golf course environmental goals, agreed to by almost all the golfing bodies and industry: *www.psr.org/golf_environment.htm.*

Books

Christians, Nick. *Fundamentals of Turfgrass Management.* Ann Arbor Press, 1998. This is a textbook for those interested in knowing more than they need to about turfgrass.

Sachs, Paul D. *Handbook of Successful Ecological Lawn Care.* The Edaphic Press, 1996. A brief book with lots of good information about growing environmentally sound lawns. Also contains a section on commercial lawncare.

Walters, Charles. *Weeds: Control Without Poisons.* Acres U.S.A., 1999. An interesting viewpoint on controlling weeds by soil science. Controversial, thought provoking.

Your State Horticultural Extension service will have lots of small monographs on lawn control. Check your telephone directory for the office nearest you.

A

abiotic plant disease, 144
aerating, 89, 90, 109–10
aeration machines, 89, 100–10
air circulation, 139
alternative turf area, 29, 241–61
anatomy of grass, 2–5
animal pests, 226–28
  moving, 226
  trapping, 226
annual weeds, 123. *See also* weeds,
  types of
antenna, 199
ants, 218, 224
aphids, 209
armadillos, 228
armyworms
  common armyworm (*Pseudaletia
    unipuncta*), 205
  fall armyworm (*Spodoptera
    frugiperda*), 205–6
artificial turf, 231
auricles, 6, *8*
  absence of, 6, *8*
  long auricles, 6, *8*
  short auricles, 6, *8*

B

bacteria, 184
bactericides, 146
bacteriostats, 146
bees, and pesticides, 225
benches, 142, 236
beneficial predators, 177
beneficials, 177
biological control of pests, 184
biotic plant disease, 144
blight, 146
blotch, 150
bluegrasses
  annual bluegrass (*Poa annua*), 15
  Canada bluegrass (*Poa compressa*),
    15–16
  Kentucky Bluegrass (*Poa pratensis*),
    14, 40
  rough bluegrass (*Poa trivialis*), 15
boundary zone, 32–33, *33*
buds, 3–4

C

Carson, Rachel, 125
caterpillars, 205
Cation Exchange Capacity (CEC), 36
CEC (Cation Exchange Capacity), 36
chemical control of pests, 186–218,
  224–28
chemical control of weeds, 120, 122
chemicals
  concerns, 215
  environmental concerns, 125
  hazards of, 224
  safety, 162
  toxicity of, 179
chewing insects
  annual bluegrass weevil (*Hyperodes
    maculicollis*), 198–99
  bluegrass billbug (*Sphenophorus
    parvulus*), 199–200
  hunting billbug (*Sphenophorus
    veratus vestitus*), 200
chinch bugs
  chinch bug (*Blissus leucopterus
    leucopterus*), 209–10
  hairy chinch bug (*Blissus
    leucopterus hirtus*), 210–11
  southern chinch bug (*Blissus
    insularis*), 211–12
clippings, 100, 111
Colborn, Dumanoski, and Myers, 125
collar, 5, *5*
compaction, 140, 168, 169
compost, 35–38, 70–71, 110, 149
  application of, 71, 73
  making, 37
contact sprays, 217
containers, 237
corn gluten, 111
cornmeal, 136
crickets. *See* mole crickets
croquet lawns, 238–39
cultivar versus species, 10
cultivation, 119
cultural controls, 201–2
cuticle, 62
cutworms
  black cutworm (*Agrostis ipsilon*),
    203–4

bronze cutworm (*Nepholodes
    minians*), 204
  variegated cutworm (*Poridroma
    saucia*), 204
Cygon, 184

D

dead patches, 169, 201
decks, 261
diamond grid pattern, *246*
Diazinon, 185, 186, 197
dimethoate, 184
disease cycle, 177
  stages of, 178, 180
disease triangle, *136*
diseases, 136–74
  air circulation and, 139
  common types of, 172–74
  diagnosing, 137–41
  droughts and, 139
  freezing temperatures, 138, 139
  fungi and, 140–41
  identifying, 141–44, 146–48, 150–52,
    154–63
  imbalances, 139
  improper fertilization, 138
  living causes, 140
  nonliving causes, 137
  shade and, 139
  signs of, 141
  stress and, 140
  symptoms, 141, 172–74
  tips on, 139
diseases, types of
  anthracnose, 142
  Bermuda grass decline, 142–43
  brown patch, 143
  centipede decline, 144
  cercospora leaf spot, 144
  common diseases, 172–74
  crown and root rot, 144, 146
  curvularia blight, 146
  dollar spot, 146–47
  fairy ring, 147
  flag smut, 159
  fusarium blight, 148
  fusarium patch, 148
  gray leaf spot, 148, 150
  gray snow mold (typhula blight), 161

leaf blotch, 150
leaf spot, 151
melting out, 150
necrotic ring spot, 152
nigrospora blight, 154
pink patch, 154
pink snow mold, 148
powdery mildew, 155
pythium blight, 155
red thread, 156
rusts, 156–57
St. Augustine decline, 157
sclerotium blight (southern blight), 158
slime mold, 158
southern blight (sclerotium blight), 158
spring dead spot, 158–59
stripe smut, 159
summer patch, 159–60
take-all patch, 160
take-all root rot, 160–61
typhula blight (gray snow mold), 161
white patch, 161
yellow patch, 162
zonate leaf spot, 162–63
dog damage, 139, 140
dog's tooth grass, 20
dormant plants, 4
dormant seeding, 43
drainage, 31
drench spray, 182, 184–86
droughts, 85–86, 124, 139
dry spots, 168

E

earwigs, 225
endophytes, 199, 203
evaporation, 82, 84
evapotranspiration, 82
evergreens, 234, 257
  planting chart for, 259
examining, 112

F

fall, 75
feeding, 60–76. *See also* fertilizers
  how much, 75–76
  overfeeding, 75
  when, 74–75
fertilizer spreader, 76, 78–79, 81

coverage, 79, 81
  spreading pattern, *80*
fertilizers, 5, 117–18
  application of, 38–39, 76, 78–79,
    81, 167
  calculating nitrogen, 77
  fall application, 75
  how much to apply, 74
  improper application of, 138
  labels, 68
  liquid, 82
  organic, 70–74
  overfeeding, 75
  spring application, 74
  starter fertilizer, 38–39
  summer application, 74
  types of, 81–82
  weed-and-feed products, 81, 122
  and weeds, 117–18
  when to apply, 74
fescues
  chewings fescue (*Festuca rubra*
    subspecies *fallax*), 12, 14
  creeping red fescue
    (*Festuca rubra*), 12
  tall fescue (*Festuca arundinacea*),
    10, 12
finish grading, 30–33
fire ants, 218, 224
firming the soil, 39
fish, 108
fleas, 225
foliar spray, 182, 184–86
food absorption, 4–5
foot traffic, 103, 234
footprints, 168
frass, 199
freezing temperatures, 138, 139
frozen grass, 138
fungi, 140–41
  helpful, 85
  as insecticide, 184
  origin of, 157
  prevention of, 161
fungicides, 71, 146
  commonly used, 164–65
  resistance to, 145
  safety, 159
fungus fighter, 136

G

garden ants, 218
gardening euphemisms, 256
gasoline, 171
gazebo, 261
germination, 43, 44–45, 108
glyphosate, 185
golf greens, 69, 230, 232–33
  designing, 233
  grass, 232–33
  mowing, 232, 233
  soil, 230, 232
  USGA guidelines and, 230, 232
grading, 28–30
grass. *See also* grass seed; grasses
  anatomy of, 2–5
  freezing temperatures, 138, 139
  of the future, 24
  in history, 22
  identifying, 5–9
  killing, 106, 108
  mixes, 18, 26, 40, 42
  mowing of, 91–100
  root depth of, 92
  sowing, 41
  species, 13, 25, 90
  types of, 10–25
  zone key, *11*
grass clippings, 89, 100, 111
grass leaves, whistling with, 23
grass seed, 18, 26
  blends and mixtures, 18, 26, 40, 42,
    118, 171
  buying, 26
  labels, 26
  reseeding, 105
  seeding, 39–46
grasses, 10–25. *See also* grass; grass seed
  annual bluegrass (*Poa annua*), 15
  annual ryegrass (*Lolium
    multiflorum*), 17
  Bahia grass (*Paspalum* species), 21
  bent grass, 16–17
  Bermuda grass (*Cynodon* species),
    18–19
  bluegrama (*Bouteloua gracilis*), 24
  bluegrasses, 14–16
  buffalo grass (*Buchloe dactyloides*), 24

Canada bluegrass (*Poa compressa*), 15–16

carpetgrass (*Axonopus affinis*), 22

centipede grass (*Eremochloa ophiuroides*), 21–22

chewings fescue (*Festuca rubra* subspecies *fallax*), 12, 14

creeping bent grass (*Agrostis palustris*), 16

creeping red fescue (*Festuca rubra*), 12

fescues, 10–14

Kentucky bluegrass (*Poa pratensis*), 14, 40

Kikuyu grass (*Pennisetum clandestinum*), 22, 24

northern lawn grasses, 10–18

perennial ryegrass (*Lolium perenne*), 18

red top (*Agrostis alba*), 17

rough bluegrass (*Poa trivialis*), 15

ryegrass, 17–18

St. Augustine grass (*Stenotaphrum secundatum*), 19–20

southern lawn grasses, 18–25

tall fescue (*Festuca arundinacea*), 10, 12

Zoysia grass (*Zoysia* species), 20–21

greenbug aphid (*Schizaphis graminum*), 209

ground covers, 242–49, 254

  aggressiveness of, 249

  feeding, 248–49

  fertilizers and, 249

  hardiness of, 247

  myths about, 242–44

  planting, 245–47

  planting chart, 251–53

  planting grid, *246*

  plants required, 247

  preparation for, 244–45

  protecting, 247

  pruning, 249

  selecting, 244

  sloping ground and, 245, 258

  watering, 247–48

  weed control, 248

  winter protection, 247

ground pearls (*Margarodes meridionalis*), 216–18

growing zones, *11*

grubs

  controlling, 195, 196, 197, 199

  damage from, 201

  identifying, 194

  threshold testing for, 193

grubs, types of

  Asiatic garden beetle (*Maladera castanea*), 190

  black turfgrass ataenius (*Ataenius spretulus*), 187, 190

  European chafer (*Rhizotrogus majalis*), 190, 192

  green June beetle (*Cotinus nitida*), 192–93

  Japanese beetle (*Popillia japonica*), 193–94

  June beetles (*Phyllophaga* species), 197–98

  northern masked chafer (*Cyclocephala borealis*), 194, 196

  Oriental beetle (*Anomala orientalis*), 196–97

  southern masked chafer (*Cyclocephala lurida*), 194, 196

H

hardscape, 261

herbicide injury, 163

herbicides, 119–20, 146

  application of, 167–68

  commonly available, 123–24, 126–27

  safety, 121

herbs, 260

horticultural glue, 205

Horticultural Latin, 14

hypha, 141

I

IBDU (Isobutyledenediurea), 63–64

infection, 178

inoculation, 178

insecticides, 146, 184–86. *See also* pesticides

  persistence and, 185

  resistance to, 185–86

  safety, 183

solubility and, 185

insects

  ants, 218, 224

  aphids, 209

  armyworms, 205–6

  chewing insects, 198–200

  chinch bugs, 209–12

  cutworms, 203–4

  earwigs, 225

  fleas, 225

  grubs, 187, 190, 192–94, 196–98

  mites, 212–15

  mole crickets, 206–9

  scales, 215–16

  wasps, 225

  webworms, 200–203

instar stage, 196

iron, 68–69

irrigating, 43–44, 52–53, 83–86

  amount of, 83

  during day, 84

  frequency, 83–84, 168

  measuring, 83

  at night, 84

  reducing, 86

  time required for, 83, 84, 85

  weeds and, 118

Isobutyledenediurea (IBDU), 63–64

L

labyrinths, 239–40, *240*

larvae, 187

Latin translations, 15, 20

lawn alternatives, 29, 241–61

lawn care companies, 112–14

lawn care summary, 99

lawn checklist, 56

lawn clippings, 89, 100, 111

lawn pest cycle, 177

lawn rollers, 39, 90–91

lawn spikes, 196

leaf cutting, 133

leaf tip, 9, *9*

  boat-keel tip, *9*, 9

  pointed tip, *9*, 9

  split boat-keel tip, *9*, 9

lesions, 142

leveling soil, 38, 104

life cycle of insects, 191

light meter, 59, 139
ligules, 6, *8*
  absence of, 6, *8*
  hairy ligule, 6, *8*
  membrane of, 6, *8*
low-maintenance lawn, 76

M

magnesium, 69
magnifying glass, 181
map of growing zones, *11*
map of temperature zones, *250*
mazes, 239–40
Mendel, Gregor, 186
metamorphosis, 191
micronutrients, 70
microorganisms, 89, 90
mildew, 155
milorganite, 72, 73, 74
minor trace nutrients, 68–70, 108
mites
  banks grass mite (*Oligonychus
    pratensis*), 214
  Bermuda grass mite (*Eriophyes
    cynodoniensis*), 212–13
  clover mite (*Bryobia praetiosa*),
    213–14
  winter grain mite (*Penthaleus
    major*), 214–15
mole crickets
  mole cricket (*Gryllotalpa
    hexadactyla*), 206–7
  short-winged mole cricket
    (*Scapteriscus abbreviatus*), 208
  southern mole cricket (*Scapteriscus
    borellii*), 208
  tawny mole cricket (*Scapteriscus
    vicinus*), 208–9
mole crickets, controlling, 209
moles, 226–27
molt, 187
monitoring techniques for pests, 180–82
  coffee can technique, 181
  cup changer technique, 182
  soap solution technique, 181
moss, 257–58
  controlling, 122–23
  tolerance of, 124, 257
mowers, 94, 96–98

blade sharpening, 97, 166
flail, 98
for golf greens, 232
hammer knife, 98
reel, 97
rotary, 94, 96–97
sickle bar, 97–98
mowing, 91–98, 108–9
  basics of, 94
  effects of, 92, 94
  frequency of, 166
  golf greens, 232, 233
  grass heights, 93, 94, 139, 161, 166, 209
  kids and, 95
  patterns for, 167
  root depth and, 92
  safety, 95, 98
  scalping, 94, 166–67
  time required for, 96
  weeds and, 117, 161
mulching, 44, 261
mushrooms, 28
mycelium, 141

N

necrotic rings, 163
nematodes, 112
nitrogen, 61–65
  application of, 76
  calculating, 77
  deficiency, 61–62, 63
  overfeeding, 61–62, 88, 89
  sources of, 62–63
  tips on, 65
nonselective controls, 120
northern lawn grasses
  annual bluegrass (*Poa annua*), 15
  annual ryegrass (*Lolium
    multiflorum*), 17
  bent grass, 16–17
  bluegrasses, 14–16
  Canada bluegrass (*Poa compressa*),
    15–16
  chewings fescue (*Festuca rubra
    subspecies fallax*), 12, 14
  creeping bent grass (*Agrostis
    palustris*), 16
  creeping red fescue
    (*Festuca rubra*), 12

fescues, 10–14
  Kentucky bluegrass (*Poa pratensis*),
    14, 40
  perennial ryegrass
    (*Lolium perenne*), 18
  red top (*Agrostis alba*), 17
  rough bluegrass (*Poa trivialis*), 15
  ryegrass, 17–18
  species of, *13*
  tall fescue (*Festuca arundinacea*),
    10, 12
nuisance pests, 218–28
nurse grass, 17, 40
nutrients, 60–76
nutritional imbalance, 139

O

organic control of pests, 186–218, 224–28
organic control of weeds, 122
organic fertilizers, 70–74, 111
organic matter, 34, 35–36
ornamental grasses, 237, 254
Our Stolen Future, 125
overfeeding, 61–62, 75, 88, 89
overseeding, 43, 110

P

pale lawns, 167
parasites, 140
pathogens, 35, 136
pathways, 103, 236–37
pavers, 261
peat moss, 35, 38
penetration, 178
perennial flowers, 254, 255–56
perennial weeds, 123. *See also* weeds,
  types of
pest control, 45–46, 107, 111
pest cycle, 177
pesticide injury, 163
pesticides, 146
  bees and, 225
  commonly used, 220–23
  guidelines for, 219
  resistance to, 185
  safe storage of, 186
  safety, 183
  types of, 146
pests, 176–228. *See also specific pests*

biological control of, 184
chemical control of, 186–218, 224–28
coffee can technique and, 181
control checklist, 228
control measures, 182–218
cup changer technique and, 182
definition of, 177
harmful pests, 188–89
identifying, 180–81
life cycle of, 191
monitoring techniques, 180–82
organic control of, 186–218, 224–28
soap solution technique and, 181
types of, 186–90, 192–94, 196–218,
    224–28
weeds and, 211
pests that hurt turf, 188–89
pet control, 107
phosphorus, 65–67
    deficiency, 66
    overdose, 66–67
photosynthesis, 16
phytotoxicity, 137
planning, 34
plant food, 60–76. *See also* feeding;
    fertilizers
play areas, 233–34
plugging, 54
post-emergence herbicides, 120
potassium, 67–68
pre-emergence herbicides, 119–20
pregrading, 28–29
preparing soil, 19, 34–39, 244–45
prepenetration, 178
problems, identifying, 166–71
professional lawn care, 112–14
propagation, 3–4, 180
pupa, 187

R

raccoons, 227
rakes, 119, 147
renovation, 105–6, 108–12
    killing grass, 106–8
    organic approach, 109–12
    versus rebuilding, 106
    sowing seeds, 108–9
    spring recipe, 105
repair of lawn, 102–5

foot traffic, 103
reseeding, 105
sodding, 103–4
resistance to chemicals, 145
rhizomes, 4, *4*
rodent pests, 226–27
rolling lawns, 39, 90–91
roots, *4*, 4–5
    depth of, 92
    injury of, 140
Roundup, 185
rust, 156–57

S

salt damage, 171
sample taking, 34
scales
    Bermuda grass scale (*Odonaspis
        ruthae*), 215–16
    turfgrass scale (*Lecanopsis
        formicarum*), 216
scalping the lawn, 94, 166–67
science project, 30
SCU (sulfur-coated urea), 64
seats, 142, 237
seaweed, 108
seed, 118. *See also* grass seed
    blends and mixtures, 18, 26, 40,
        42, 171
    versus sod, 47
seedhead, 22
seeding, 39–46
    checklist for, 56
    germination, 43
    reseeding, 105
    sowing seeds, 42
    weather for, 39–40, 43
septic tank, 169
shade, 59–60, 234–36
    level of, 139, 170
    moss and, 257–58
shade-tolerant grass, 234, 235
sheaths, 6, *6*
    closed sheath, 6, *6*
    partially split sheath, 6, *6*
    split sheath, 6, *6*
shoots, 2–3, *3*
shrubs, 258
    deciduous, 258

evergreen, 258
    planting chart, 259
    sloping ground and, 258
signs of disease, 141
Silent Spring, 125
skunks, 227
sloping ground
    ground covers and, 245, 258
    shrubs and, 258
snow mold, 150
sod, 46, 48–53
    checklist for, 56
    laying, 49, *50*, *51*, 51–52
    plugging, 54
    preparation for, 48–49
    versus seed, 47
    stolonizing, 54, 56
    strip sodding, 54
    walking on, 53
    watering, 52–53
soil, 28–39
    care for, 21
    checklist for, 56
    compaction of, 140, 168, 169
    firming, 39
    grading, 28–33
    leveling, 38, 104
    preparing, 19, 34–39, 244–45
    testing, 33–34
solarization, 109
southern lawn grasses
    Bahia grass (*Paspalum* species), 21
    Bermuda grass (*Cynodon* species),
        18–19
    bluegrama (*Bouteloua gracilis*), 24
    buffalo grass (*Buchloe dactyloides*), 24
    carpetgrass (*Axonopus affinis*), 22
    centipede grass (*Eremochloa
        ophiuroides*), 21–22
    Kikuyu grass (*Pennisetum
        clandestinum*), 22, 24
    St. Augustine grass (*Stenotaphrum
        secundatum*), 19–20
    species of, 25
    Zoysia grass (*Zoysia* species), 20–21
southern soil care, 21
sowing machines, 42
sowing seeds, 41, 42, 108–9
species versus cultivar, 10

spores, 71
spray injury, 163
sprays
    caution with, 40
    contact spray, 217
    drench spray, 182, 184–86
    foliar spray, 182, 184–86
    guidelines for, 219
    injury and, 163
    labels on, 218
spring, 74, 105
standing water, 169
starter fertilizer, 38–39
stolonizing, 54, 56
stolons, 3–4, *4*
strip sodding, 54
subgrading, 29–30
subsoil, 32–33
subsurface grading, 29–30
sugar esters, 184
sulfur, 69–70
sulfur-coated urea (SCU), 64
summer, 74
summer drought, 85–86, 124, 139
sun levels, 59
sun scald, 140
sunscreen, 86
sunshine, 59–60
symptoms of disease, 141
systemic fungicides, 145
systemic insect controls, 217

T

temperature zones, *250*
temperatures for seeding, 39–40
temperatures, freezing, 138, 139
tennis courts, 237–38
termites, 29
testing soil, 33–34
thatch, 17, 87–90
    causes of, 87–89
    controlling, 89–90
    problems, 87
    tendencies, 87
threshold, 177
threshold testing, 193
tillers, 3, *4*
topdressing, 12, 110
    tips for, 143

topsoil, 29, 30, 32–33, 34, 35, 36
trace nutrients, 68–70
transpiration, 82
trees, 170
turf, 29, 69. *See also* grass
    alternative areas, 29, 241–61
    artificial turf, 231
    golf courses and, 69, 230, 232–33
    wonders of, 7

U

urea, 64–65
USGA guidelines, 230, 232

V

VAM (Vesicular Arbuscular
    Mycorrhizae), 85
vector, 178
vernation, 9, *9*
    folded vernation, 9, *9*
    rolled vernation, 9, *9*
Vesicular Arbuscular Mycorrhizae
    (VAM), 85
vines, 260
voles, 226–27

W

walking on sod, 53
warm season lawn, 75–76
wasps, 225
watering, 43–44, 52–53, 83–86
    amount of, 83
    during day, 84
    frequency of, 83–84, 168
    measuring, 83
    at night, 84
    reducing, 86
    time required for, 83, 84, 85
    weeds and, 118
webworms
    bluegrass sod webworm
        (*Parapediasia teterrella*), 202
    sod webworm (*Crambus teterrellus*),
        200–202
    tropical sod webworm
        (*Herpetogramma phaeopteralis*),
        202–3
weed-and-feed products, 81, 122

weed control, 28, 116–24
weed rakes, 119
weed seed, 2, 118
weed spuds, 119
weeds, 116–34
    chemical controls, 119–20, 122
    classes of, 123
    common types of, 129
    cultivation and, 119
    cultural controls, 117–19
    fertilizer analysis, 117–18
    grass seed and, 2, 118
    herbicides, 119–20
    identifying, 118
    irrigation and, 118
    mowing, 117
    organic controls, 122
    pests and, 211
    as symptoms, 117
    watering and, 118
weeds, types of
    annual weeds, 123
    bunch-type grasses, 130
    chickweed, 128, 130
    clover, 124, 128
    common weeds, 129
    knotweed, 130
    nut sedge, 132, 134
    perennial weeds, 123
    plantains, 128
    sorrels, 128
    spreading grasses, 131–32
    spurges, 128
    white clover, 124
whistling with grass leaves, 23
wildflowers, 254, 255–57
wilt, 4
winter overseeding, 43
worms, 71, 111

Z

zone key
    growing map, *11*
    temperature map, *250*

THE EVERYTHING GARDENING BOOK

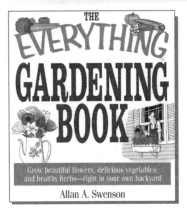

By Allan A. Swenson

You don't have to have a green thumb to enjoy fragrant flowers, nutritious vegetables, healthy herbs, and tasty fruits. In *The Everything® Gardening Book*, noted gardener and author Allan A. Swenson presents down-to-earth advice for choosing the right tools, improving your soil, picking the best plant varieties, fending off unwanted bugs, knowing when to water, and much more. Featuring an eight-page color insert and useful illustrations throughout, *The Everything® Gardening Book* is the only book you need to start reaping the benefits of Mother Nature's rich bounty right in your own backyard.

Trade paperback,
$14.95 ($22.95 CAN)
1-58062-860-5, 320 pages

OTHER *EVERYTHING*® BOOKS BY ADAMS MEDIA CORPORATION

Everything® **Civil War Book**
Everything® **World War II Book**

HOBBIES

Everything® **Bridge Book**
Everything® **Candlemaking Book**
Everything® **Casino Gambling Book**
Everything® **Chess Basics Book**
Everything® **Collectibles Book**
Everything® **Crossword and Puzzle Book**
Everything® **Digital Photography Book**
Everything® **Drums Book (with CD),**
        $19.95, ($31.95 CAN)
Everything® **Family Tree Book**
Everything® **Games Book**
Everything® **Guitar Book**
Everything® **Knitting Book**
Everything® **Magic Book**
Everything® **Motorcycle Book**
Everything® **Online Genealogy Book**
Everything® **Playing Piano and**
        Keyboards Book
Everything® **Rock & Blues Guitar**
        Book (with CD), $19.95,
        ($31.95 CAN)
Everything® **Scrapbooking Book**

HOME IMPROVEMENT

Everything® **Feng Shui Book**
Everything® **Gardening Book**
Everything® **Home Decorating Book**
Everything® **Landscaping Book**
Everything® **Lawn Care Book**
Everything® **Organize Your Home Book**

KIDS' STORY BOOKS

Everything® **Bedtime Story Book**
Everything® **Bible Stories Book**
Everything® **Fairy Tales Book**
Everything® **Mother Goose Book**

NEW AGE

Everything® **Astrology Book**

Everything® **Divining the Future Book**
Everything® **Dreams Book**
Everything® **Ghost Book**
Everything® **Meditation Book**
Everything® **Numerology Book**
Everything® **Palmistry Book**
Everything® **Spells and Charms Book**
Everything® **Tarot Book**
Everything® **Wicca and Witchcraft Book**

PARENTING

Everything® **Baby Names Book**
Everything® **Baby Shower Book**
Everything® **Baby's First Food Book**
Everything® **Baby's First Year Book**
Everything® **Breastfeeding Book**
Everything® **Get Ready for Baby Book**
Everything® **Homeschooling Book**
Everything® **Potty Training Book,**
        $9.95, ($15.95 CAN)
Everything® **Pregnancy Book**
Everything® **Pregnancy Organizer,**
        $15.00, ($22.95 CAN)
Everything® **Toddler Book**
Everything® **Tween Book**

PERSONAL FINANCE

Everything® **Budgeting Book**
Everything® **Get Out of Debt Book**
Everything® **Get Rich Book**
Everything® **Investing Book**
Everything® **Homebuying Book, 2nd Ed.**
Everything® **Homeselling Book**
Everything® **Money Book**
Everything® **Mutual Funds Book**
Everything® **Online Investing Book**
Everything® **Personal Finance Book**

PETS

Everything® **Cat Book**
Everything® **Dog Book**
Everything® **Dog Training and Tricks**
Everything® **Horse Book**
Everything® **Puppy Book**
Everything® **Tropical Fish Book**

REFERENCE

Everything® **Astronomy Book**
Everything® **Car Care Book**
Everything® **Christmas Book, $15.00,**
        ($21.95 CAN)
Everything® **Classical Mythology Book**
Everything® **Divorce Book**
Everything® **Etiquette Book**
Everything® **Great Thinkers Book**
Everything® **Learning French Book**
Everything® **Learning German Book**
Everything® **Learning Italian Book**
Everything® **Learning Latin Book**
Everything® **Learning Spanish Book**
Everything® **Mafia Book**
Everything® **Philosophy Book**
Everything® **Shakespeare Book**
Everything® **Tall Tales, Legends, &**
        Other Outrageous Lies Book
Everything® **Toasts Book**
Everything® **Trivia Book**
Everything® **Weather Book**
Everything® **Wills & Estate Planning**
        Book

RELIGION

Everything® **Angels Book**
Everything® **Buddhism Book**
Everything® **Catholicism Book**
Everything® **Judaism Book**
Everything® **Saints Book**
Everything® **World's Religions Book**
Everything® **Understanding Islam Book**

SCHOOL & CAREERS

Everything® **After College Book**
Everything® **College Survival Book**
Everything® **Cover Letter Book**
Everything® **Get-a-Job Book**
Everything® **Hot Careers Book**
Everything® **Job Interview Book**
Everything® **Online Job Search Book**
Everything® **Resume Book, 2nd Ed.**
Everything® **Study Book**

All Everything® books are priced at $12.95 or $14.95, unless otherwise stated. Prices subject to change without notice.
Canadian prices range from $11.95–$22.95 and are subject to change without notice.

WE HAVE EVERYTHING . . . .

SPORTS/FITNESS

Everything® **Bicycle Book**
Everything® **Fishing Book**
Everything® **Fly Fishing Book**
Everything® **Golf Book**
Everything® **Golf Instruction Book**
Everything® **Pilates Book**
Everything® **Running Book**
Everything® **Sailing Book, 2nd Ed.**
Everything® **T'ai Chi and QiGong Book**
Everything® **Total Fitness Book**
Everything® **Weight Training Book**
Everything® **Yoga Book**

TRAVEL

Everything® **Guide to Las Vegas**
Everything® **Guide to New England**
Everything® **Guide to New York City**
Everything® **Guide to Washington D.C.**

Everything® **Travel Guide to The Disneyland Resort®, California Adventure®, Universal Studios®, and the Anaheim Area**
Everything® **Travel Guide to the Walt Disney World® Resort, Universal Studios®, and Greater Orlando, 3rd Ed.**

WEDDINGS & ROMANCE

Everything® **Creative Wedding Ideas Book**
Everything® **Dating Book**
Everything® **Jewish Wedding Book**
Everything® **Romance Book**
Everything® **Wedding Book, 2nd Ed.**
Everything® **Wedding Organizer, $15.00 ($22.95 CAN)**

Everything® **Wedding Checklist, $7.95 ($11.95 CAN)**
Everything® **Wedding Etiquette Book, $7.95 ($11.95 CAN)**
Everything® **Wedding Shower Book, $7.95 ($12.95 CAN)**
Everything® **Wedding Vows Book, $7.95 ($11.95 CAN)**
Everything® **Weddings on a Budget Book, $9.95 ($15.95 CAN)**

WRITING

Everything® **Creative Writing Book**
Everything® **Get Published Book**
Everything® **Grammar and Style Book**
Everything® **Grant Writing Book**
Everything® **Guide to Writing Children's Books**
Everything® **Writing Well Book**

ALSO AVAILABLE:

THE EVERYTHING®  KIDS' SERIES!

Each book is 8" x 9¼", 144 pages, and two-color throughout.

Everything® **Kids' Baseball Book, 2nd Edition, $6.95** ($10.95 CAN)
Everything® **Kids' Bugs Book, $6.95** ($10.95 CAN)
Everything® **Kids' Cookbook, $6.95** ($10.95 CAN)
Everything® **Kids' Joke Book, $6.95** ($10.95 CAN)
Everything® **Kids' Math Puzzles Book, $6.95** ($10.95 CAN)
Everything® **Kids' Mazes Book, $6.95** ($10.95 CAN)
Everything® **Kids' Money Book, $6.95** ($11.95 CAN)

Everything® **Kids' Monsters Book, $6.95** ($10.95 CAN)
Everything® **Kids' Nature Book, $6.95** ($11.95 CAN)
Everything® **Kids' Puzzle Book $6.95** ($10.95 CAN)
Everything® **Kids' Science Experiments Book, $6.95** ($10.95 CAN)
Everything® **Kids' Soccer Book, $6.95** ($10.95 CAN)
Everything® **Kids' Travel Activity Book, $6.95** ($10.95 CAN)

Available wherever books are sold!
To order, call 800-872-5627, or visit us at everything.com

Everything® and everything.com® are registered trademarks of Adams Media Corporation.